GIANTS

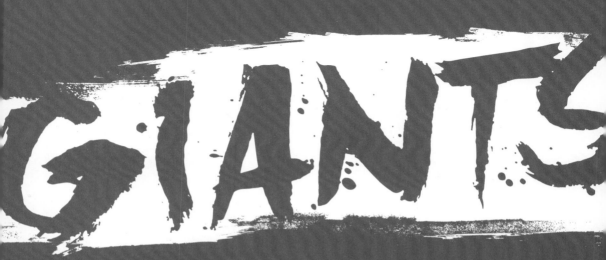

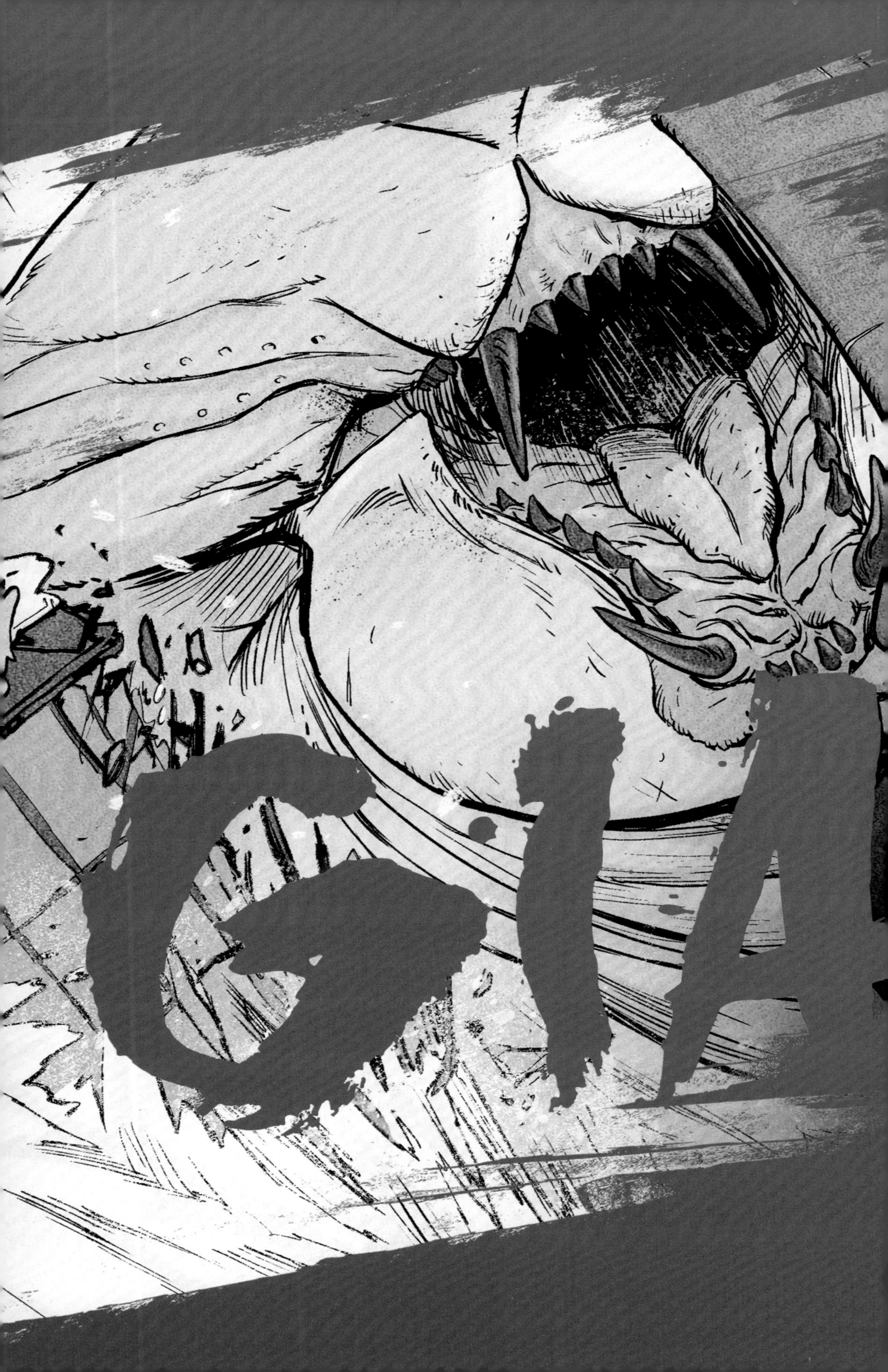
GIA

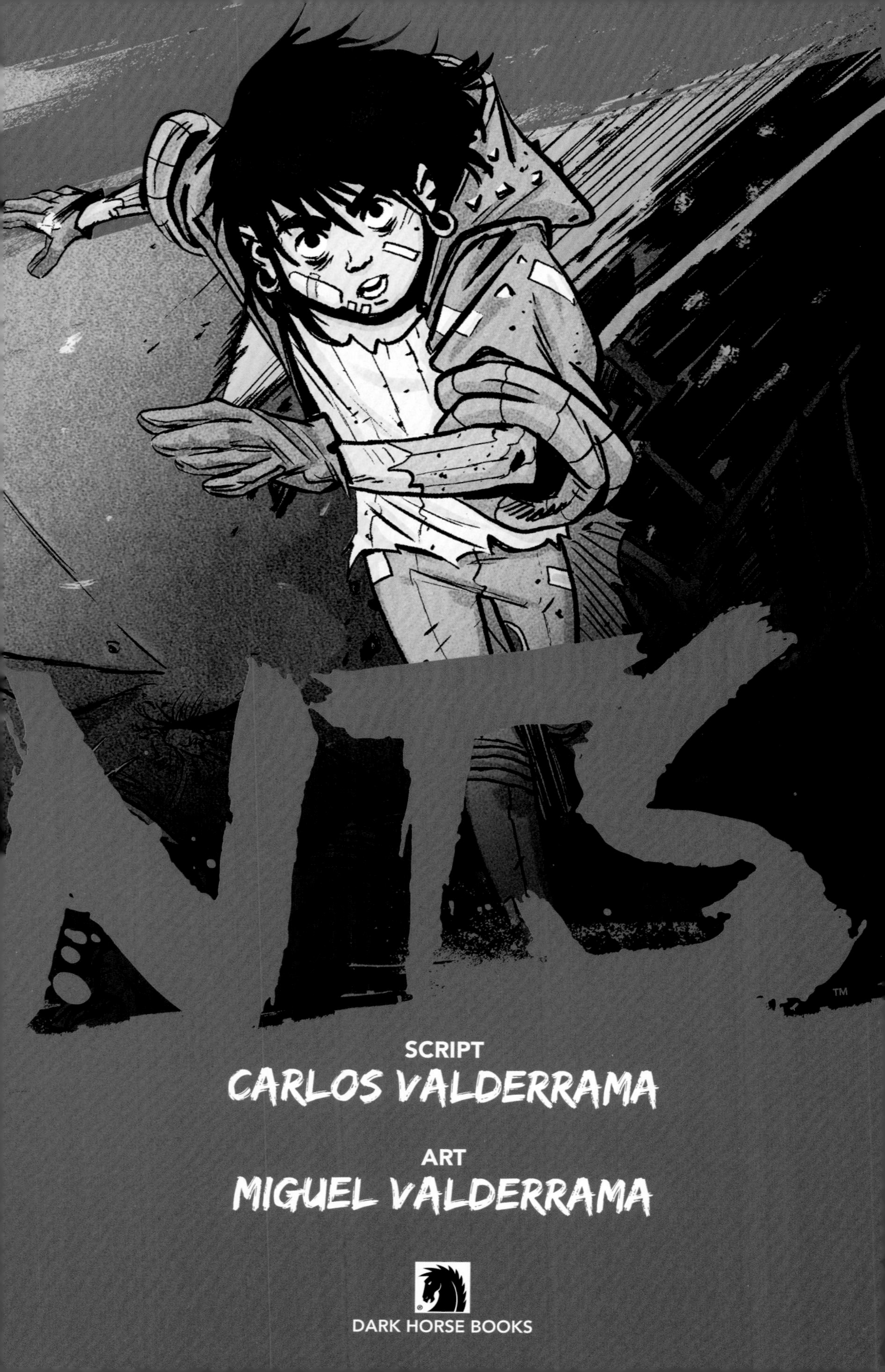

SCRIPT
CARLOS VALDERRAMA

ART
MIGUEL VALDERRAMA

DARK HORSE BOOKS

PRESIDENT AND PUBLISHER **MIKE RICHARDSON**   EDITOR **RANDY STRADLEY**

ASSISTANT EDITORS **KEVIN BURKHALTER** AND **KONNER KNUDSEN**

COLLECTION DESIGNER **ETHAN KIMBERLING**   DIGITAL ART TECHNICIAN **CHRISTINA McKENZIE**

Neil Hankerson *Executive Vice President* Tom Weddle *Chief Financial Officer* Randy Stradley *Vice President of Publishing* Nick McWhorter *Chief Business Development Officer* Matt Parkinson *Vice President of Marketing* Dale LaFountain *Vice President of Information Technology* Cara Niece *Vice President of Production and Scheduling* Mark Bernardi *Vice President of Book Trade and Digital Sales* Ken Lizzi *General Counsel* Dave Marshall *Editor in Chief* Davey Estrada *Editorial Director* Chris Warner *Senior Books Editor* Cary Grazzini *Director of Specialty Projects* Lia Ribacchi *Art Director* Vanessa Todd-Holmes *Director of Print Purchasing* Matt Dryer *Director of Digital Art and Prepress* Michael Gombos *Director of International Publishing and Licensing* Kari Yadro *Director of Custom Programs*

GIANTS

This volume collects the Dark Horse comic book series *Giants* #1–#5, originally published December 2017–April 2018.

Published by Dark Horse Books
A division of Dark Horse Comics, Inc.
10956 SE Main Street
Milwaukie, OR 97222

DarkHorse.com

To find a comics shop in your area, visit comicshoplocator.com

First edition: August 2018
ISBN 978-1-50670-624-5
Digital ISBN 978-1-50670-625-2

1 3 5 7 9 10 8 6 4 2
Printed in China

Library of Congress Cataloging-in-Publication Data

Names: Valderrama, Carlos, 1984- author, artist. | Valderrama, Miguel, 1988-
   author, artist.
Title: Giants / Carlos and Miguel Valderrama.
Description: First edition. | Milwaukie, OR : Dark Horse Books, August 2018.
Identifiers: LCCN 2018011863 | ISBN 9781506706245 (alk. paper)
Subjects: LCSH: Graphic novels.
Classification: LCC PN6728.G486 V35 2018 | DDC 741.5/973--dc23
LC record available at https://lccn.loc.gov/2018011863

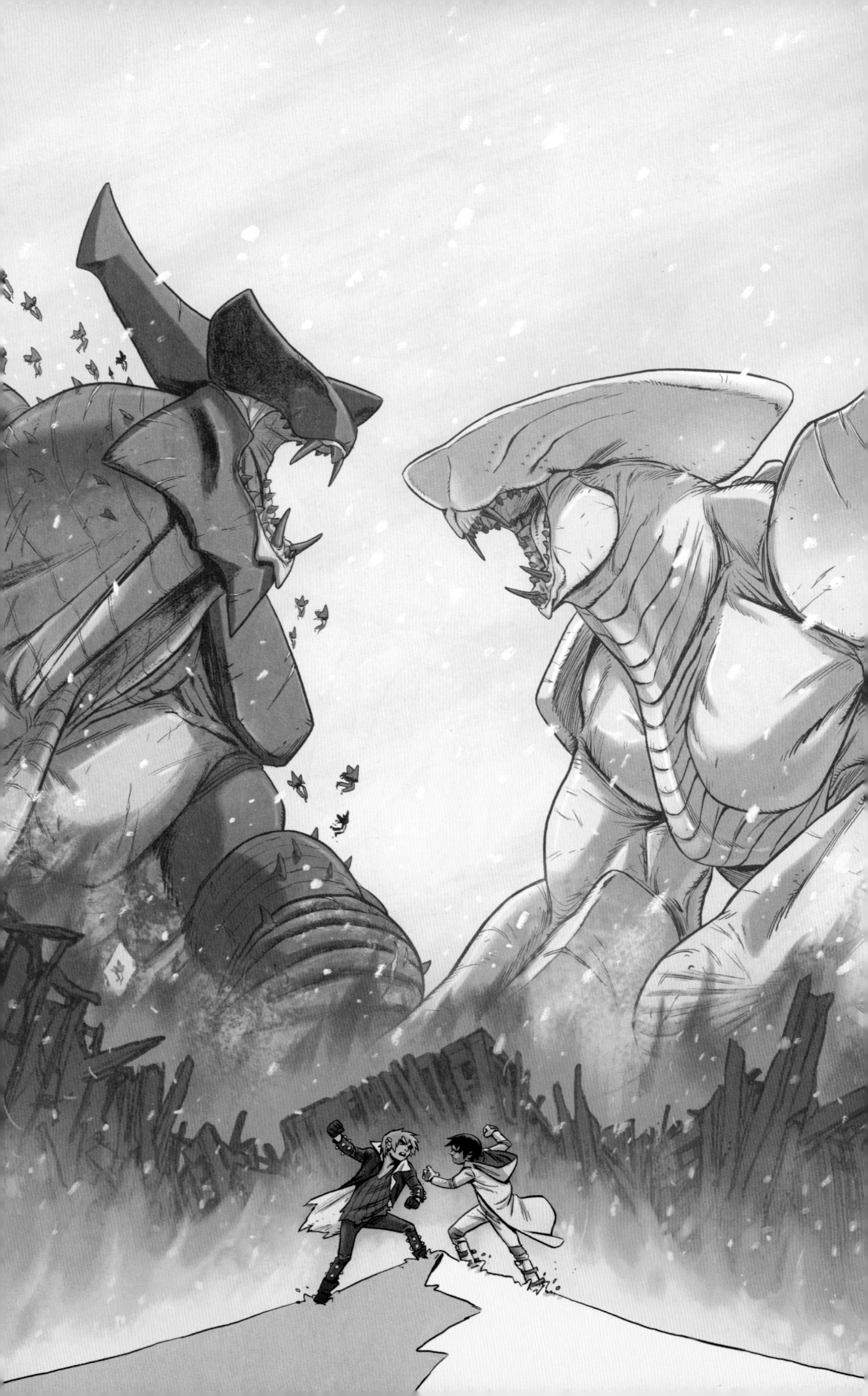

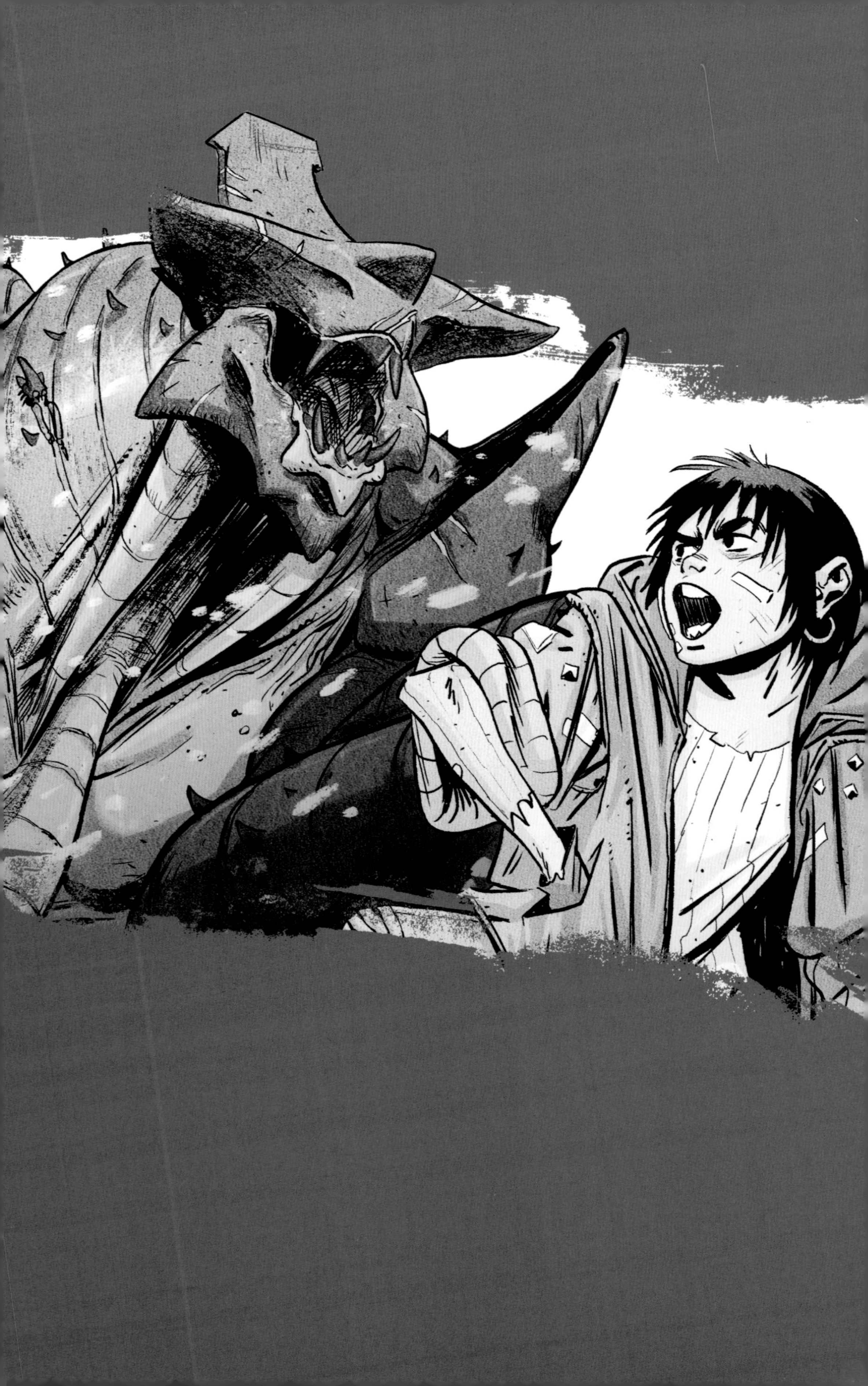

"SMALL THINGS DON'T MATTER.

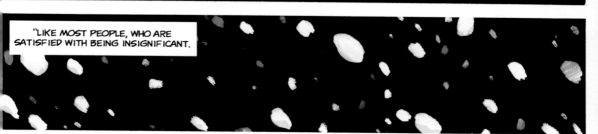

"LIKE MOST PEOPLE, WHO ARE SATISFIED WITH BEING INSIGNIFICANT.

"BUT THERE ARE ALWAYS THOSE WHO RISE ABOVE THE OTHERS.

"AND I'M SICK OF BEING JUST ANOTHER INSECT LIVING AMONG LARGER BEASTS, LIVING UNDER THEIR SHADOW.

"TODAY I FIGHT MY WAY TO THE TOP.

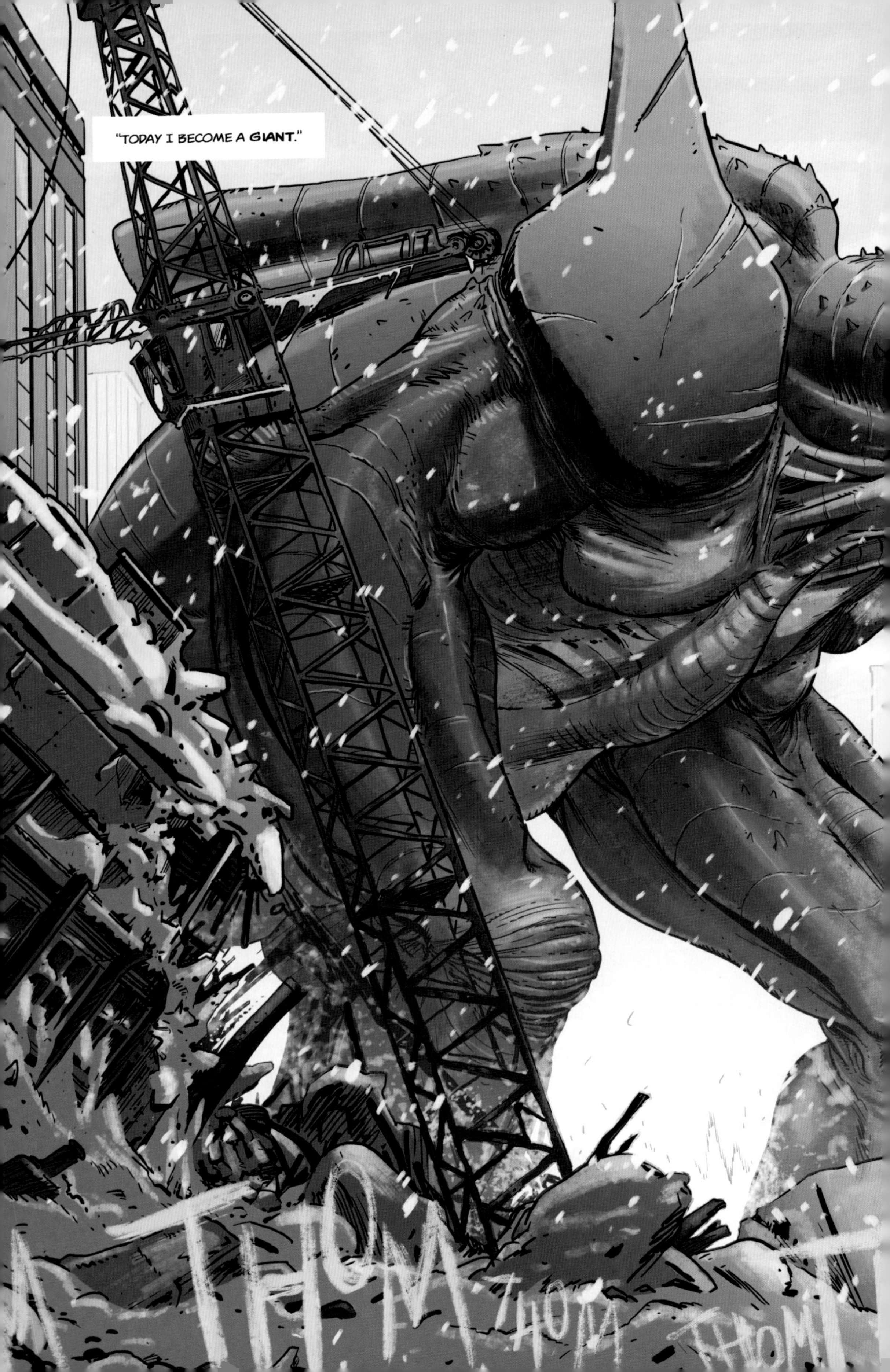
"TODAY I BECOME A GIANT."
THOM
THOM
THOM

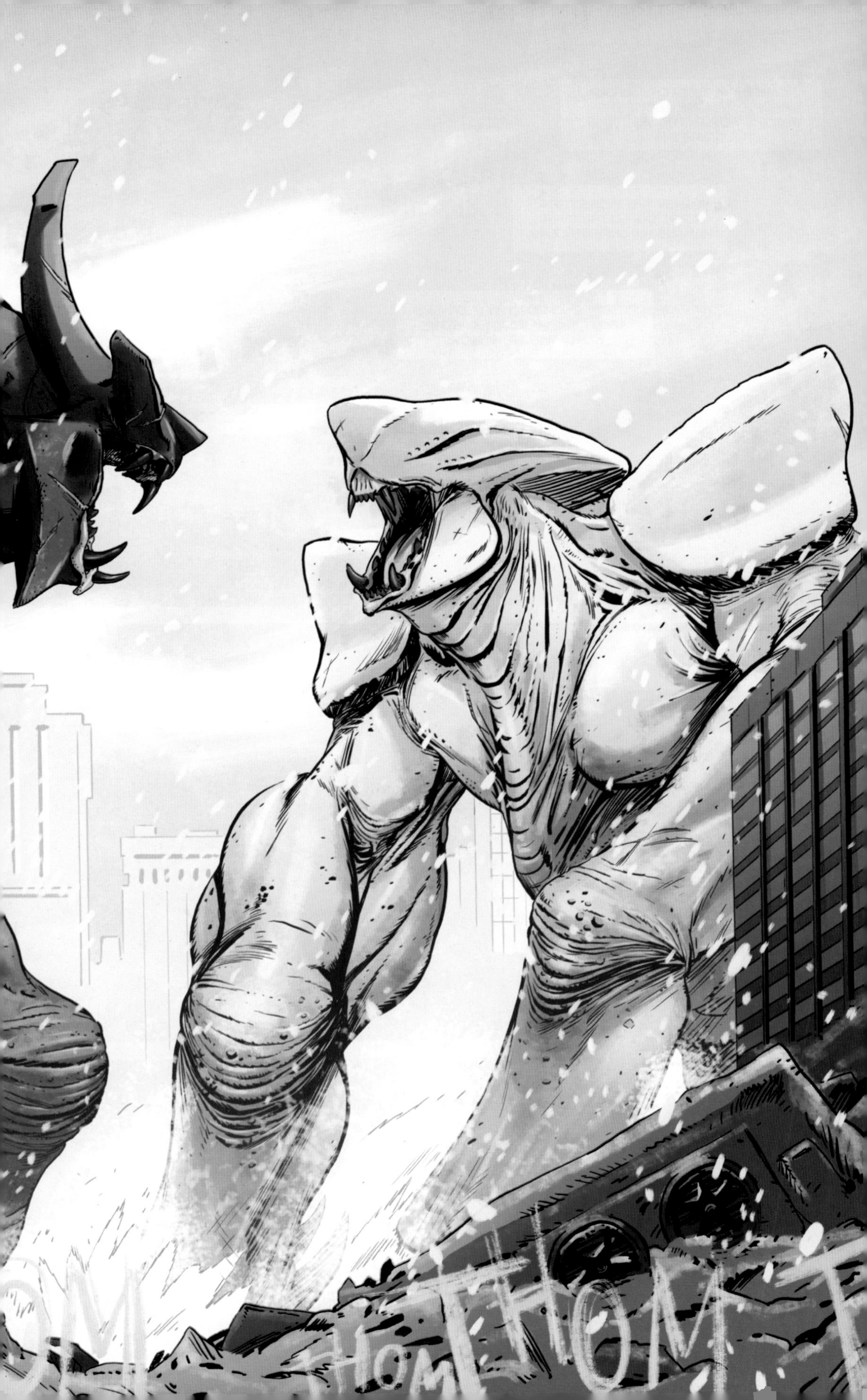
OM
THOM
THOM

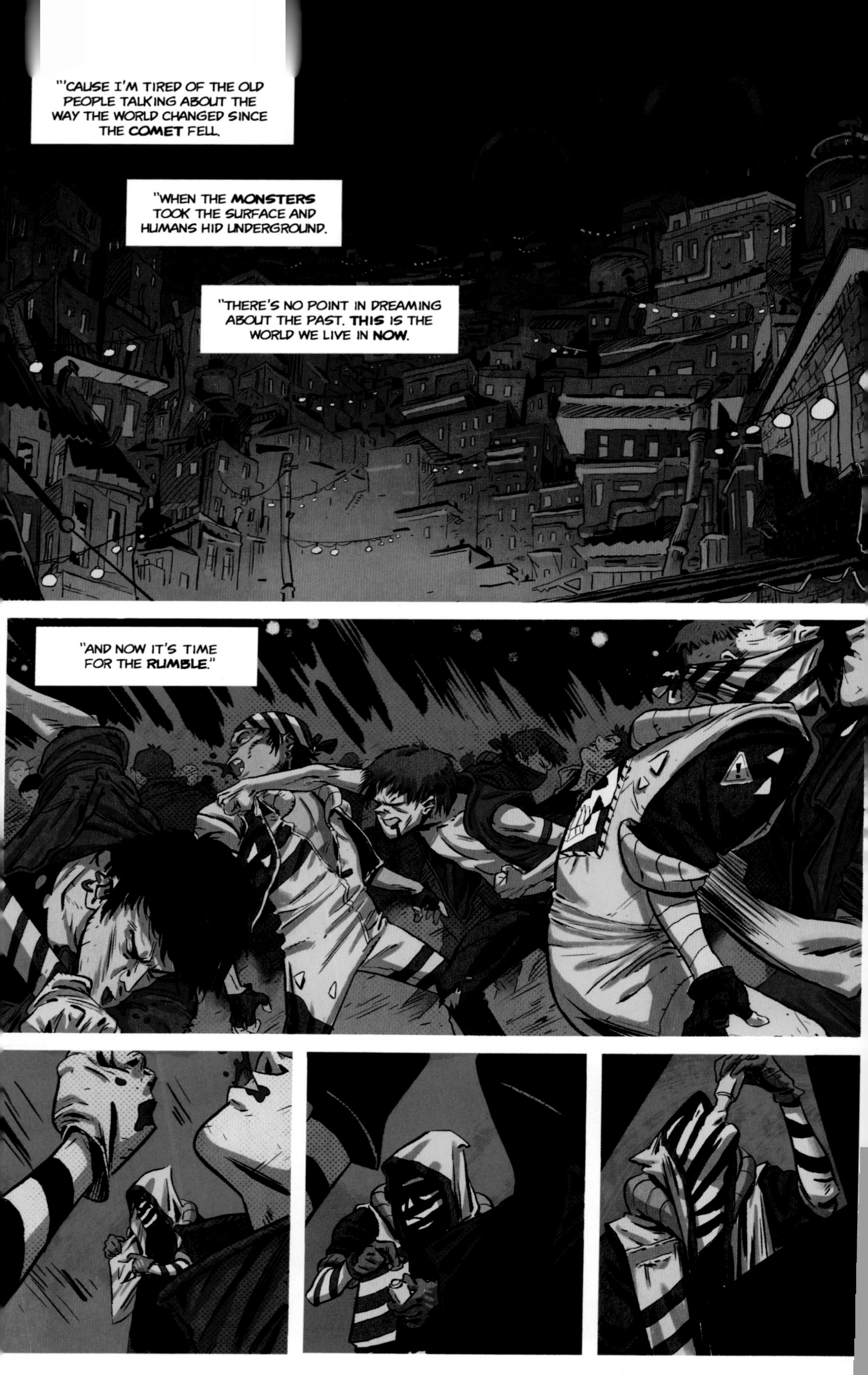
"'CAUSE I'M TIRED OF THE OLD PEOPLE TALKING ABOUT THE WAY THE WORLD CHANGED SINCE THE **COMET** FELL.
"WHEN THE **MONSTERS** TOOK THE SURFACE AND HUMANS HID UNDERGROUND.
"THERE'S NO POINT IN DREAMING ABOUT THE PAST. **THIS** IS THE WORLD WE LIVE IN **NOW**.
"AND NOW IT'S TIME FOR THE **RUMBLE**."

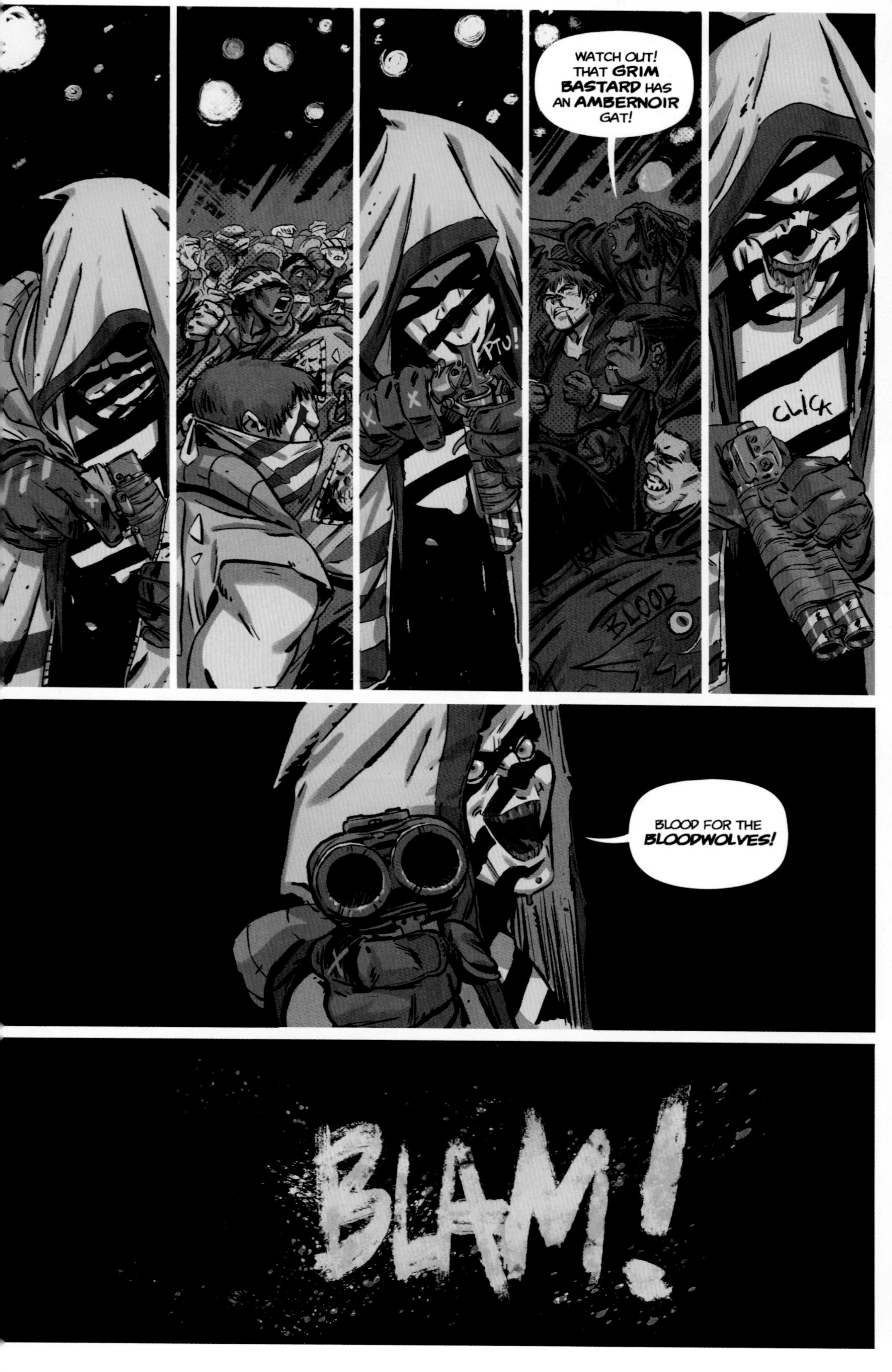
WATCH OUT! THAT GRIM BASTARD HAS AN AMBERNOIR GAT!
PTU!
BLOOD
CLICK
BLOOD FOR THE BLOODWOLVES!
BLAM!

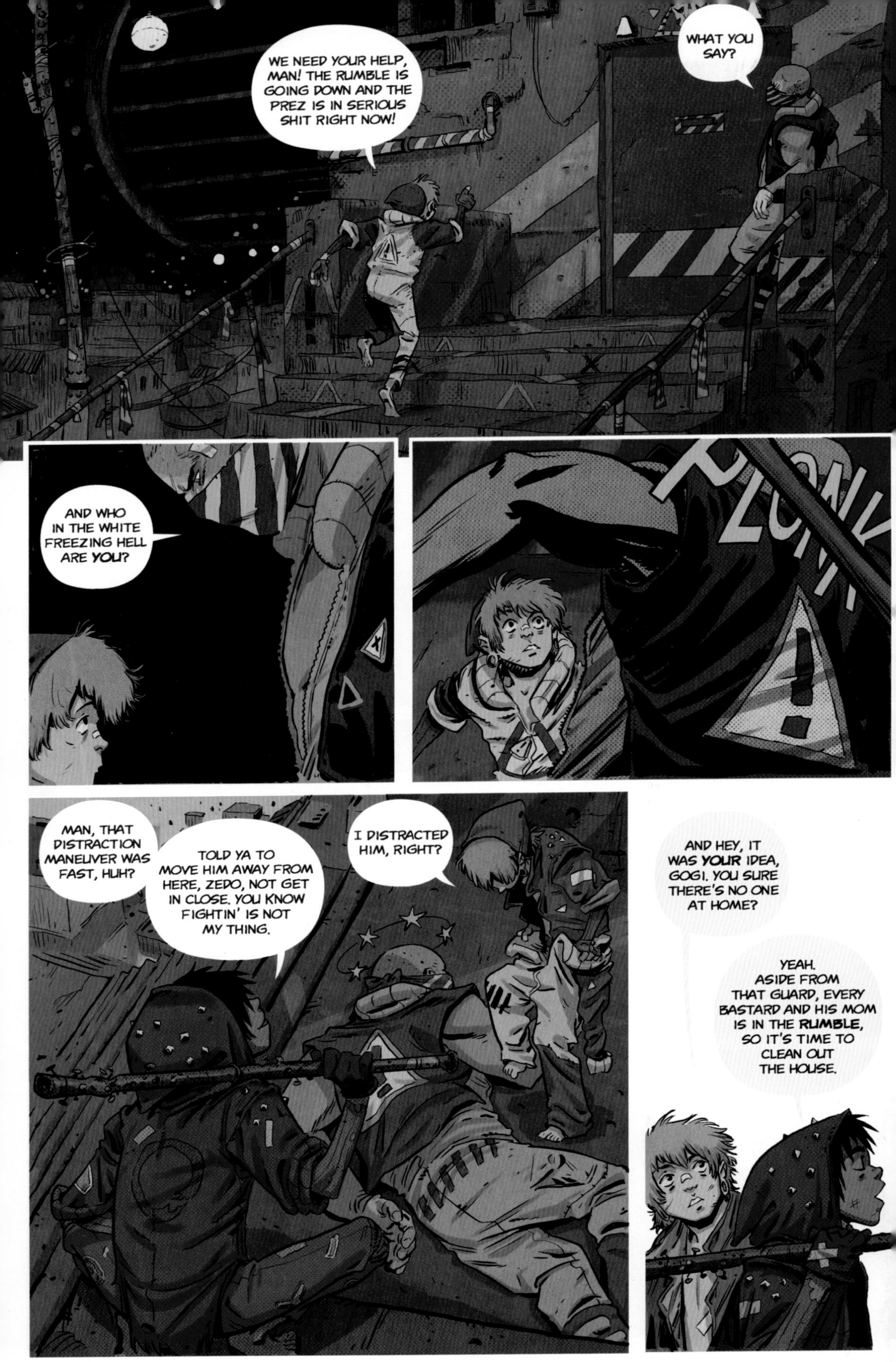
WE NEED YOUR HELP, MAN! THE RUMBLE IS GOING DOWN AND THE PREZ IS IN SERIOUS SHIT RIGHT NOW!
WHAT YOU SAY?
AND WHO IN THE WHITE FREEZING HELL ARE YOU?
PLONK
MAN, THAT DISTRACTION MANEUVER WAS FAST, HUH?
TOLD YA TO MOVE HIM AWAY FROM HERE, ZEDO, NOT GET IN CLOSE. YOU KNOW FIGHTIN' IS NOT MY THING.
I DISTRACTED HIM, RIGHT?
AND HEY, IT WAS YOUR IDEA, GOGI. YOU SURE THERE'S NO ONE AT HOME?
YEAH. ASIDE FROM THAT GUARD, EVERY BASTARD AND HIS MOM IS IN THE RUMBLE, SO IT'S TIME TO CLEAN OUT THE HOUSE.

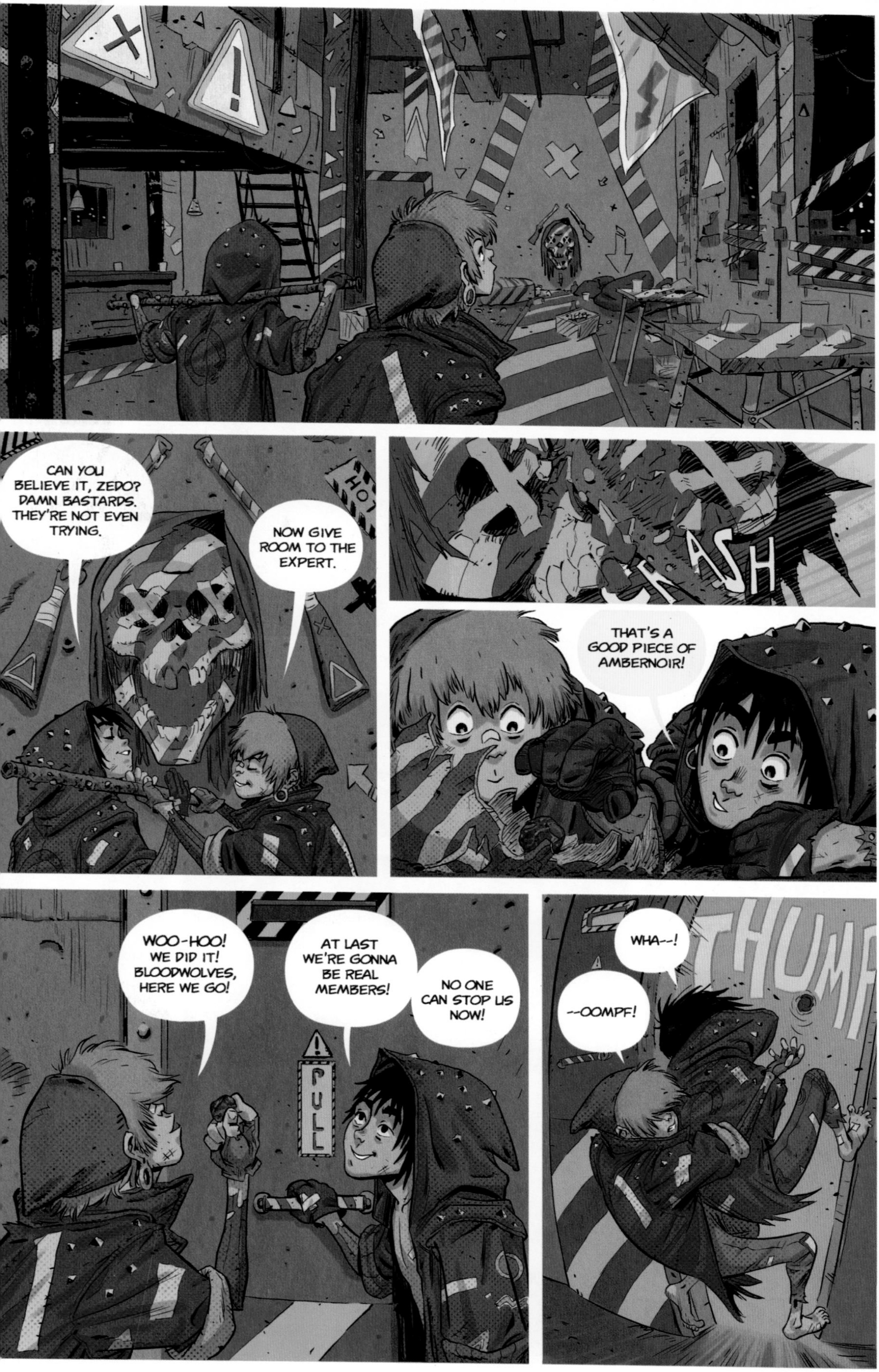
CAN YOU BELIEVE IT, ZEDO? DAMN BASTARDS. THEY'RE NOT EVEN TRYING.
NOW GIVE ROOM TO THE EXPERT.
CRASH
THAT'S A GOOD PIECE OF AMBERNOIR!
WOO-HOO! WE DID IT! BLOODWOLVES, HERE WE GO!
AT LAST WE'RE GONNA BE REAL MEMBERS!
PULL
NO ONE CAN STOP US NOW!
THUMP
WHA--!
--OOMPF!

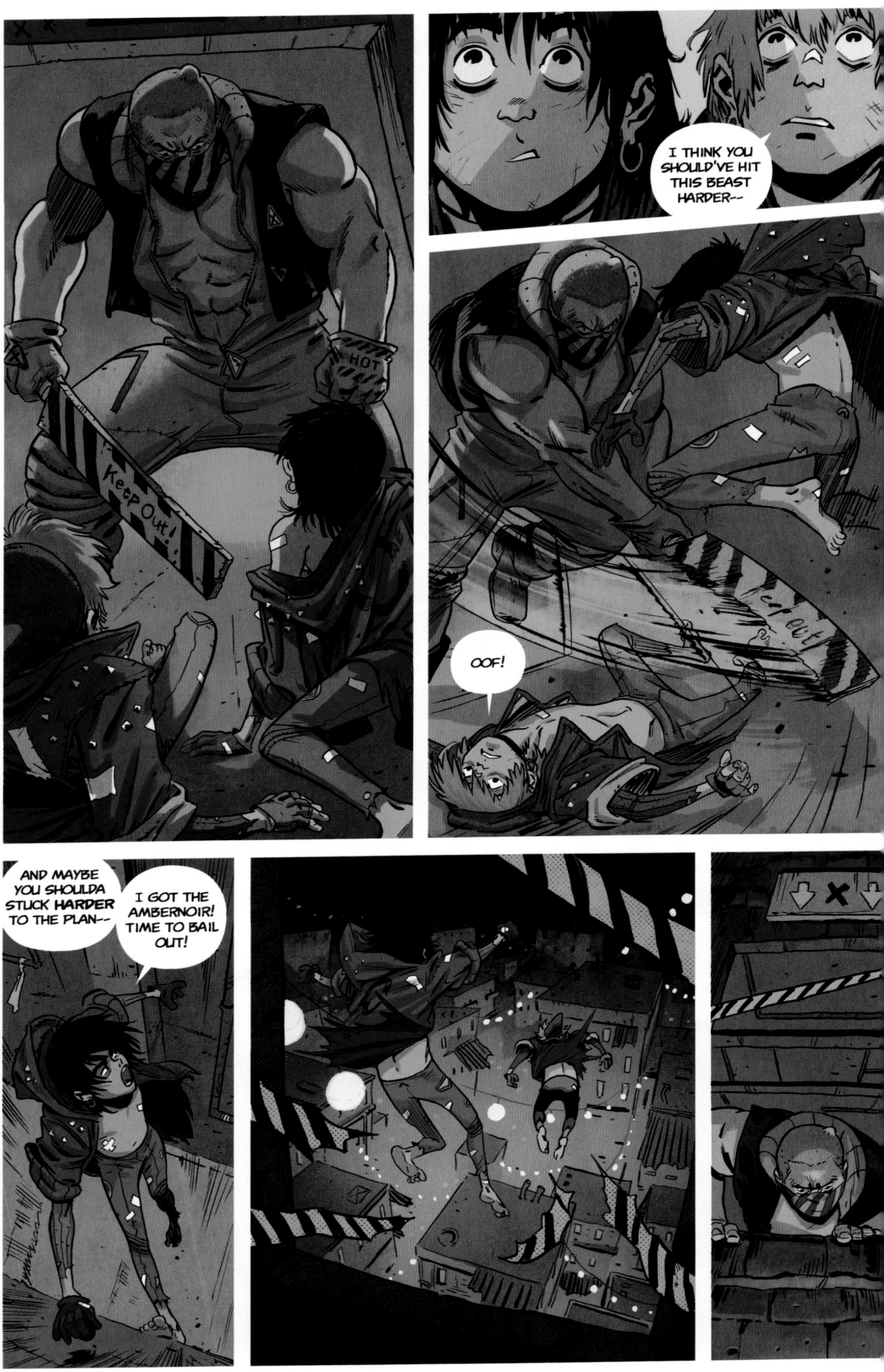
HOT
Keep Out!
I THINK YOU SHOULD'VE HIT THIS BEAST HARDER--
Keep Out
OOF!
AND MAYBE YOU SHOULDA STUCK HARDER TO THE PLAN--
I GOT THE AMBERNOIR! TIME TO BAIL OUT!

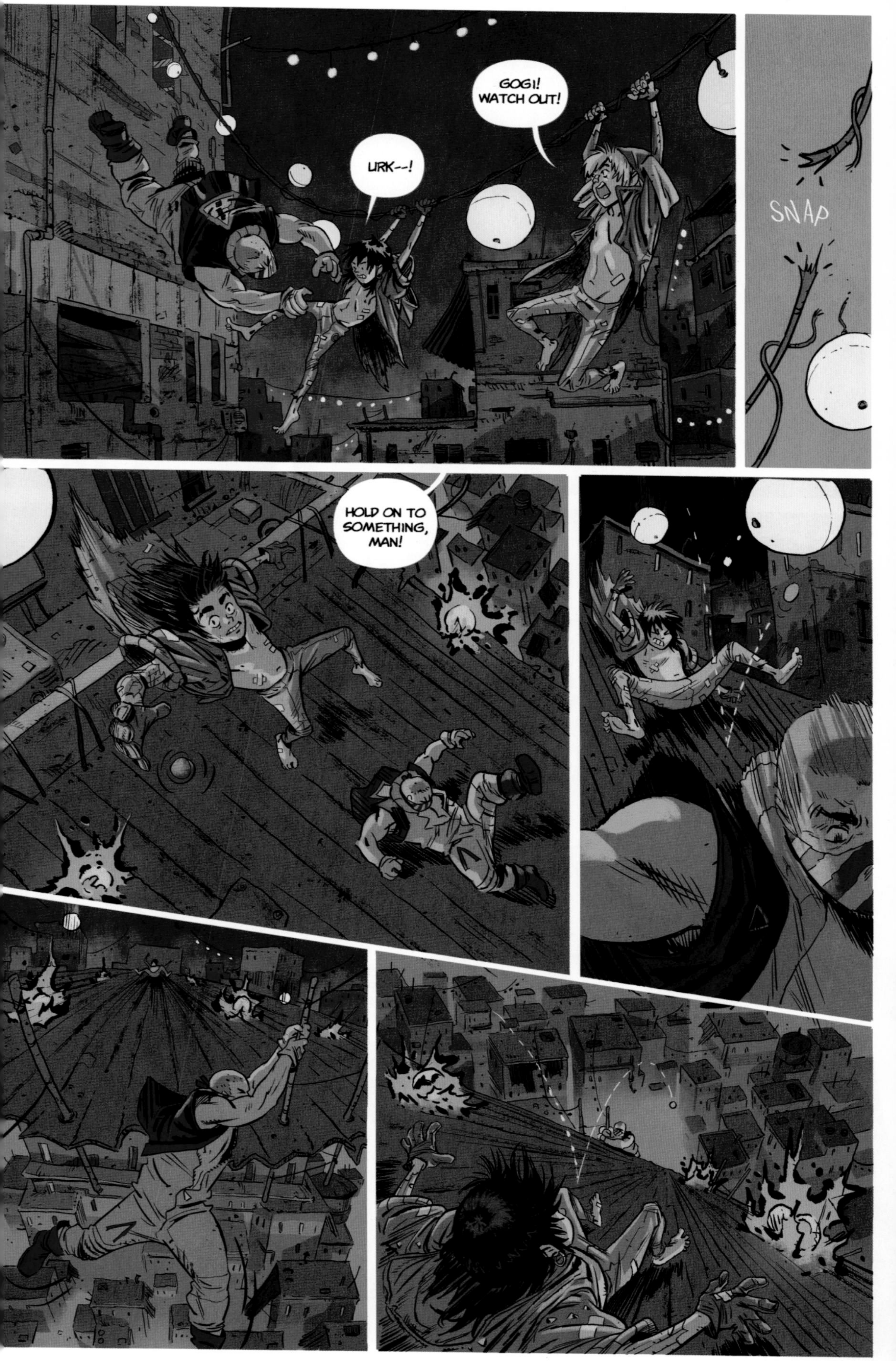
URK--!
GOGI! WATCH OUT!
SNAP
HOLD ON TO SOMETHING, MAN!

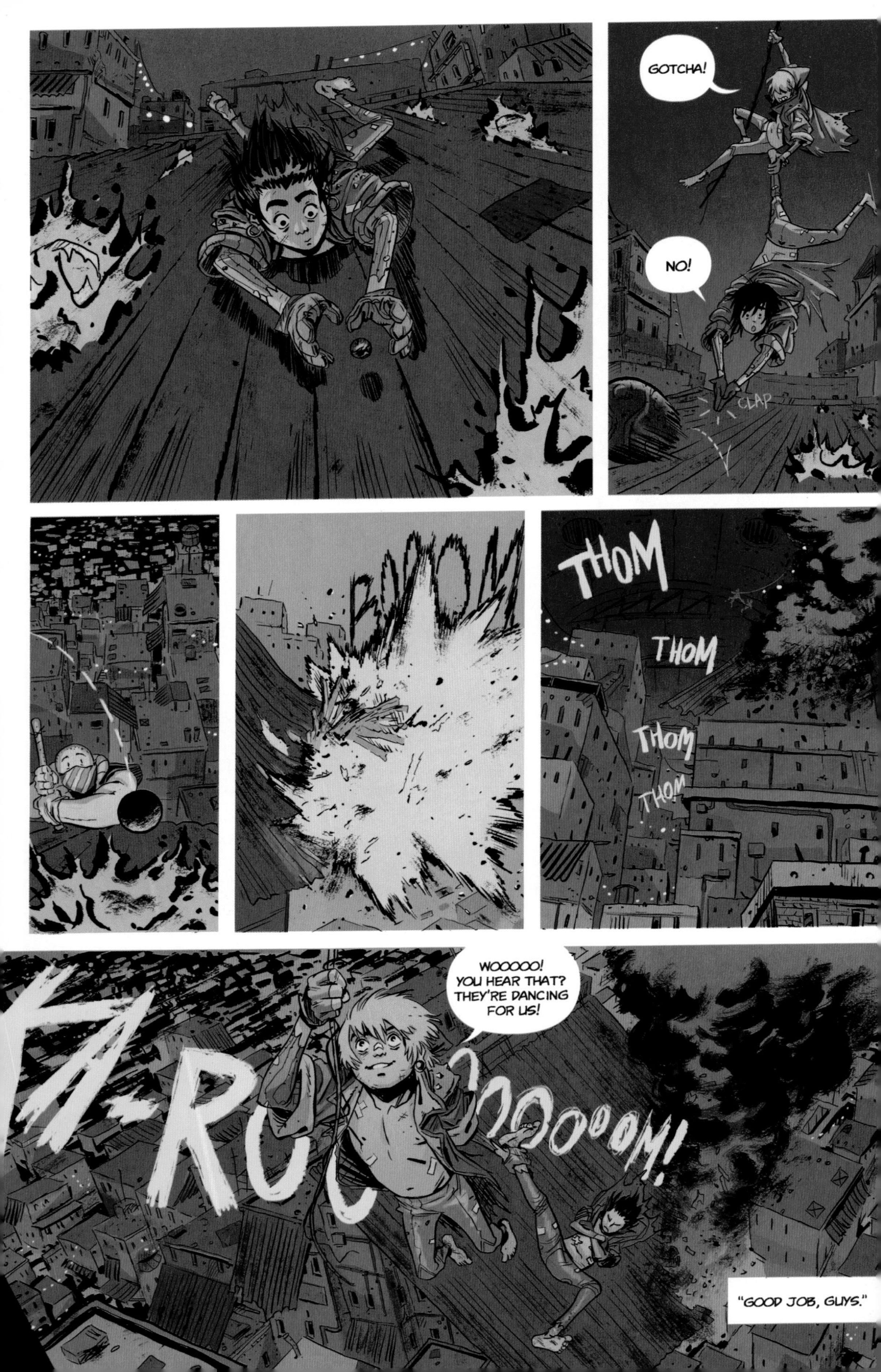
GOTCHA!
NO!
CLAP
BOOOM
THOM
THOM
THOM
THOM
WOOOOO! YOU HEAR THAT? THEY'RE DANCING FOR US!
KA-ROOOOOOOM!
"GOOD JOB, GUYS."

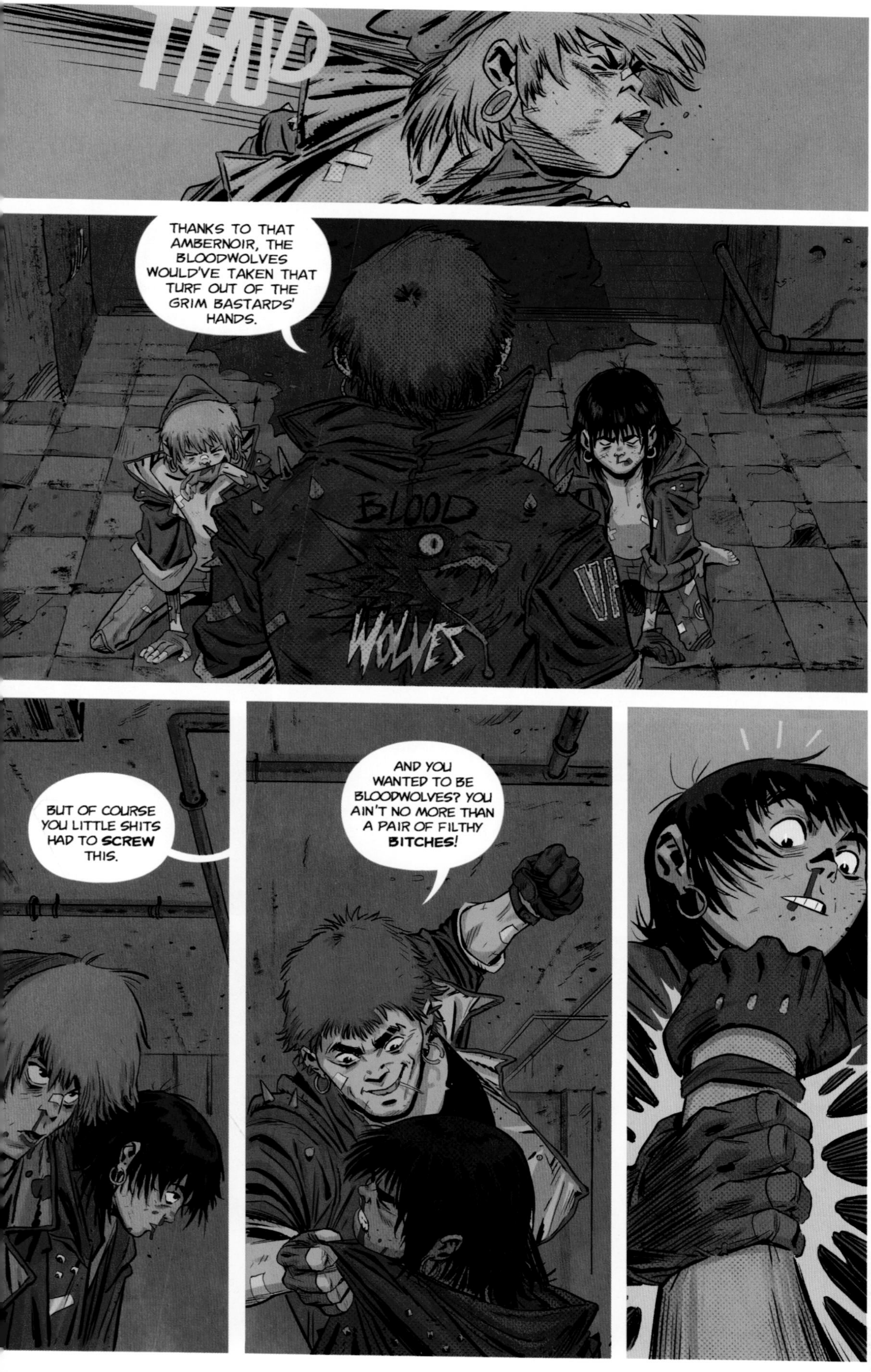
THUD
THANKS TO THAT AMBERNOIR, THE BLOODWOLVES WOULD'VE TAKEN THAT TURF OUT OF THE GRIM BASTARDS' HANDS.
BLOOD
WOLVES
BUT OF COURSE YOU LITTLE SHITS HAD TO **SCREW** THIS.
AND YOU WANTED TO BE BLOODWOLVES? YOU AIN'T NO MORE THAN A PAIR OF FILTHY **BITCHES**!

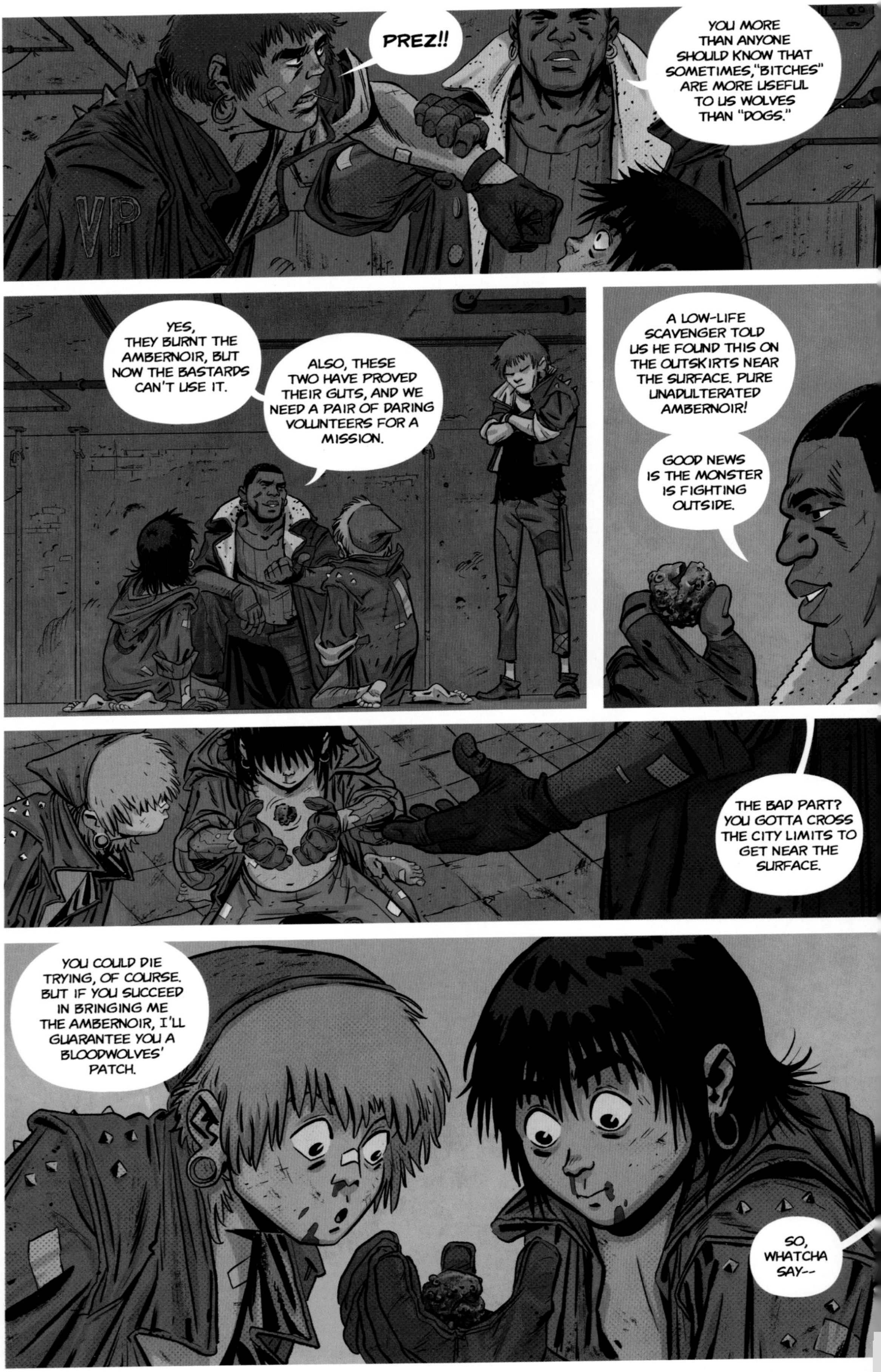
PREZ!!
YOU MORE THAN ANYONE SHOULD KNOW THAT SOMETIMES, "BITCHES" ARE MORE USEFUL TO US WOLVES THAN "DOGS."
YES, THEY BURNT THE AMBERNOIR, BUT NOW THE BASTARDS CAN'T USE IT.
ALSO, THESE TWO HAVE PROVED THEIR GUTS, AND WE NEED A PAIR OF DARING VOLUNTEERS FOR A MISSION.
A LOW-LIFE SCAVENGER TOLD US HE FOUND THIS ON THE OUTSKIRTS NEAR THE SURFACE. PURE UNADULTERATED AMBERNOIR!
GOOD NEWS IS THE MONSTER IS FIGHTING OUTSIDE.
THE BAD PART? YOU GOTTA CROSS THE CITY LIMITS TO GET NEAR THE SURFACE.
YOU COULD DIE TRYING, OF COURSE. BUT IF YOU SUCCEED IN BRINGING ME THE AMBERNOIR, I'LL GUARANTEE YOU A BLOODWOLVES' PATCH.
SO, WHATCHA SAY--

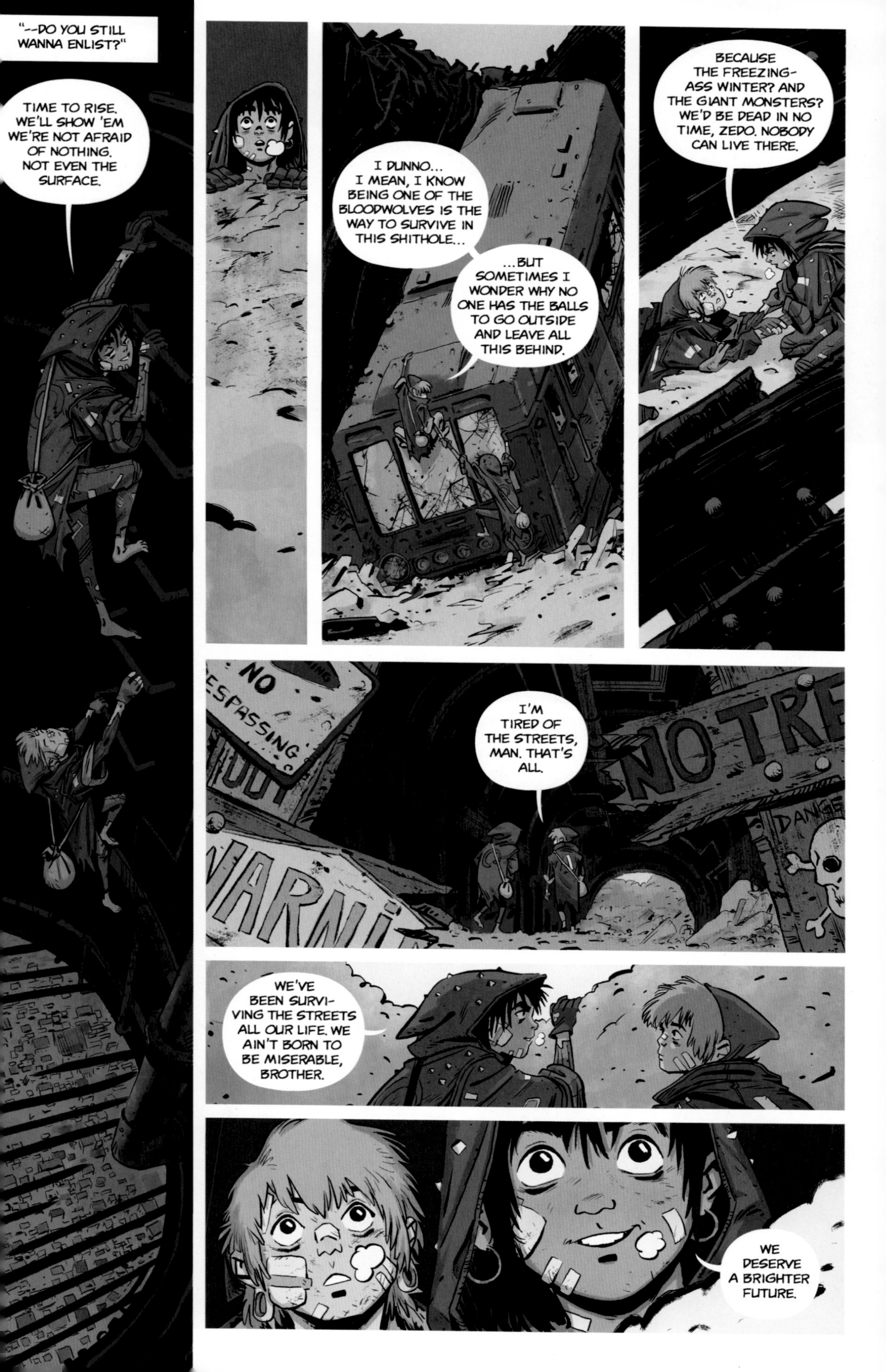
"--DO YOU STILL WANNA ENLIST?"
TIME TO RISE. WE'LL SHOW 'EM WE'RE NOT AFRAID OF NOTHING. NOT EVEN THE SURFACE.
I DUNNO... I MEAN, I KNOW BEING ONE OF THE BLOODWOLVES IS THE WAY TO SURVIVE IN THIS SHITHOLE...
...BUT SOMETIMES I WONDER WHY NO ONE HAS THE BALLS TO GO OUTSIDE AND LEAVE ALL THIS BEHIND.
BECAUSE THE FREEZING-ASS WINTER? AND THE GIANT MONSTERS? WE'D BE DEAD IN NO TIME, ZEDO. NOBODY CAN LIVE THERE.
NO TRESPASSING
NO TRE
WARNI
DANGE
I'M TIRED OF THE STREETS, MAN. THAT'S ALL.
WE'VE BEEN SURVIVING THE STREETS ALL OUR LIFE. WE AIN'T BORN TO BE MISERABLE, BROTHER.
WE DESERVE A BRIGHTER FUTURE.

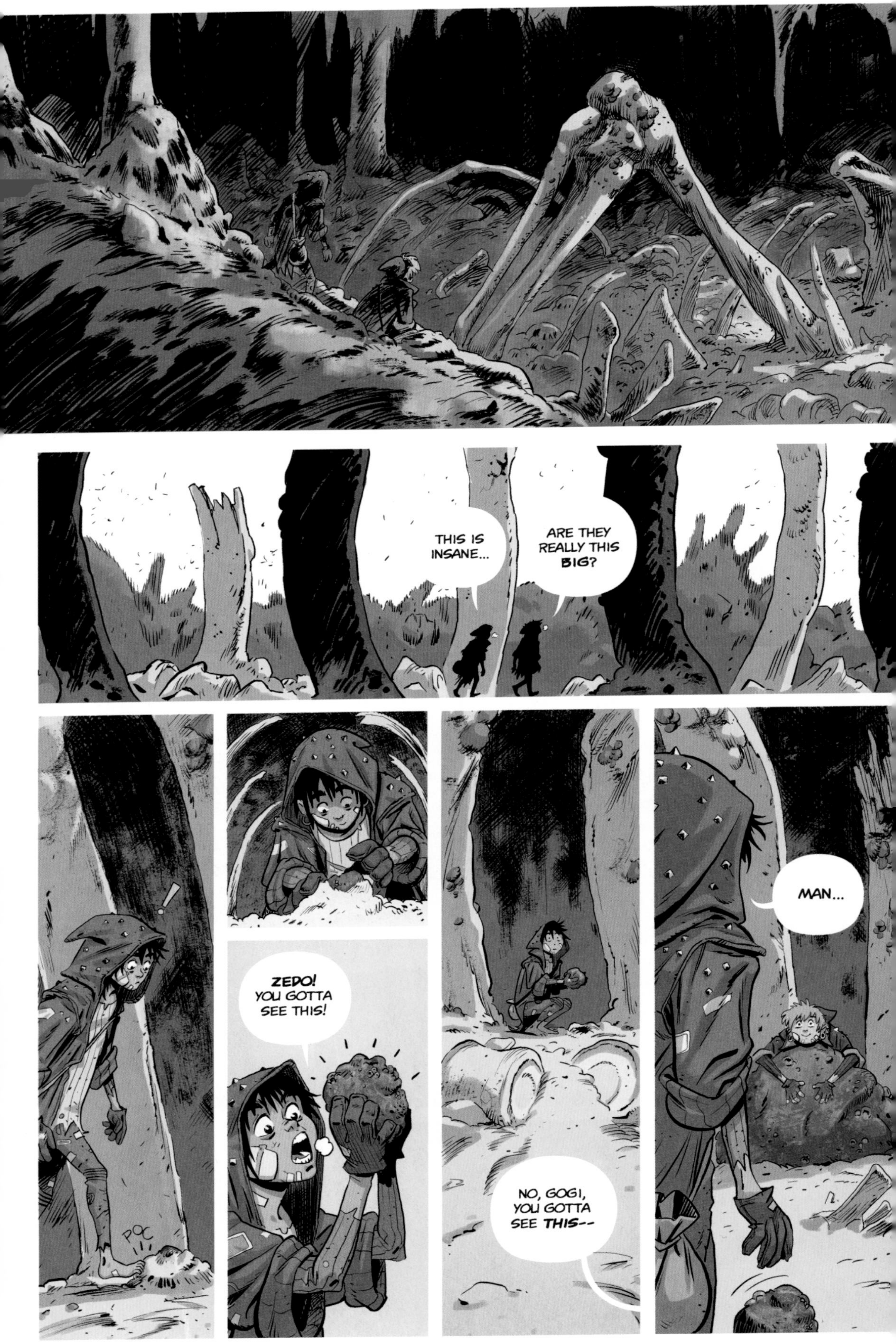
THIS IS INSANE...
ARE THEY REALLY THIS BIG?
POC
ZEDO! YOU GOTTA SEE THIS!
NO, GOGI, YOU GOTTA SEE THIS--
MAN...

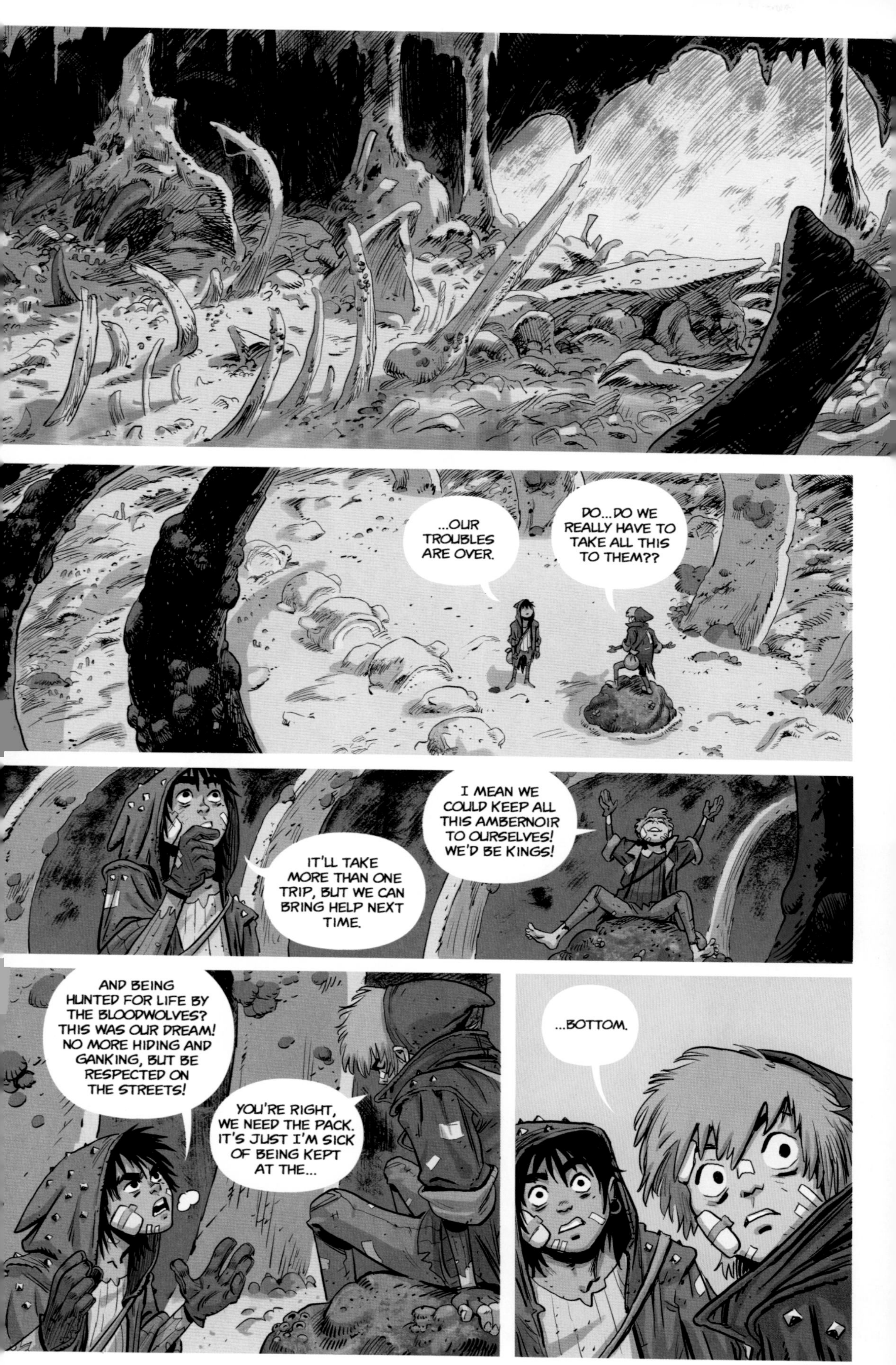
...OUR TROUBLES ARE OVER.
DO...DO WE REALLY HAVE TO TAKE ALL THIS TO THEM??
I MEAN WE COULD KEEP ALL THIS AMBERNOIR TO OURSELVES! WE'D BE KINGS!
IT'LL TAKE MORE THAN ONE TRIP, BUT WE CAN BRING HELP NEXT TIME.
AND BEING HUNTED FOR LIFE BY THE BLOODWOLVES? THIS WAS OUR DREAM! NO MORE HIDING AND GANKING, BUT BE RESPECTED ON THE STREETS!
YOU'RE RIGHT, WE NEED THE PACK. IT'S JUST I'M SICK OF BEING KEPT AT THE...
...BOTTOM.

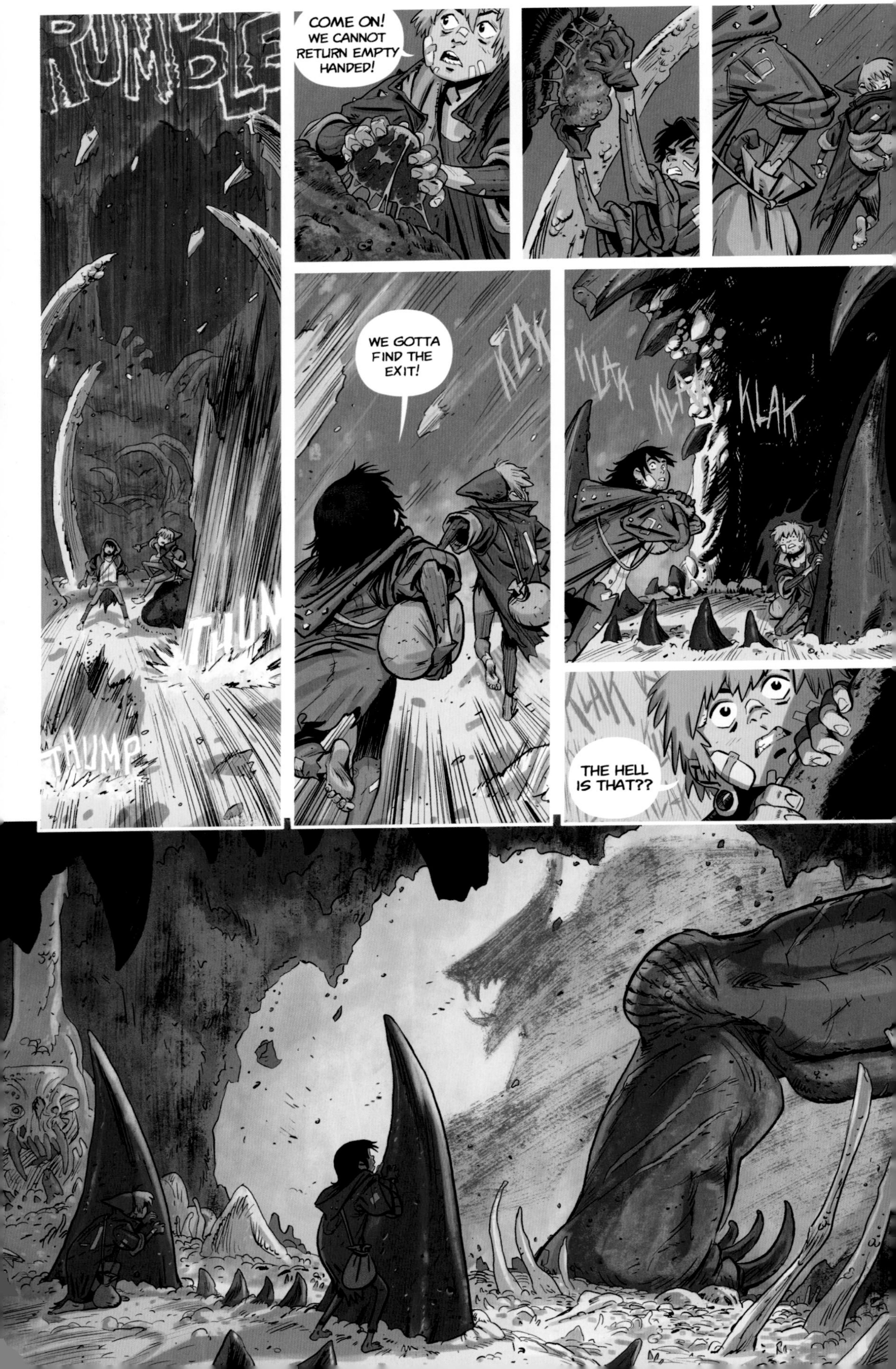

RUMBLE
THUMP
THUMP
COME ON! WE CANNOT RETURN EMPTY HANDED!
WE GOTTA FIND THE EXIT!
KLAK
KLAK
KLAK
KLAK
THE HELL IS THAT??

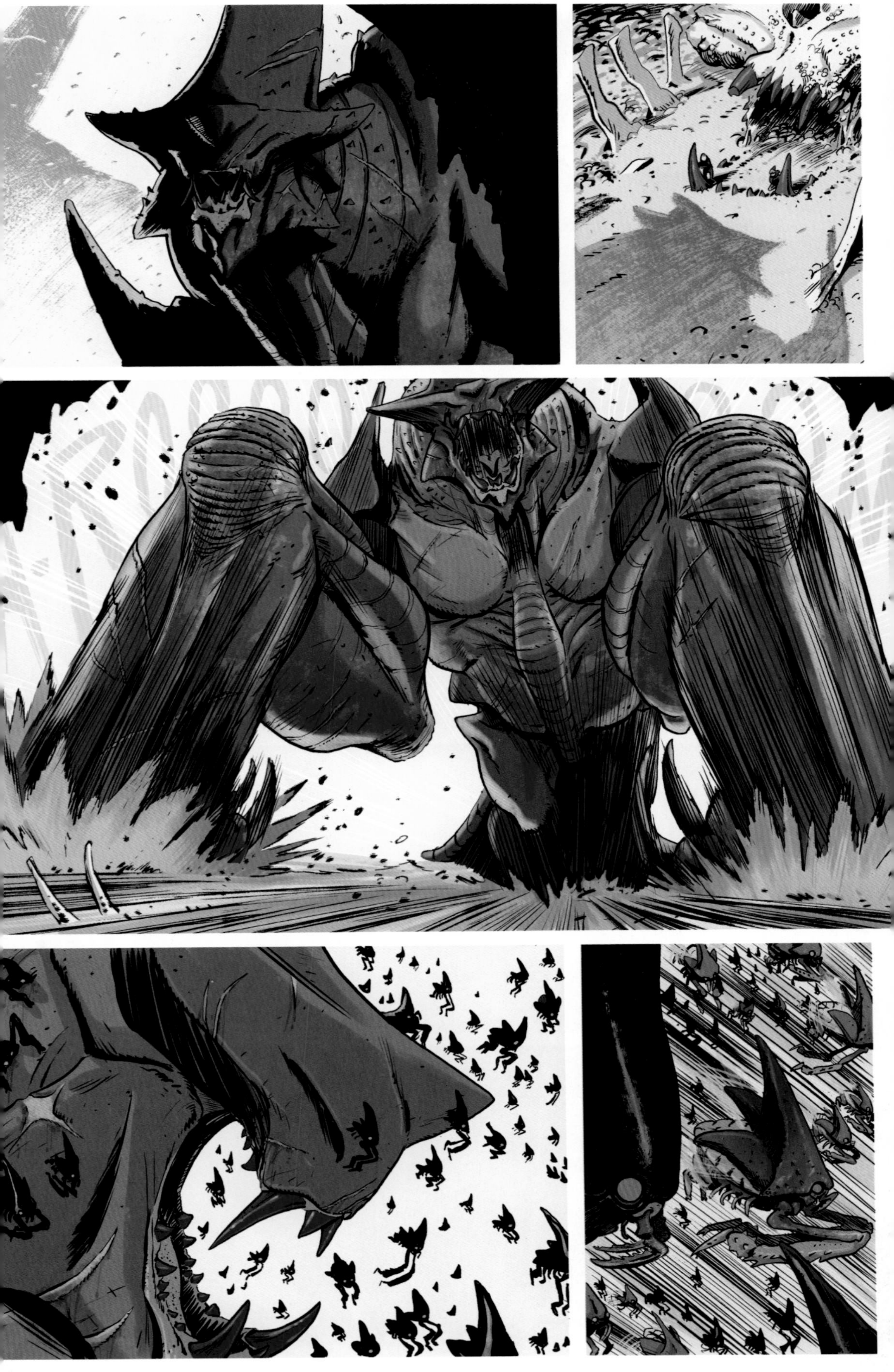

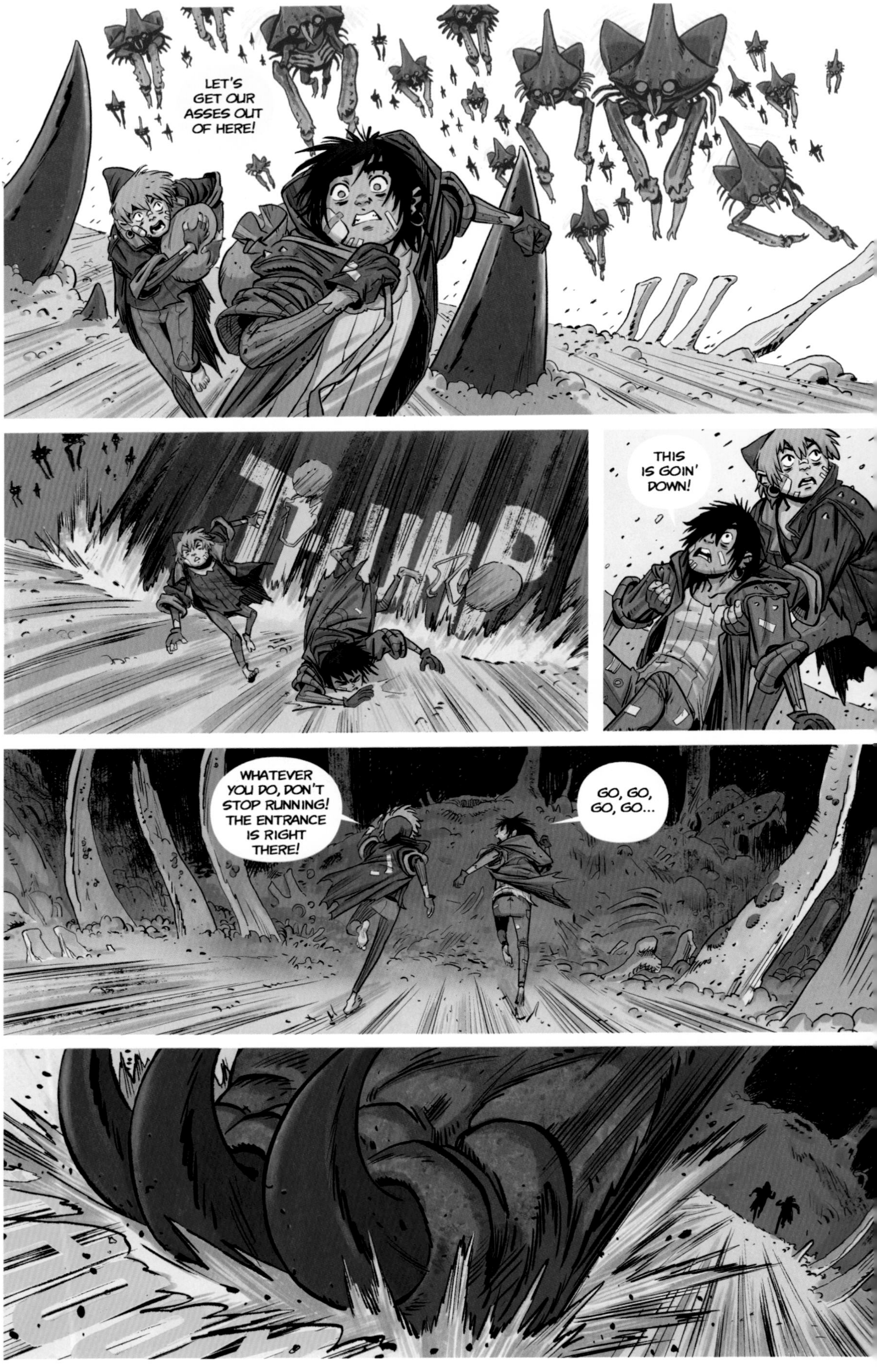
LET'S GET OUR ASSES OUT OF HERE!
THUMP
THIS IS GOIN' DOWN!
WHATEVER YOU DO, DON'T STOP RUNNING! THE ENTRANCE IS RIGHT THERE!
GO, GO, GO, GO...

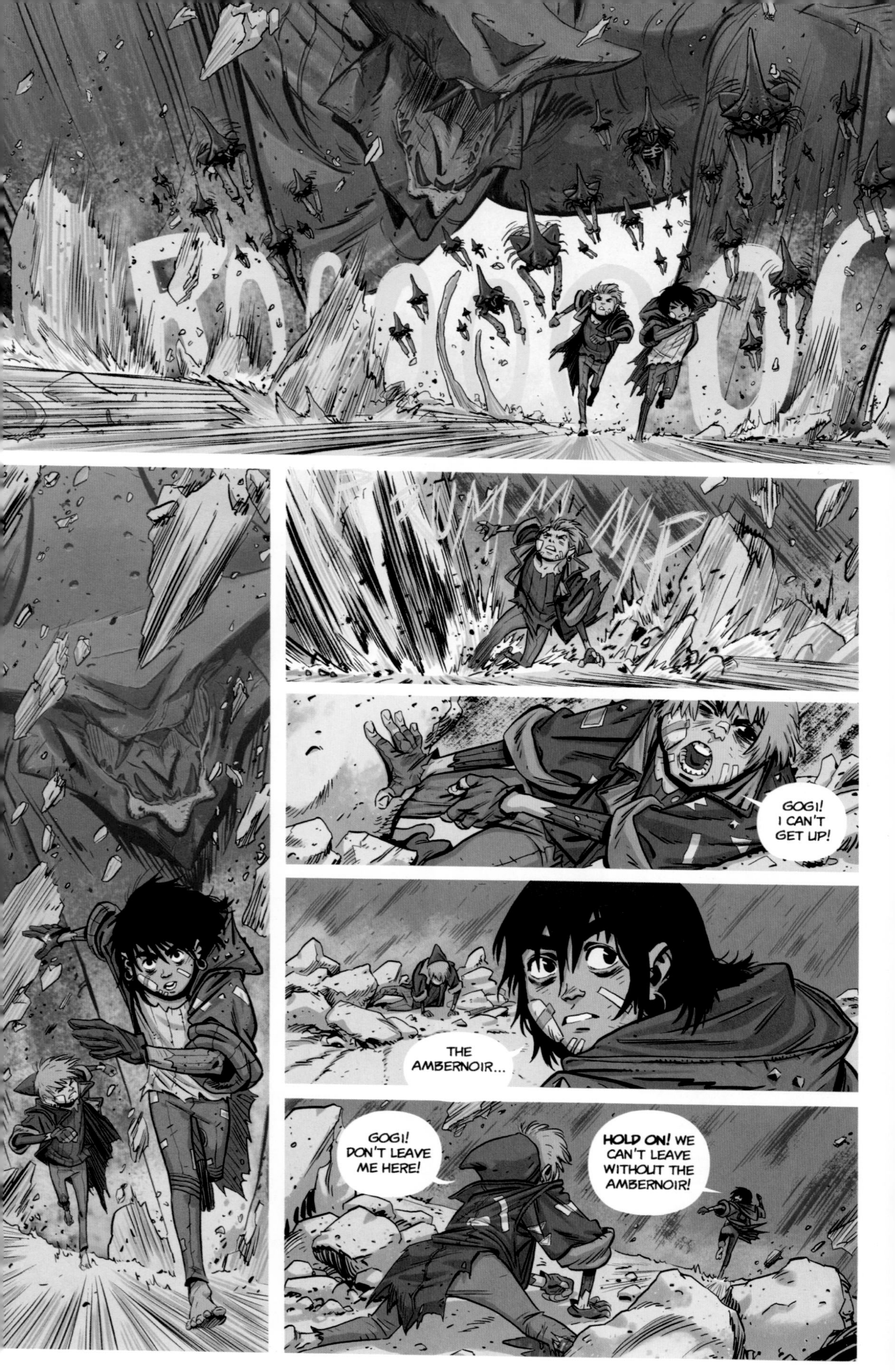
ROOOOOOOO
BRUMMMP
GOGI! I CAN'T GET UP!
THE AMBERNOIR...
GOGI! DON'T LEAVE ME HERE!
HOLD ON! WE CAN'T LEAVE WITHOUT THE AMBERNOIR!

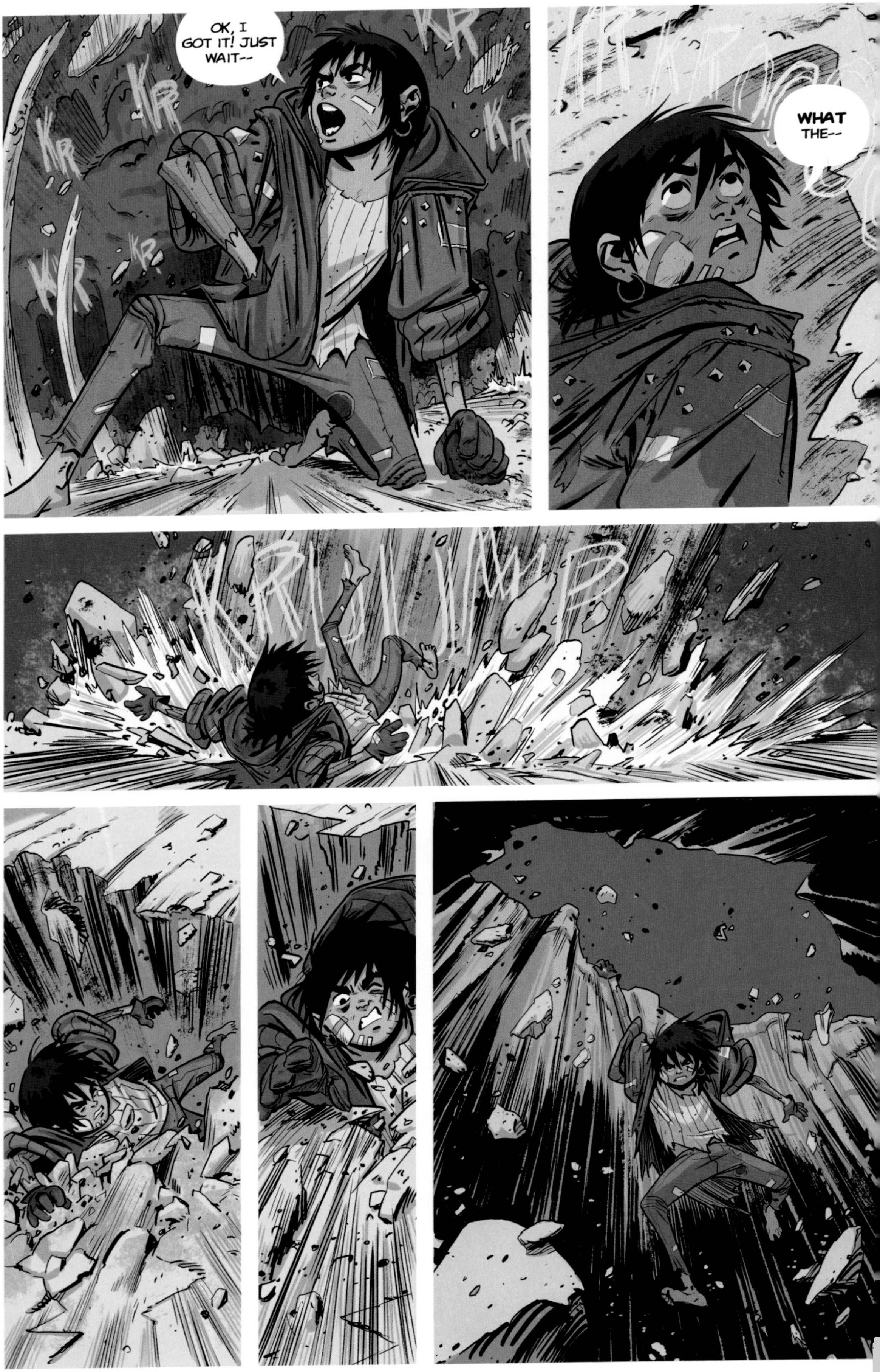
OK, I GOT IT! JUST WAIT--
KR
KR
KR
KR
KR
KR
KR
KR
WHAT THE--
KRUMP

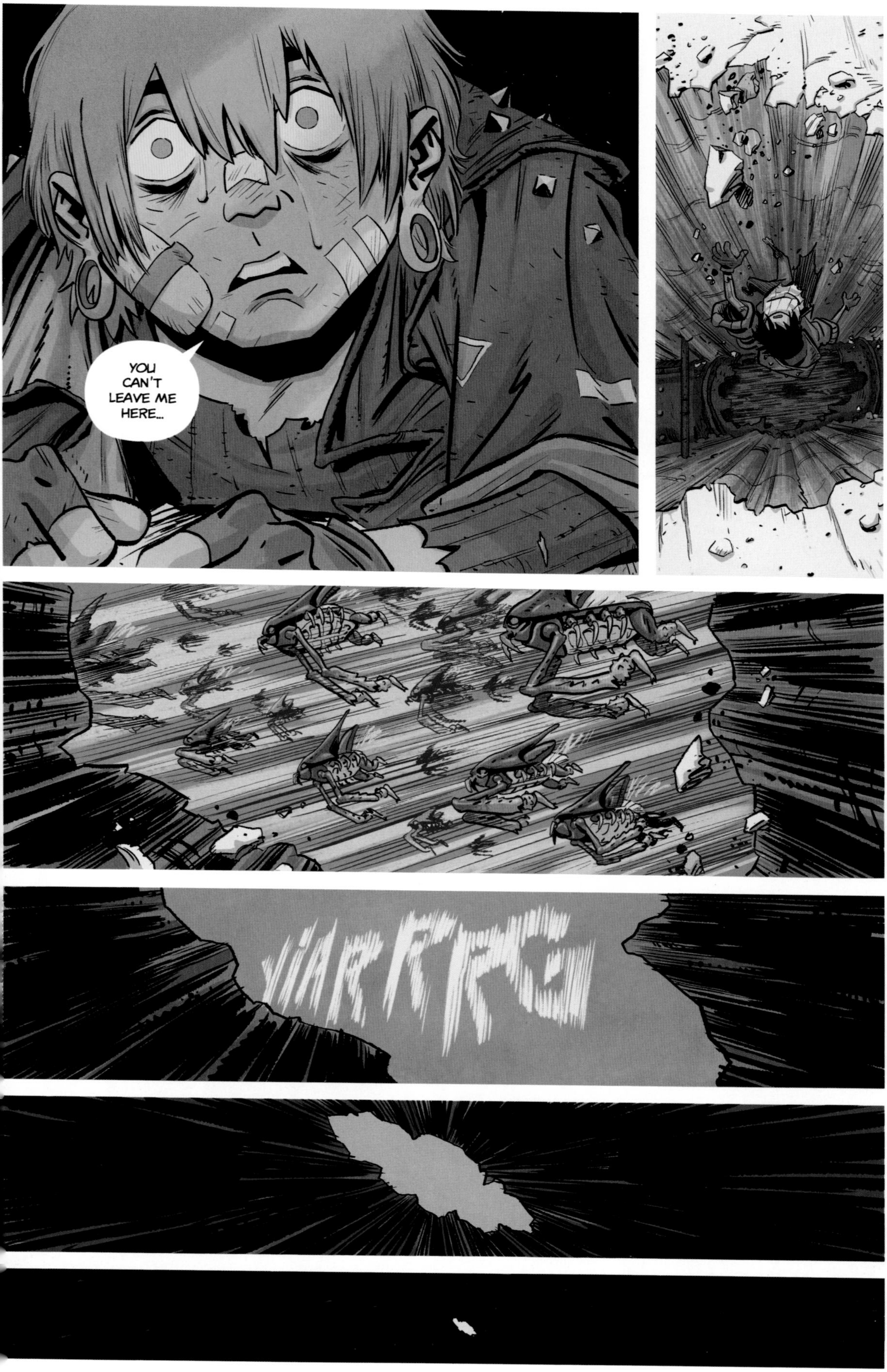
YOU CAN'T LEAVE ME HERE...
VRRRRG

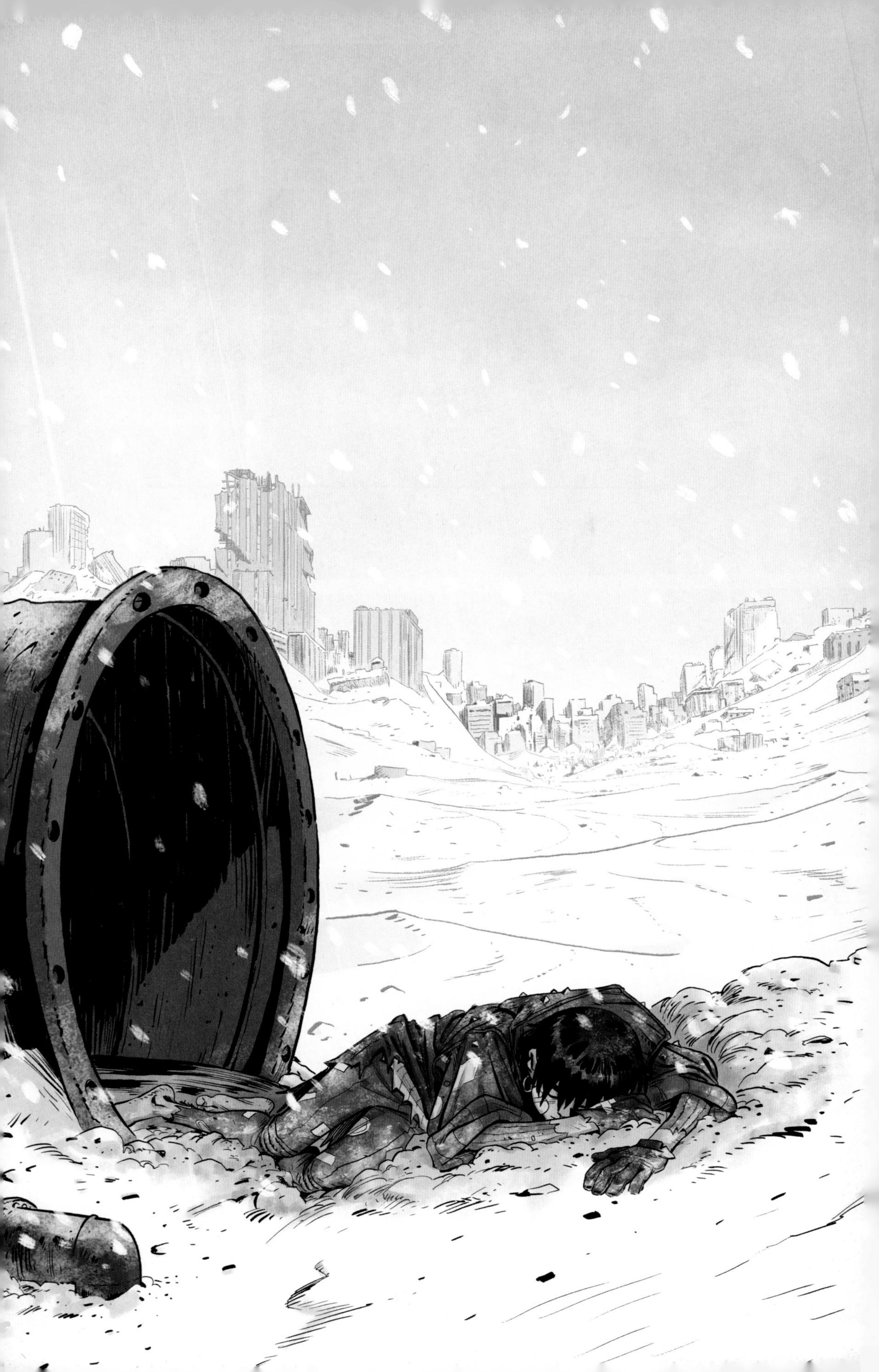

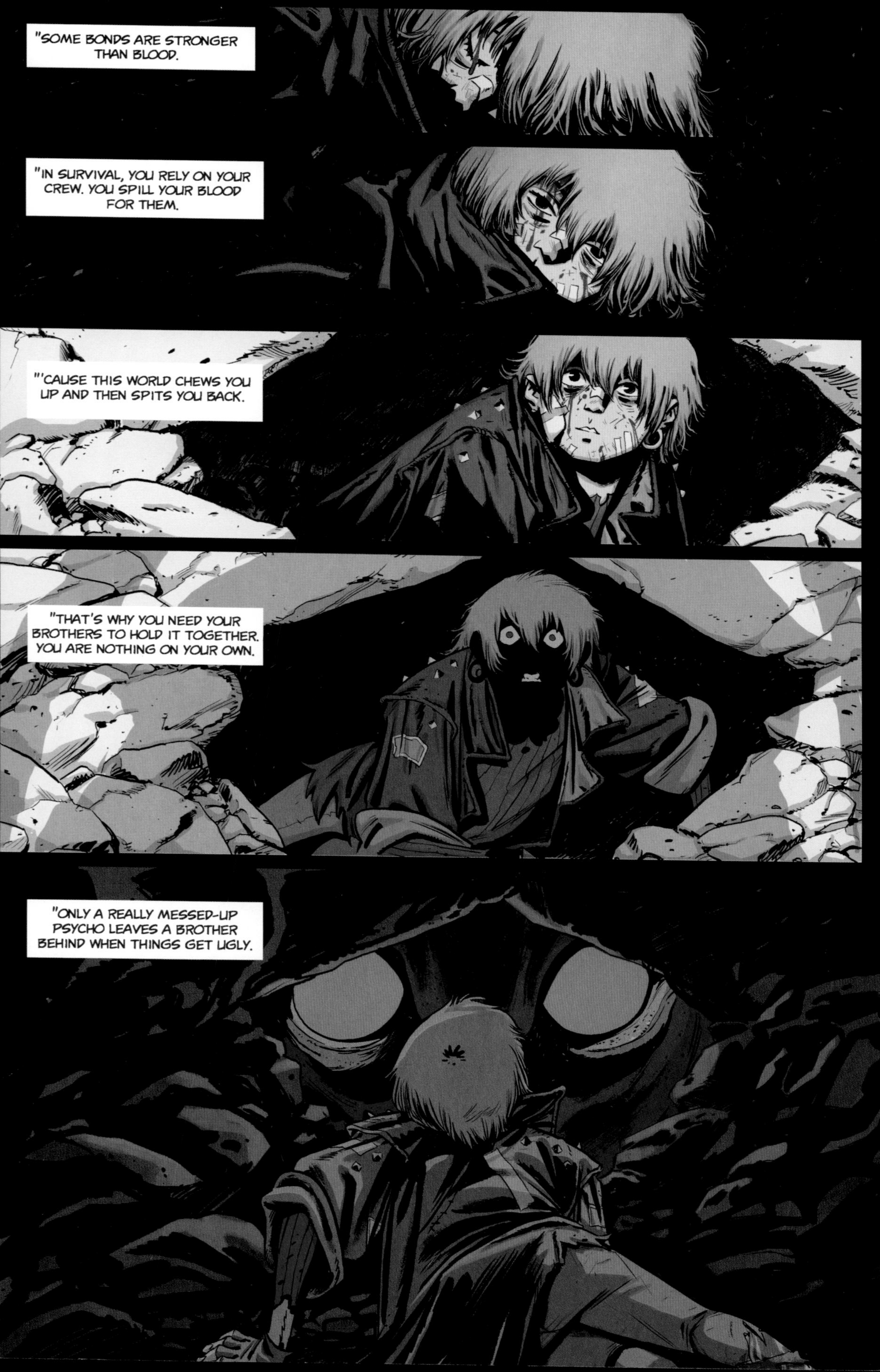
"SOME BONDS ARE STRONGER THAN BLOOD.
"IN SURVIVAL, YOU RELY ON YOUR CREW. YOU SPILL YOUR BLOOD FOR THEM.
"'CAUSE THIS WORLD CHEWS YOU UP AND THEN SPITS YOU BACK.
"THAT'S WHY YOU NEED YOUR BROTHERS TO HOLD IT TOGETHER. YOU ARE NOTHING ON YOUR OWN.
"ONLY A REALLY MESSED-UP PSYCHO LEAVES A BROTHER BEHIND WHEN THINGS GET UGLY.

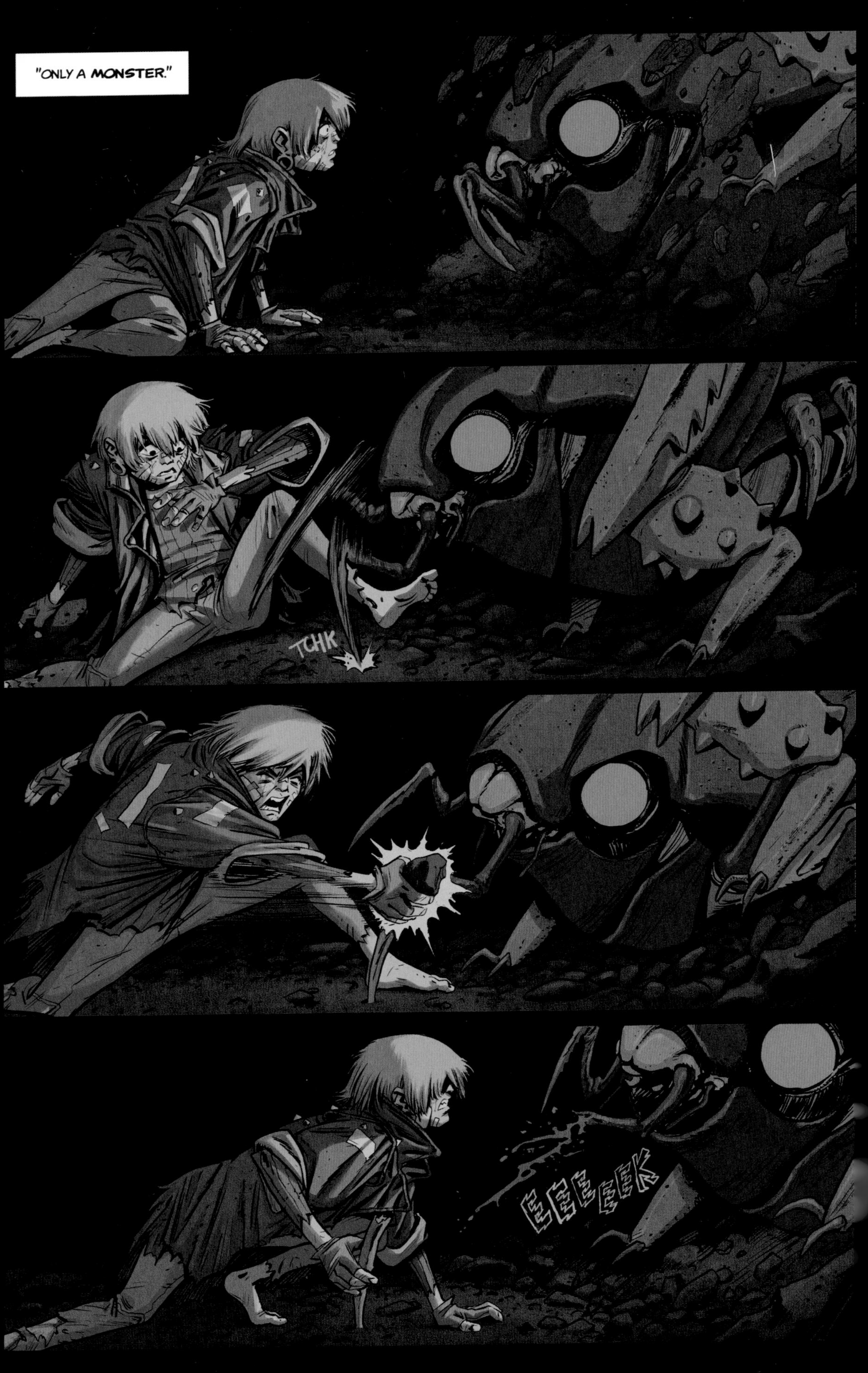
"ONLY A MONSTER."
TCHK
EEEEEK

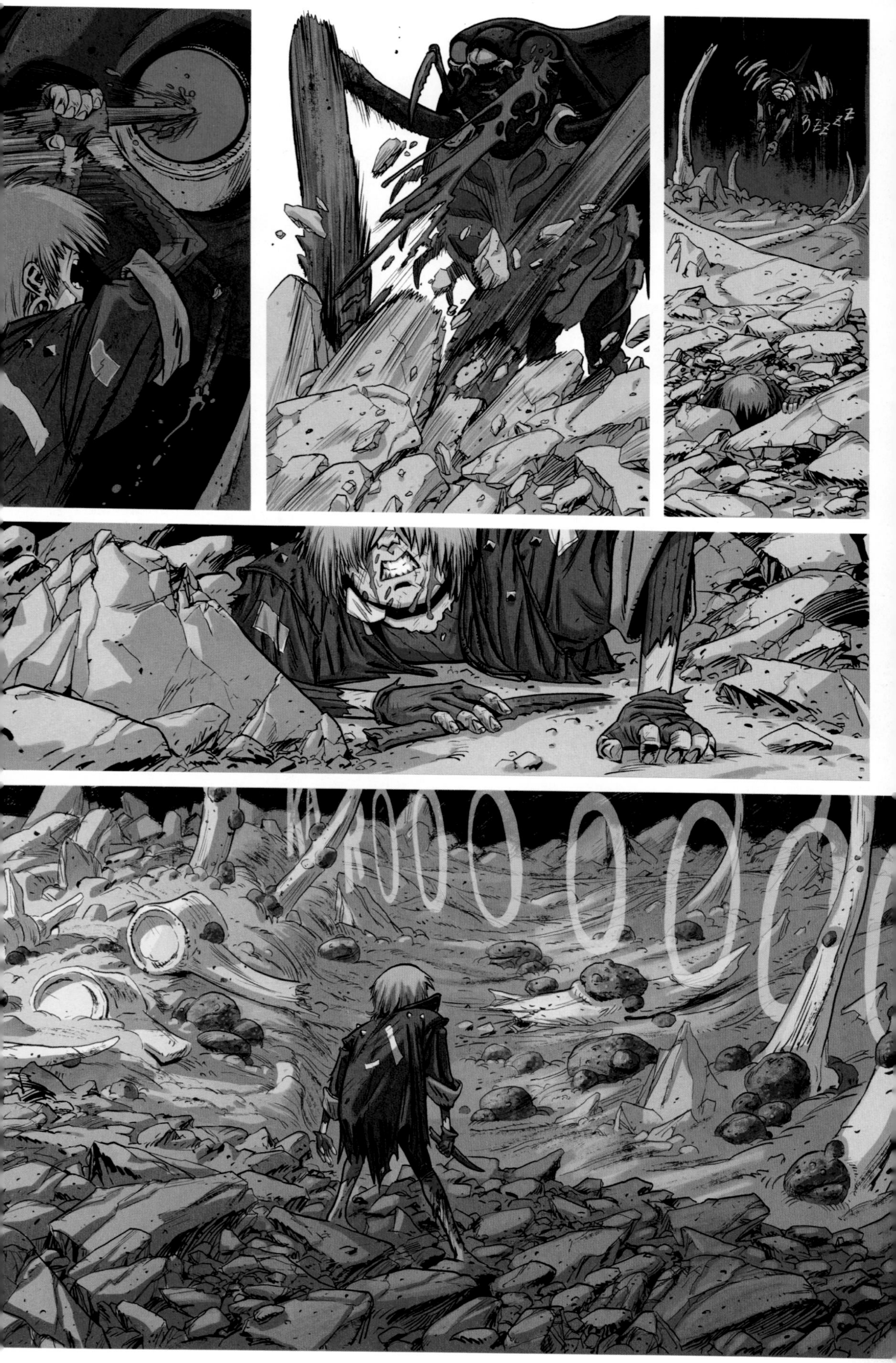
BZZZZ
KAROOOOOOO

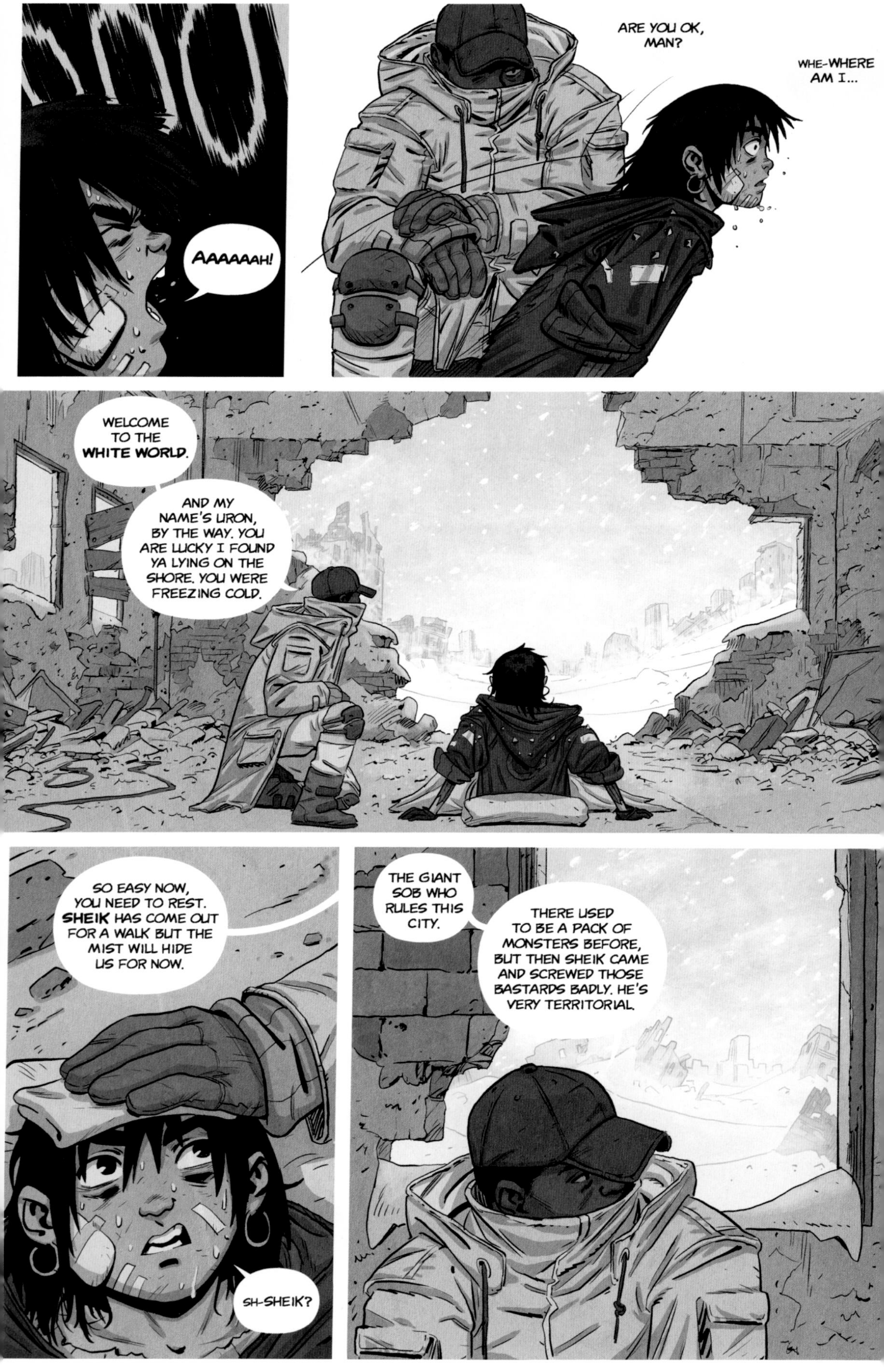
AAAAAAH!
ARE YOU OK, MAN?
WHE-WHERE AM I...
WELCOME TO THE WHITE WORLD.
AND MY NAME'S URON, BY THE WAY. YOU ARE LUCKY I FOUND YA LYING ON THE SHORE. YOU WERE FREEZING COLD.
SO EASY NOW, YOU NEED TO REST. SHEIK HAS COME OUT FOR A WALK BUT THE MIST WILL HIDE US FOR NOW.
SH-SHEIK?
THE GIANT SOB WHO RULES THIS CITY.
THERE USED TO BE A PACK OF MONSTERS BEFORE, BUT THEN SHEIK CAME AND SCREWED THOSE BASTARDS BADLY. HE'S VERY TERRITORIAL.

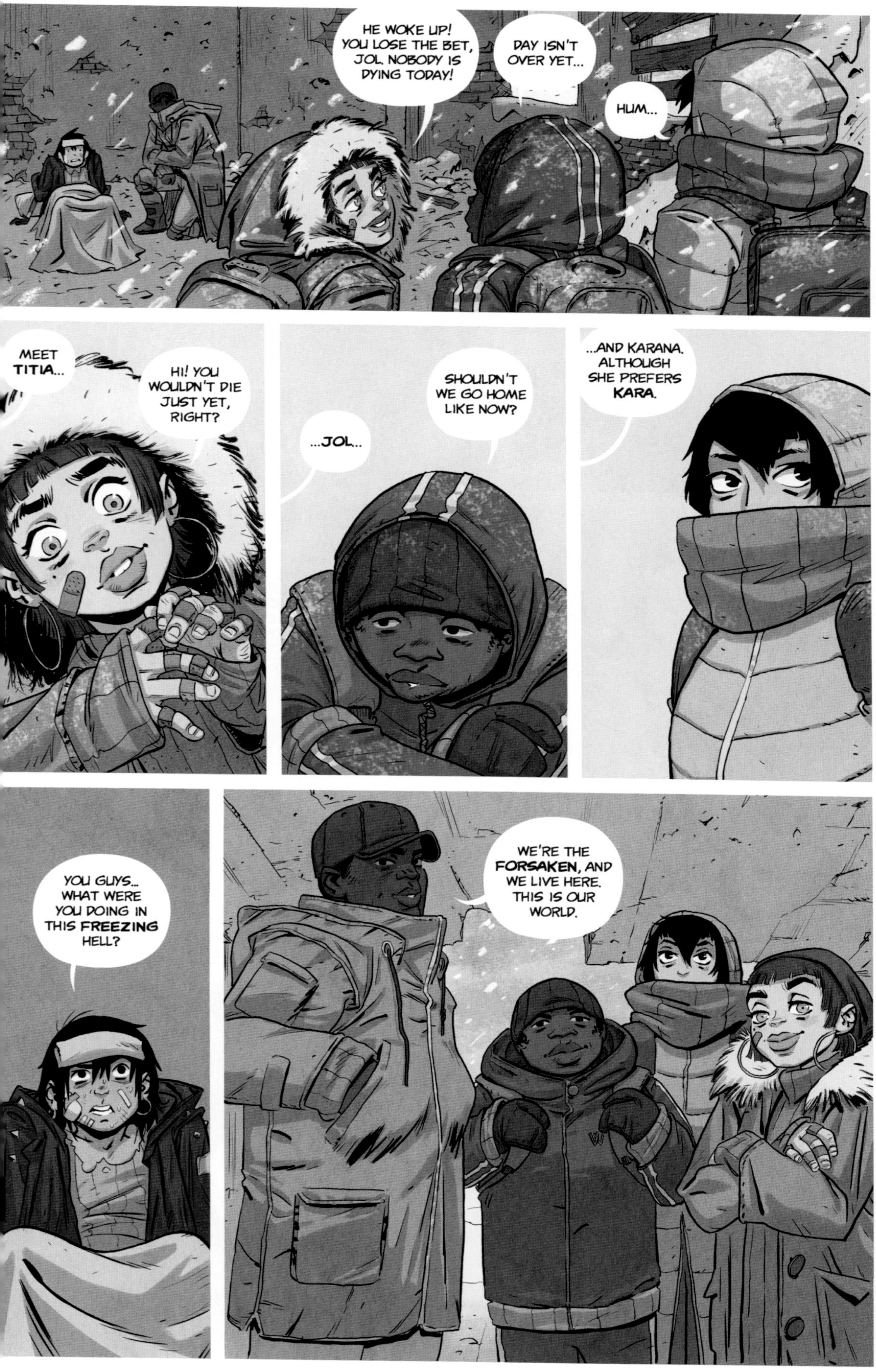
HE WOKE UP! YOU LOSE THE BET, JOL. NOBODY IS DYING TODAY!
DAY ISN'T OVER YET...
HUM...
MEET TITIA...
HI! YOU WOULDN'T DIE JUST YET, RIGHT?
...JOL...
SHOULDN'T WE GO HOME LIKE NOW?
...AND KARANA. ALTHOUGH SHE PREFERS KARA.
YOU GUYS... WHAT WERE YOU DOING IN THIS FREEZING HELL?
WE'RE THE FORSAKEN, AND WE LIVE HERE. THIS IS OUR WORLD.

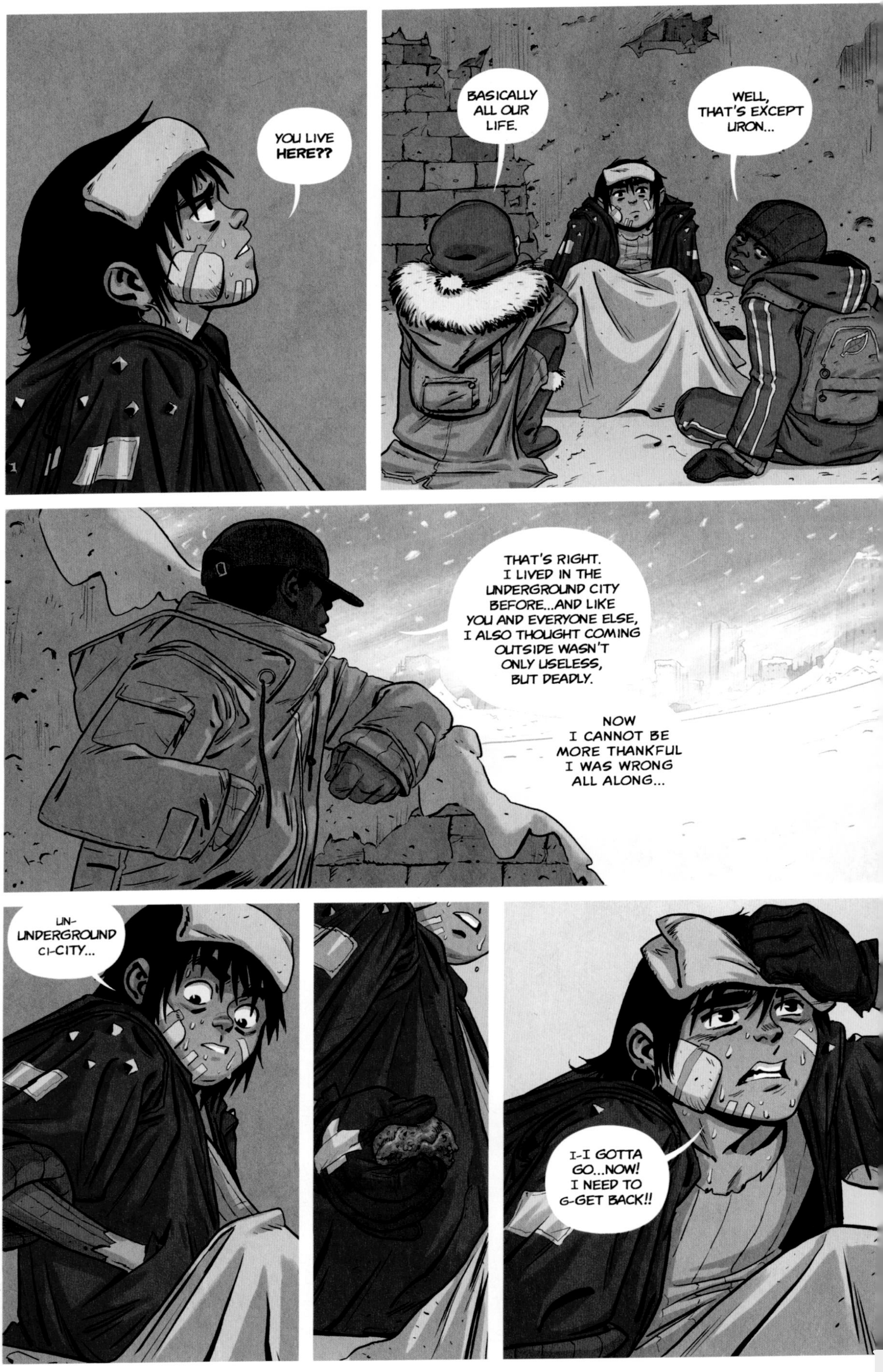
YOU LIVE HERE??
BASICALLY ALL OUR LIFE.
WELL, THAT'S EXCEPT URON...
THAT'S RIGHT. I LIVED IN THE UNDERGROUND CITY BEFORE...AND LIKE YOU AND EVERYONE ELSE, I ALSO THOUGHT COMING OUTSIDE WASN'T ONLY USELESS, BUT DEADLY.
NOW I CANNOT BE MORE THANKFUL I WAS WRONG ALL ALONG...
UN-UNDERGROUND CI-CITY...
I-I GOTTA GO...NOW! I NEED TO G-GET BACK!!

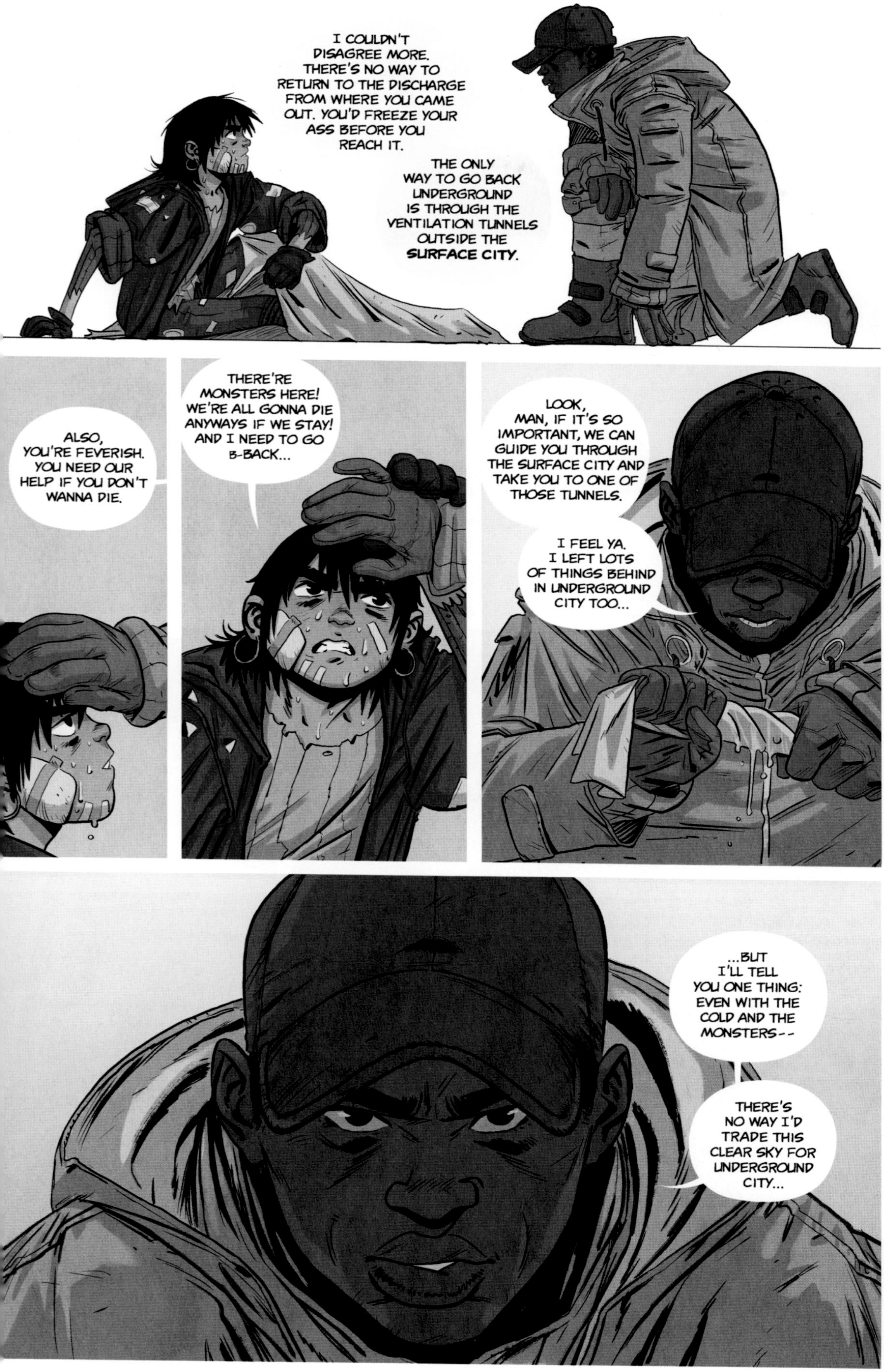
I COULDN'T DISAGREE MORE. THERE'S NO WAY TO RETURN TO THE DISCHARGE FROM WHERE YOU CAME OUT. YOU'D FREEZE YOUR ASS BEFORE YOU REACH IT.
THE ONLY WAY TO GO BACK UNDERGROUND IS THROUGH THE VENTILATION TUNNELS OUTSIDE THE **SURFACE CITY**.
ALSO, YOU'RE FEVERISH. YOU NEED OUR HELP IF YOU DON'T WANNA DIE.
THERE'RE MONSTERS HERE! WE'RE ALL GONNA DIE ANYWAYS IF WE STAY! AND I NEED TO GO B-BACK...
LOOK, MAN, IF IT'S SO IMPORTANT, WE CAN GUIDE YOU THROUGH THE SURFACE CITY AND TAKE YOU TO ONE OF THOSE TUNNELS.
I FEEL YA. I LEFT LOTS OF THINGS BEHIND IN UNDERGROUND CITY TOO...
...BUT I'LL TELL YOU ONE THING: EVEN WITH THE COLD AND THE MONSTERS--
THERE'S NO WAY I'D TRADE THIS CLEAR SKY FOR UNDERGROUND CITY...

"...AND AFTER A WHILE, I ASSURE YOU YOU'D PREFER THIS TO THAT HOPELESS PRISON DOWN THERE."

...AND WHO'S GONNA FIND MORE AMBERNOIR, YOU? YOU HEARD? THOSE GRIM BASTARDS, THEY'RE GETTING DESPERATE.

YEAH, THAT'S WHY THEY GO VISIT YOUR MOMMA.

WHAT...

...THE F...!?

LOOK WHO WE HAVE HERE! YOU GOTTA BE A REAL BADASS IF YOU'VE MANAGED TO COME BACK!

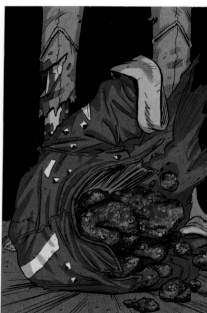

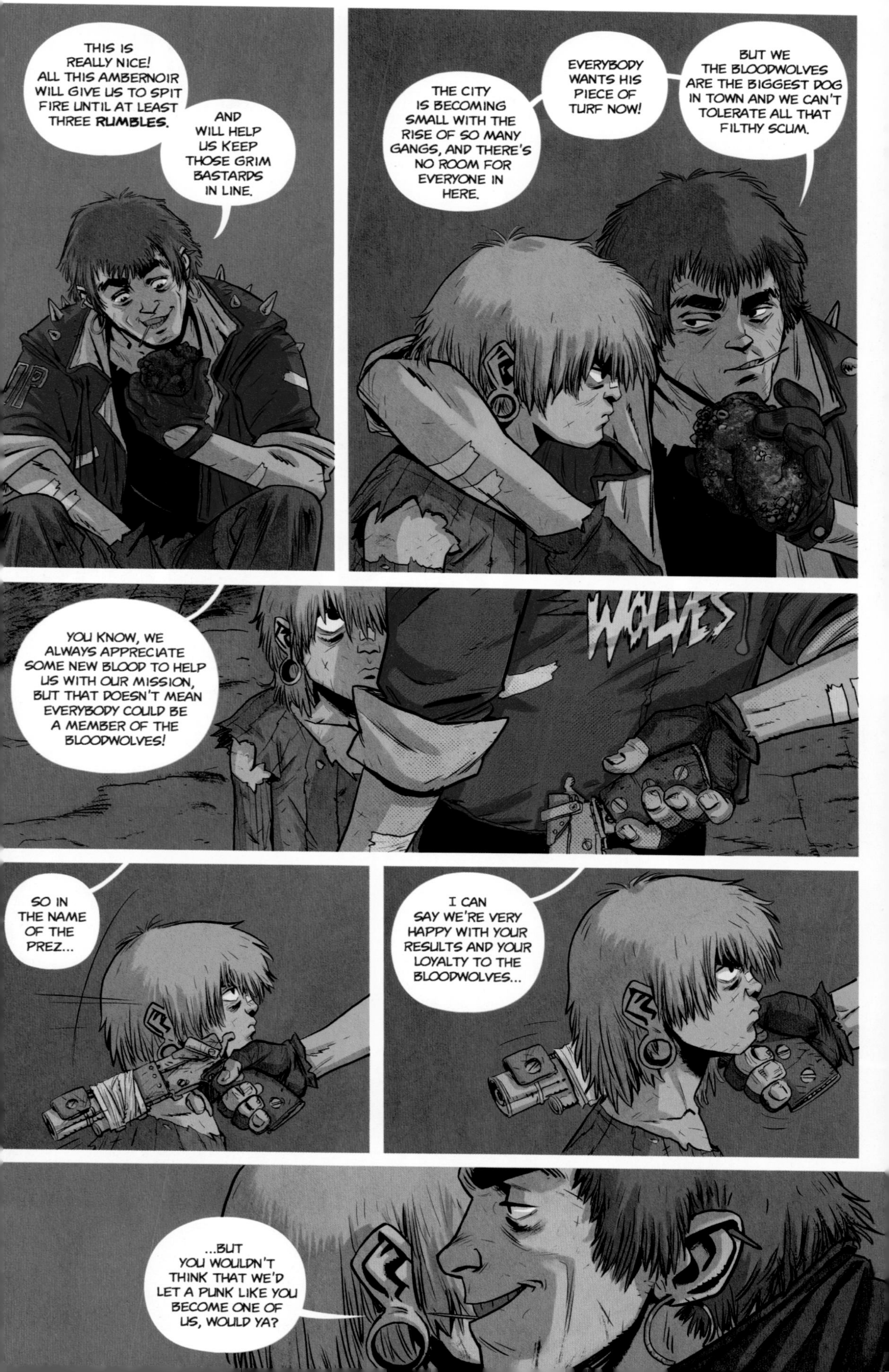
THIS IS REALLY NICE! ALL THIS AMBERNOIR WILL GIVE US TO SPIT FIRE UNTIL AT LEAST THREE **RUMBLES**.
AND WILL HELP US KEEP THOSE GRIM BASTARDS IN LINE.
THE CITY IS BECOMING SMALL WITH THE RISE OF SO MANY GANGS, AND THERE'S NO ROOM FOR EVERYONE IN HERE.
EVERYBODY WANTS HIS PIECE OF TURF NOW!
BUT WE THE BLOODWOLVES ARE THE BIGGEST DOG IN TOWN AND WE CAN'T TOLERATE ALL THAT FILTHY SCUM.
WOLVES
YOU KNOW, WE ALWAYS APPRECIATE SOME NEW BLOOD TO HELP US WITH OUR MISSION, BUT THAT DOESN'T MEAN EVERYBODY COULD BE A MEMBER OF THE BLOODWOLVES!
SO IN THE NAME OF THE PREZ...
I CAN SAY WE'RE VERY HAPPY WITH YOUR RESULTS AND YOUR LOYALTY TO THE BLOODWOLVES...
...BUT YOU WOULDN'T THINK THAT WE'D LET A PUNK LIKE YOU BECOME ONE OF US, WOULD YA?

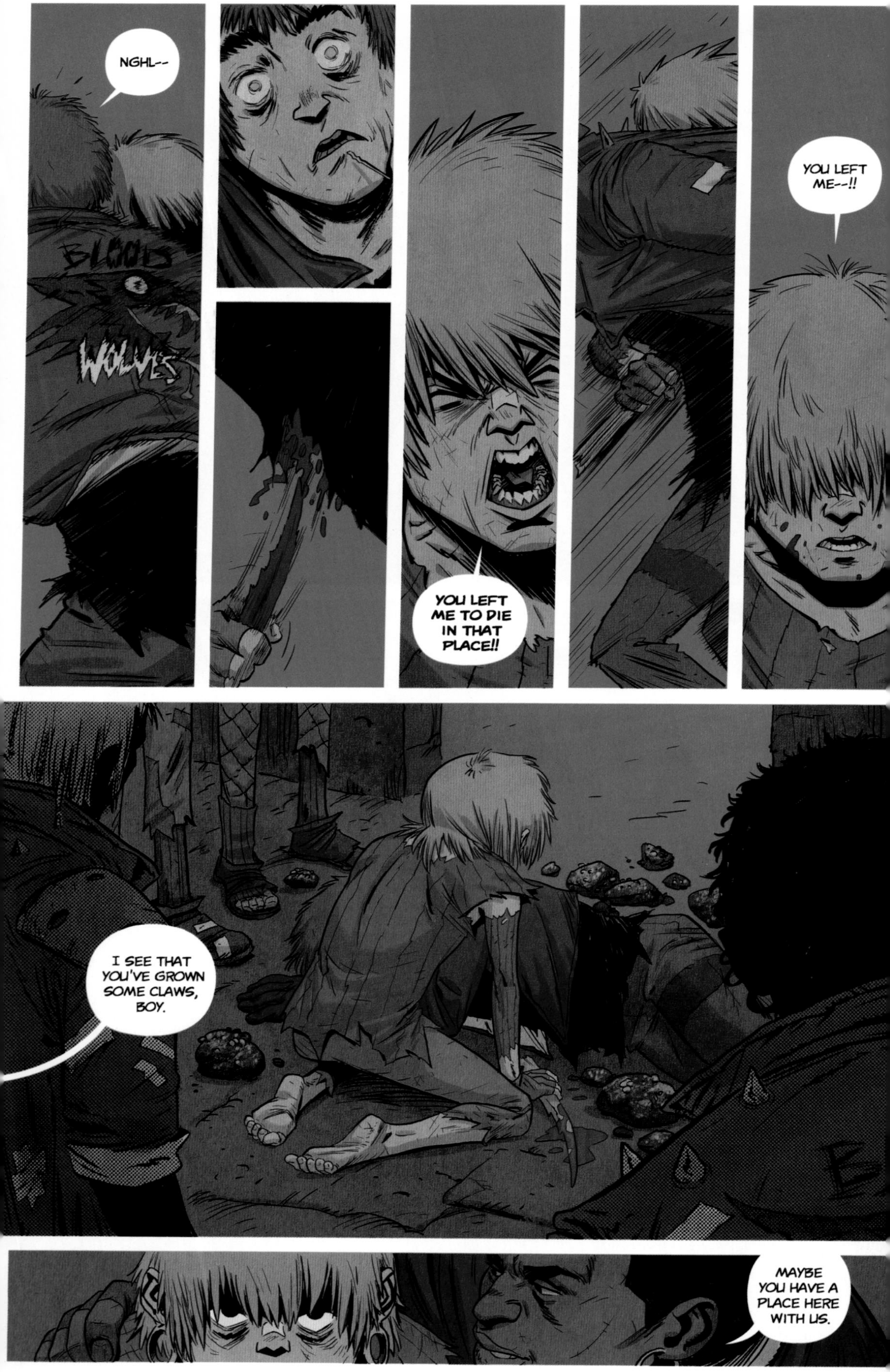
NGHL--
YOU LEFT ME TO DIE IN THAT PLACE!!
YOU LEFT ME--!!
I SEE THAT YOU'VE GROWN SOME CLAWS, BOY.
MAYBE YOU HAVE A PLACE HERE WITH US.

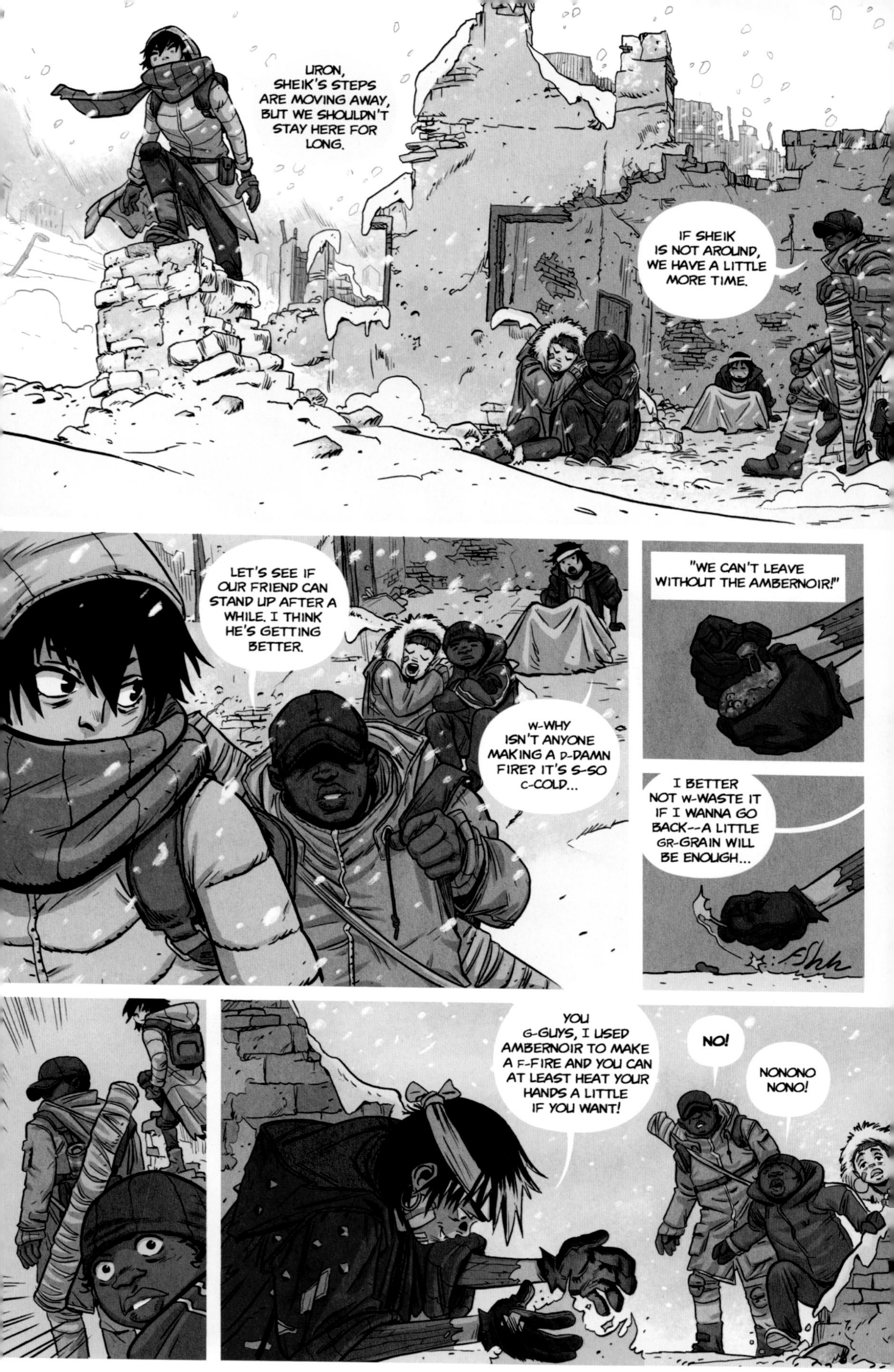
URON, SHEIK'S STEPS ARE MOVING AWAY, BUT WE SHOULDN'T STAY HERE FOR LONG.
IF SHEIK IS NOT AROUND, WE HAVE A LITTLE MORE TIME.
LET'S SEE IF OUR FRIEND CAN STAND UP AFTER A WHILE. I THINK HE'S GETTING BETTER.
W-WHY ISN'T ANYONE MAKING A D-DAMN FIRE? IT'S S-SO C-COLD...
"WE CAN'T LEAVE WITHOUT THE AMBERNOIR!"
I BETTER NOT W-WASTE IT IF I WANNA GO BACK--A LITTLE GR-GRAIN WILL BE ENOUGH...
FSHH
YOU G-GUYS, I USED AMBERNOIR TO MAKE A F-FIRE AND YOU CAN AT LEAST HEAT YOUR HANDS A LITTLE IF YOU WANT!
NO!
NONONO NONO!

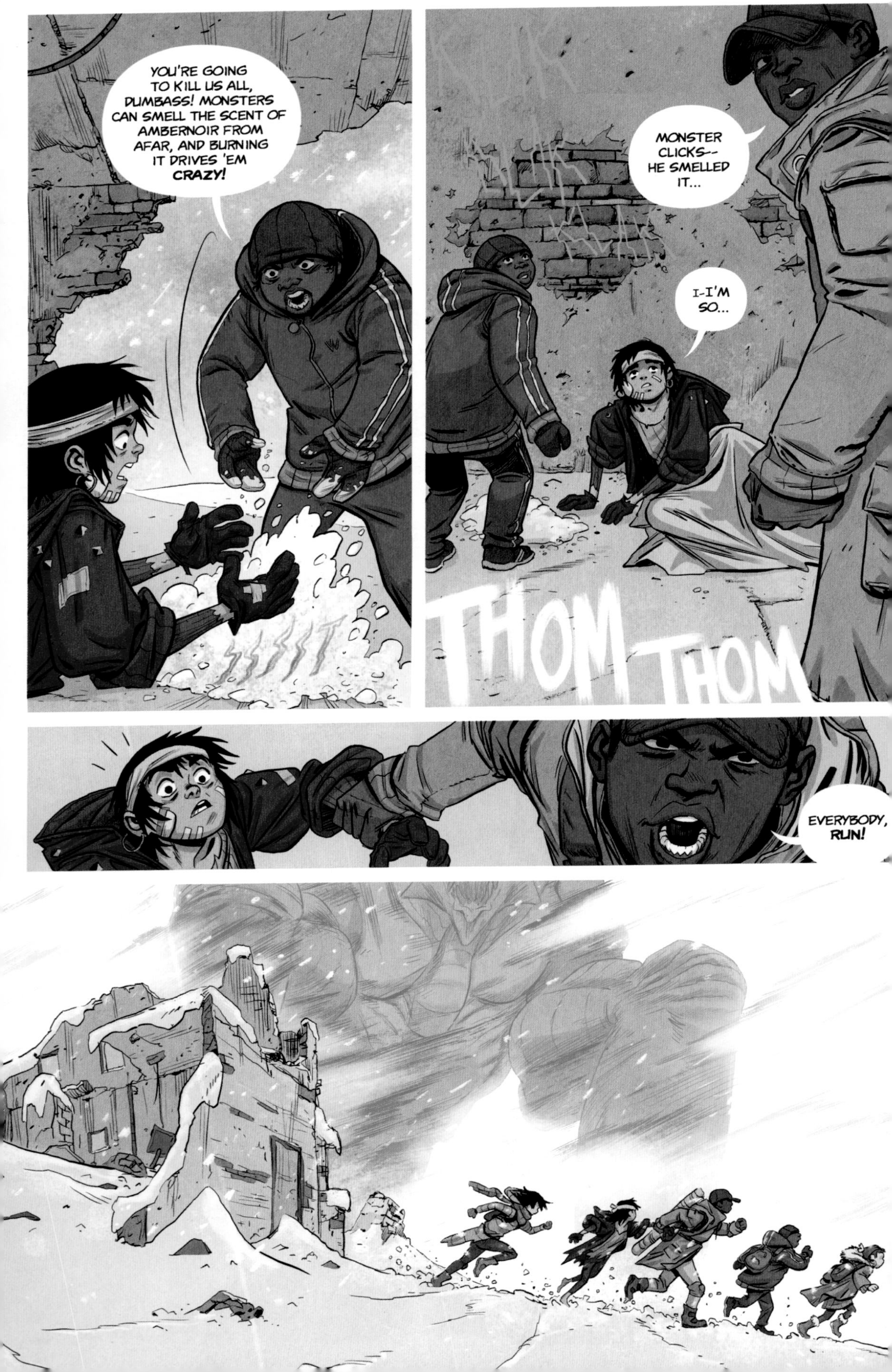

YOU'RE GOING TO KILL US ALL, DUMBASS! MONSTERS CAN SMELL THE SCENT OF AMBERNOIR FROM AFAR, AND BURNING IT DRIVES 'EM CRAZY!
SSSSST
MONSTER CLICKS-- HE SMELLED IT...
I-I'M SO...
THOM THOM
EVERYBODY, RUN!

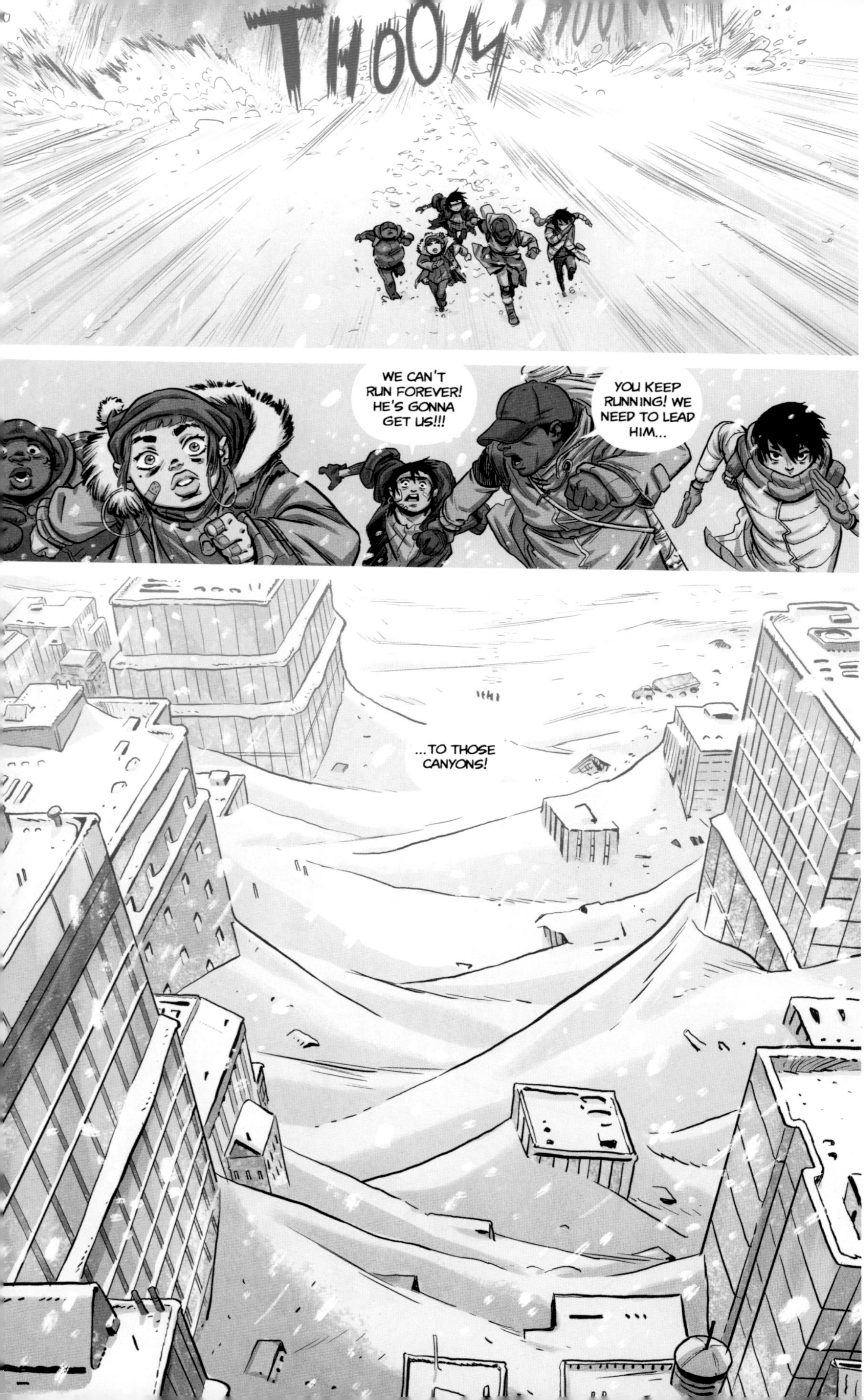
THOOM
WE CAN'T RUN FOREVER! HE'S GONNA GET US!!!
YOU KEEP RUNNING! WE NEED TO LEAD HIM...
...TO THOSE CANYONS!

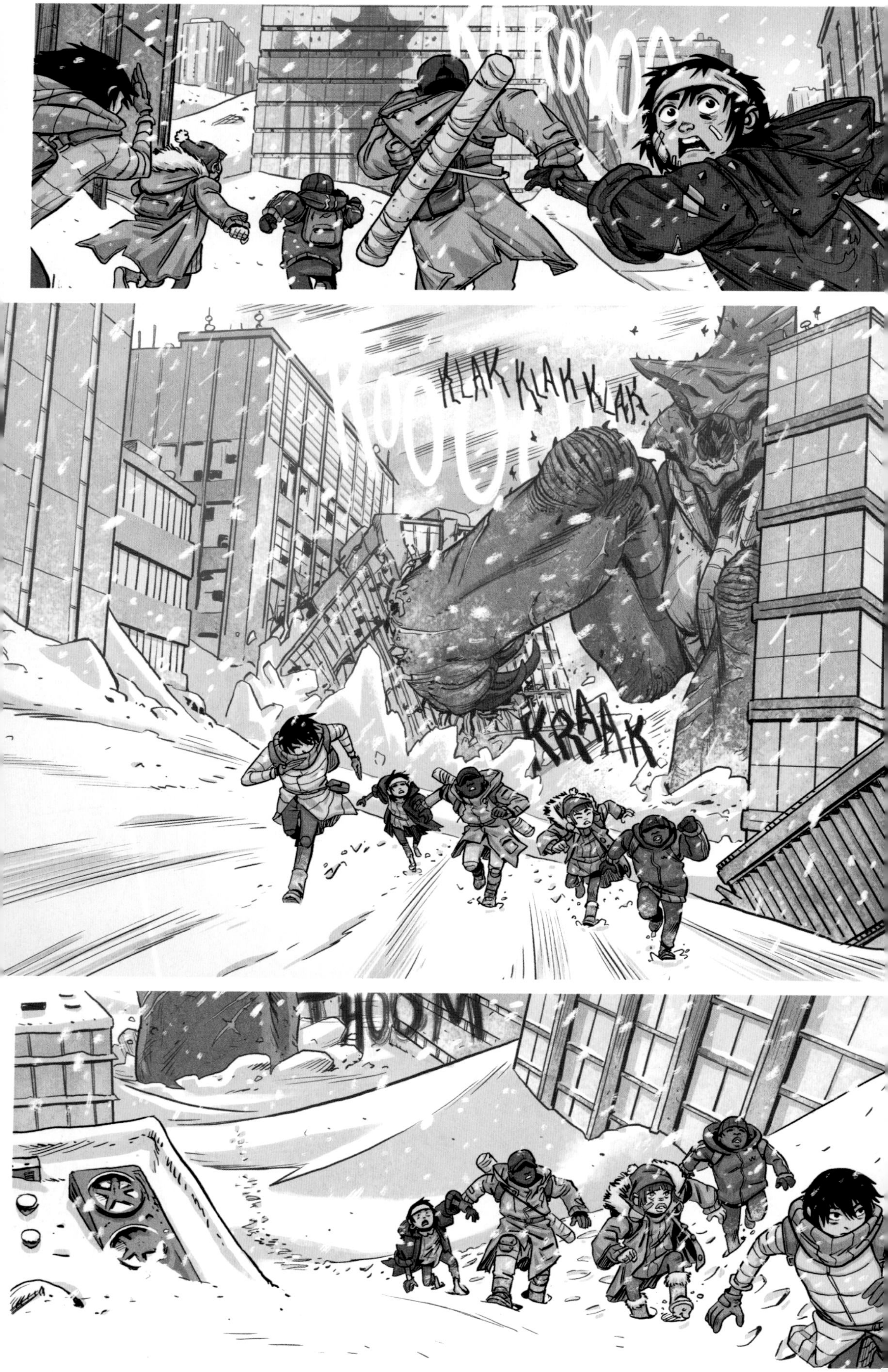
KAROOOO
KLAK KLAK KLAK
KRAAK
THOOM

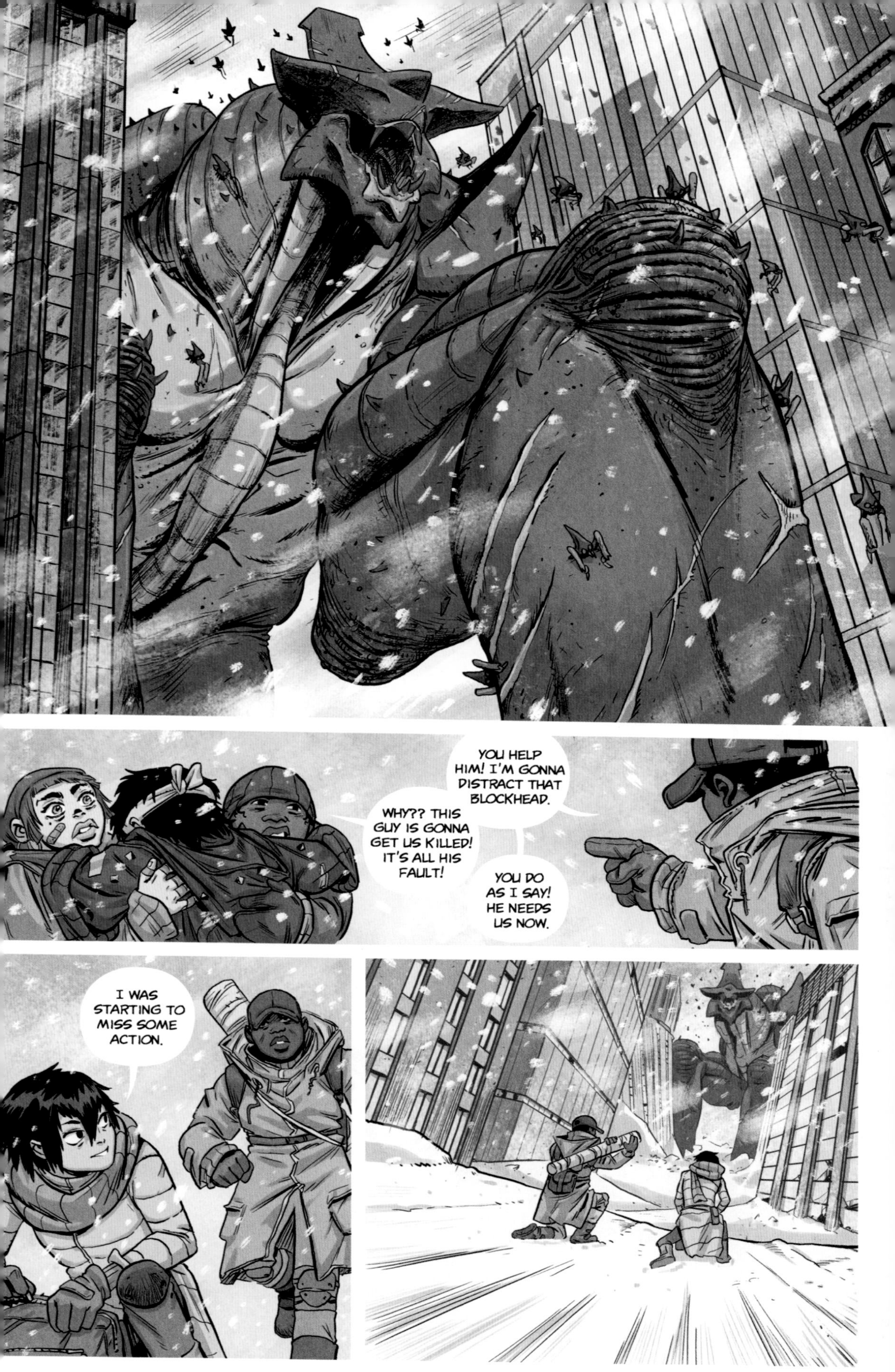
YOU HELP HIM! I'M GONNA DISTRACT THAT BLOCKHEAD.
WHY?? THIS GUY IS GONNA GET US KILLED! IT'S ALL HIS FAULT!
YOU DO AS I SAY! HE NEEDS US NOW.
I WAS STARTING TO MISS SOME ACTION.

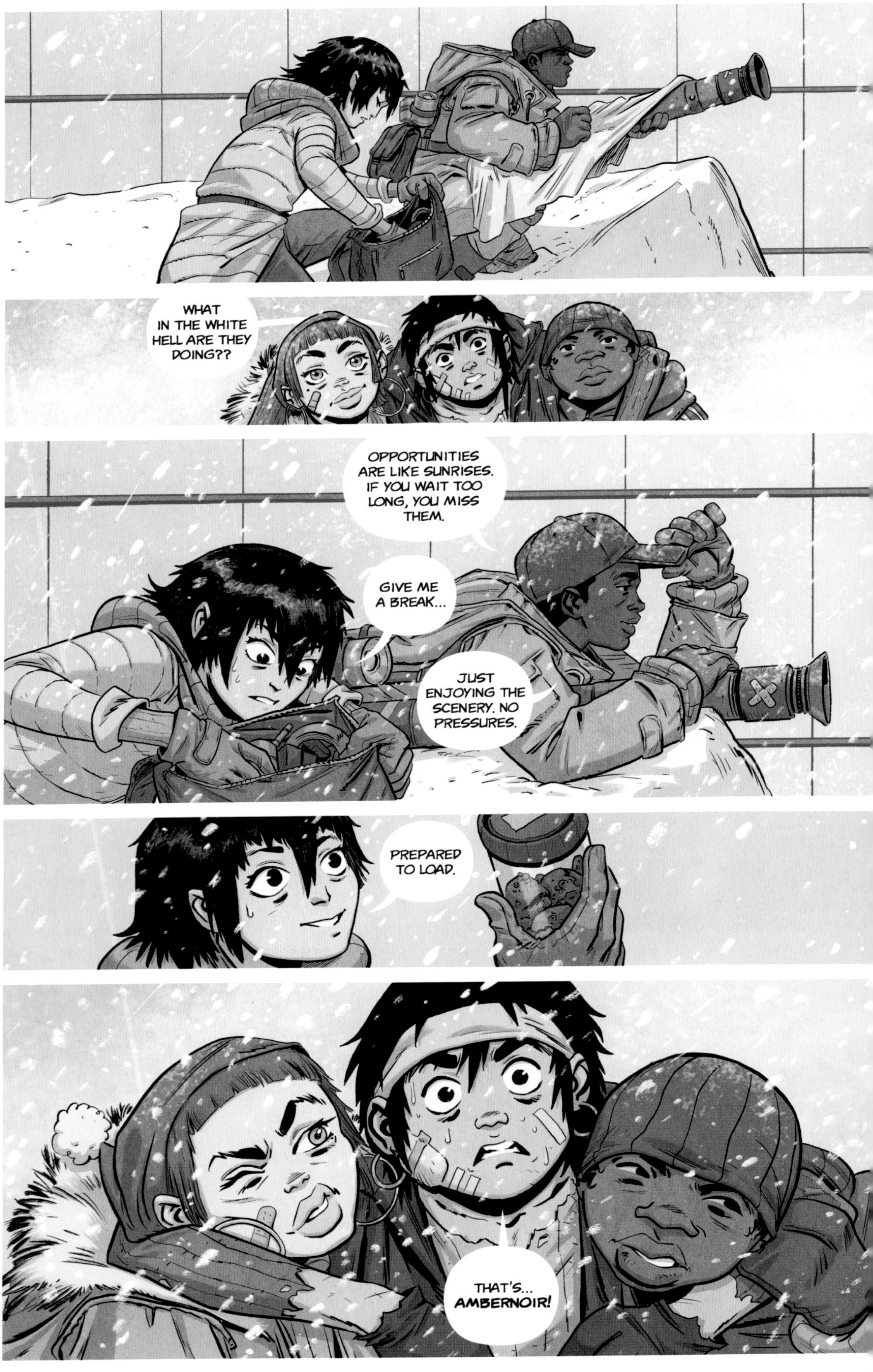
WHAT IN THE WHITE HELL ARE THEY DOING??
OPPORTUNITIES ARE LIKE SUNRISES. IF YOU WAIT TOO LONG, YOU MISS THEM.
GIVE ME A BREAK...
JUST ENJOYING THE SCENERY. NO PRESSURES.
PREPARED TO LOAD.
THAT'S... AMBERNOIR!

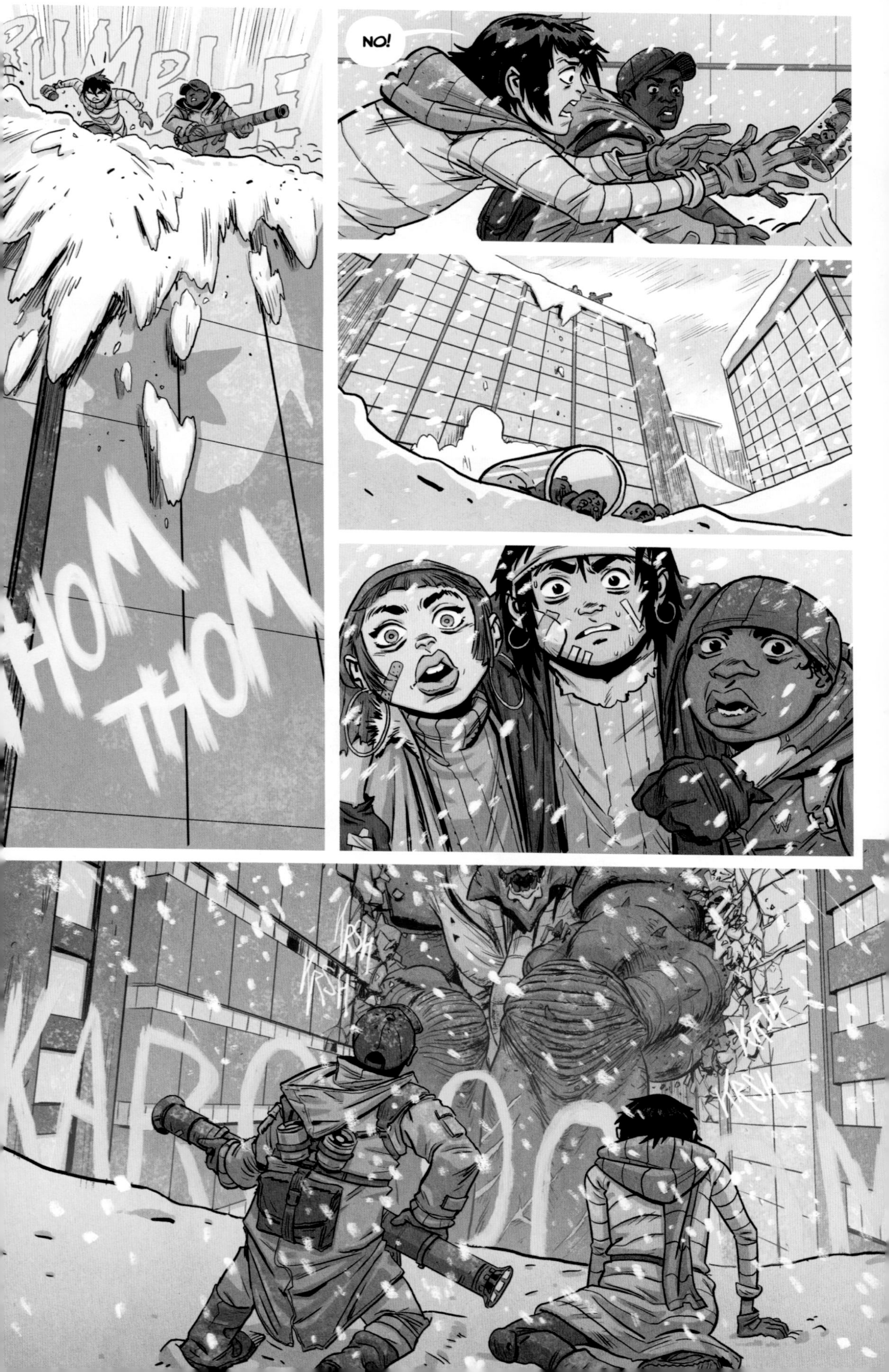
RUMBLE
THOM
THOM
NO!
KRSH
KRSH
KAROOM
KRSH
KRSH

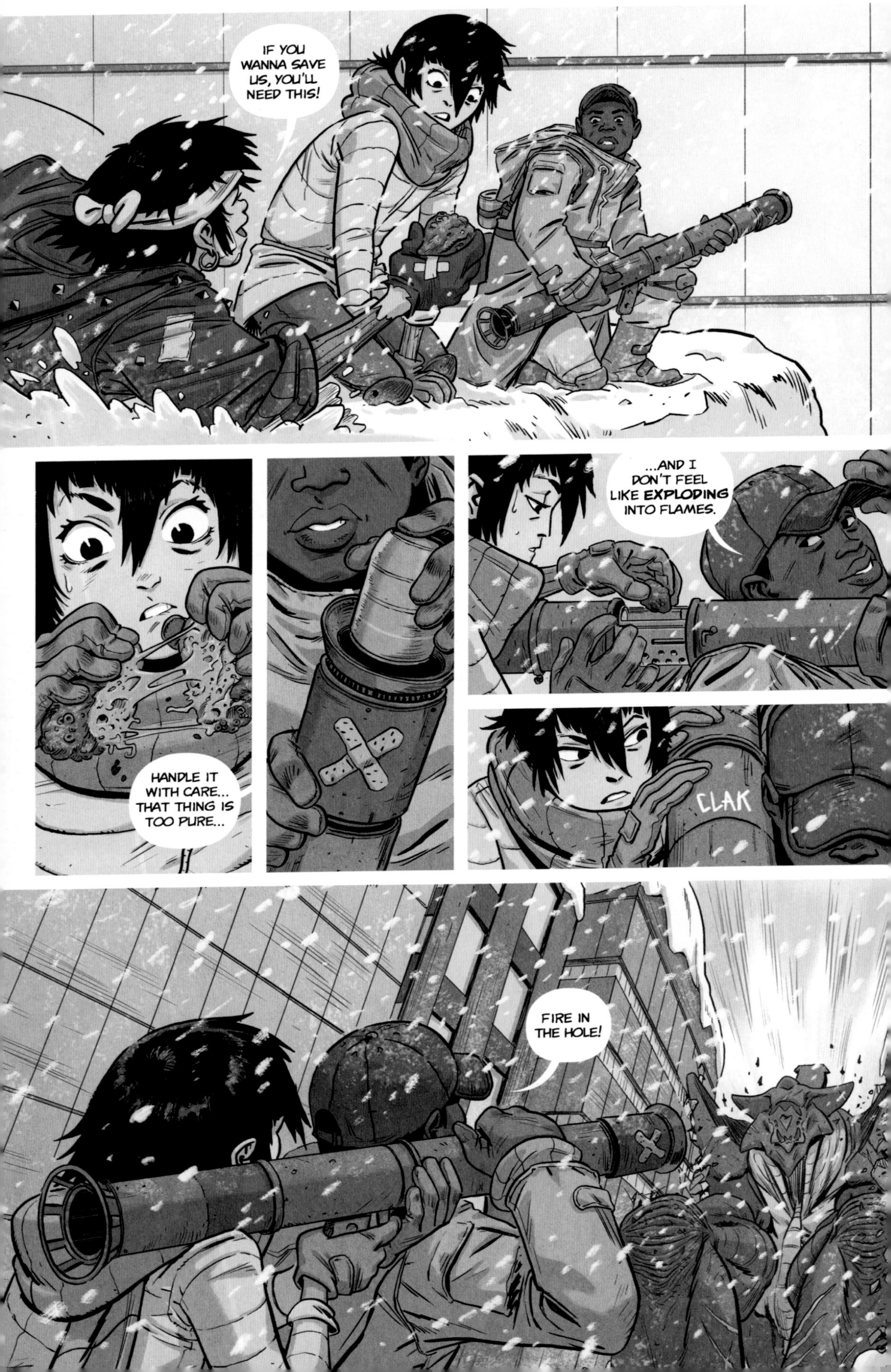

IF YOU WANNA SAVE US, YOU'LL NEED THIS!
HANDLE IT WITH CARE... THAT THING IS TOO PURE...
...AND I DON'T FEEL LIKE **EXPLODING** INTO FLAMES.
CLAK
FIRE IN THE HOLE!

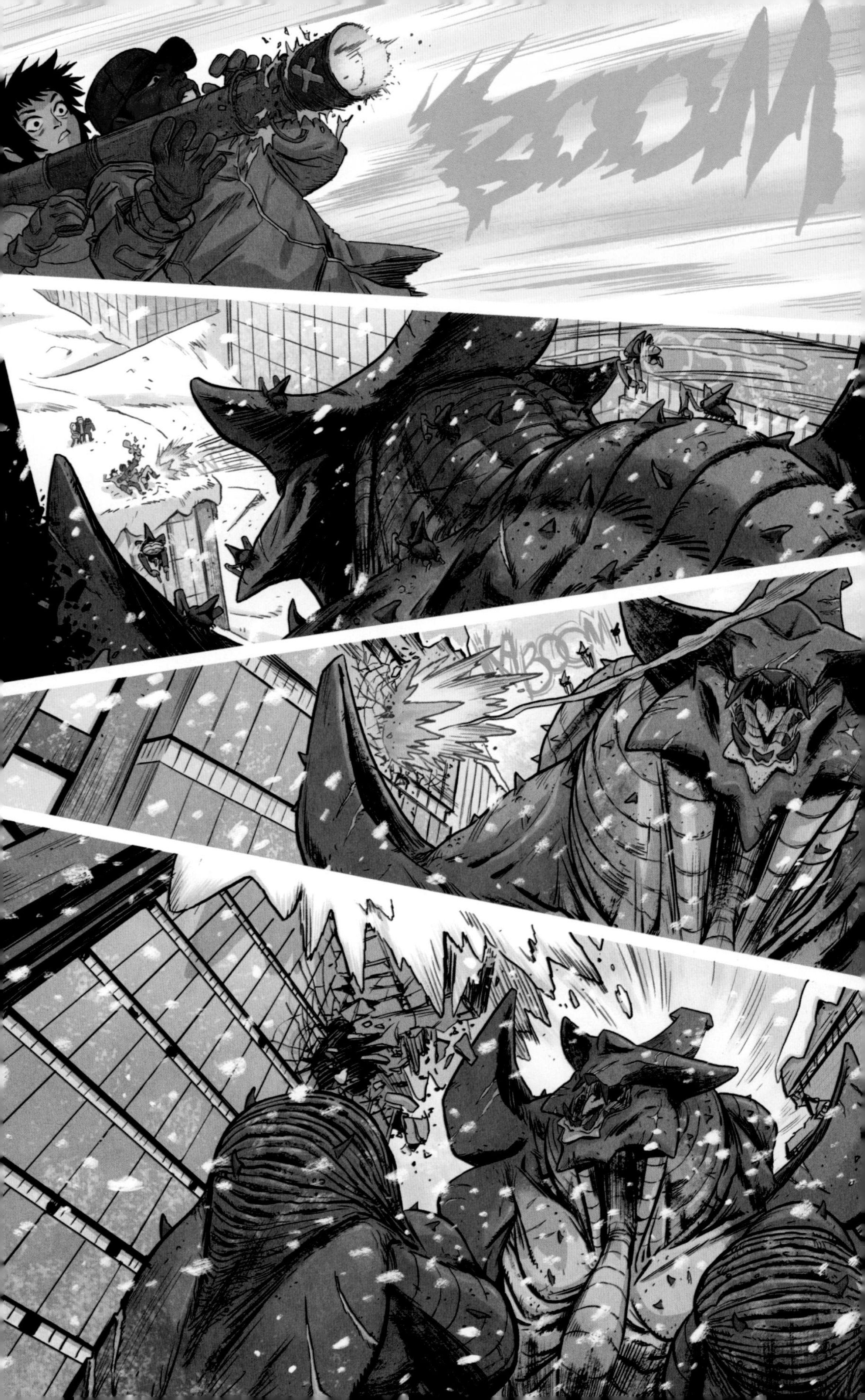
BOOM
KABOOM

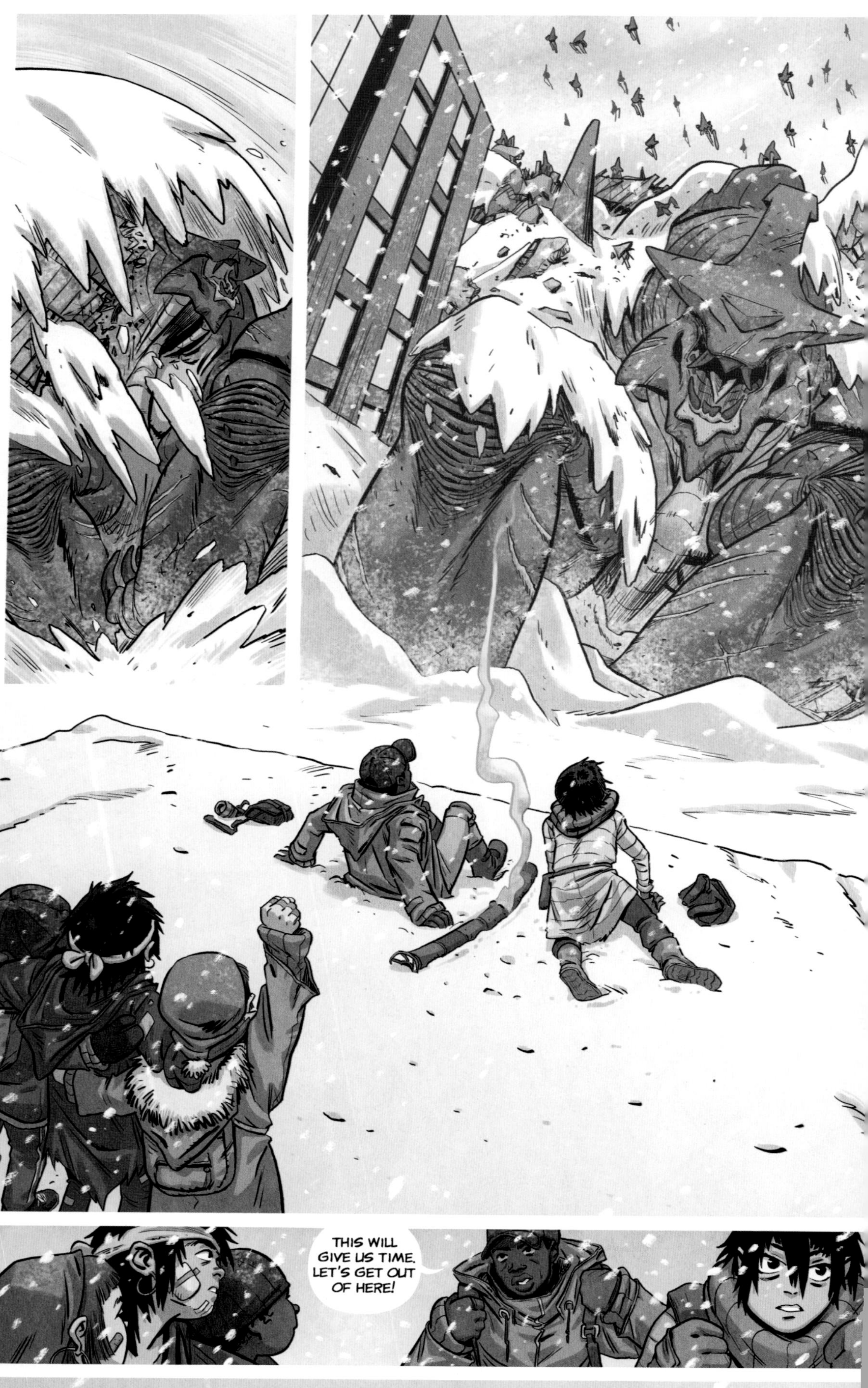
THIS WILL
GIVE US TIME.
LET'S GET OUT
OF HERE!

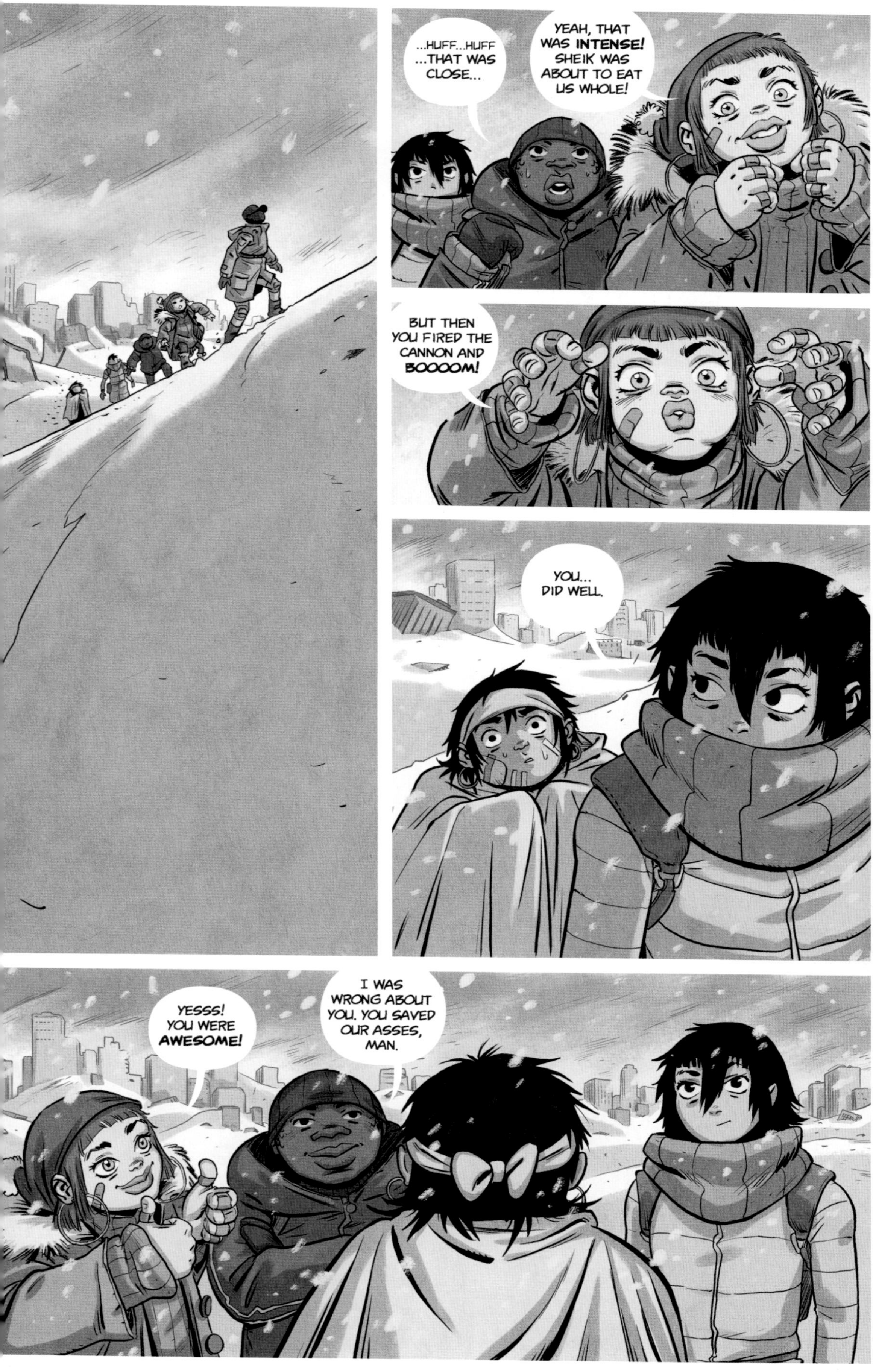
...HUFF...HUFF ...THAT WAS CLOSE...
YEAH, THAT WAS INTENSE! SHEIK WAS ABOUT TO EAT US WHOLE!
BUT THEN YOU FIRED THE CANNON AND BOOOOM!
YOU... DID WELL.
YESSS! YOU WERE AWESOME!
I WAS WRONG ABOUT YOU. YOU SAVED OUR ASSES, MAN.

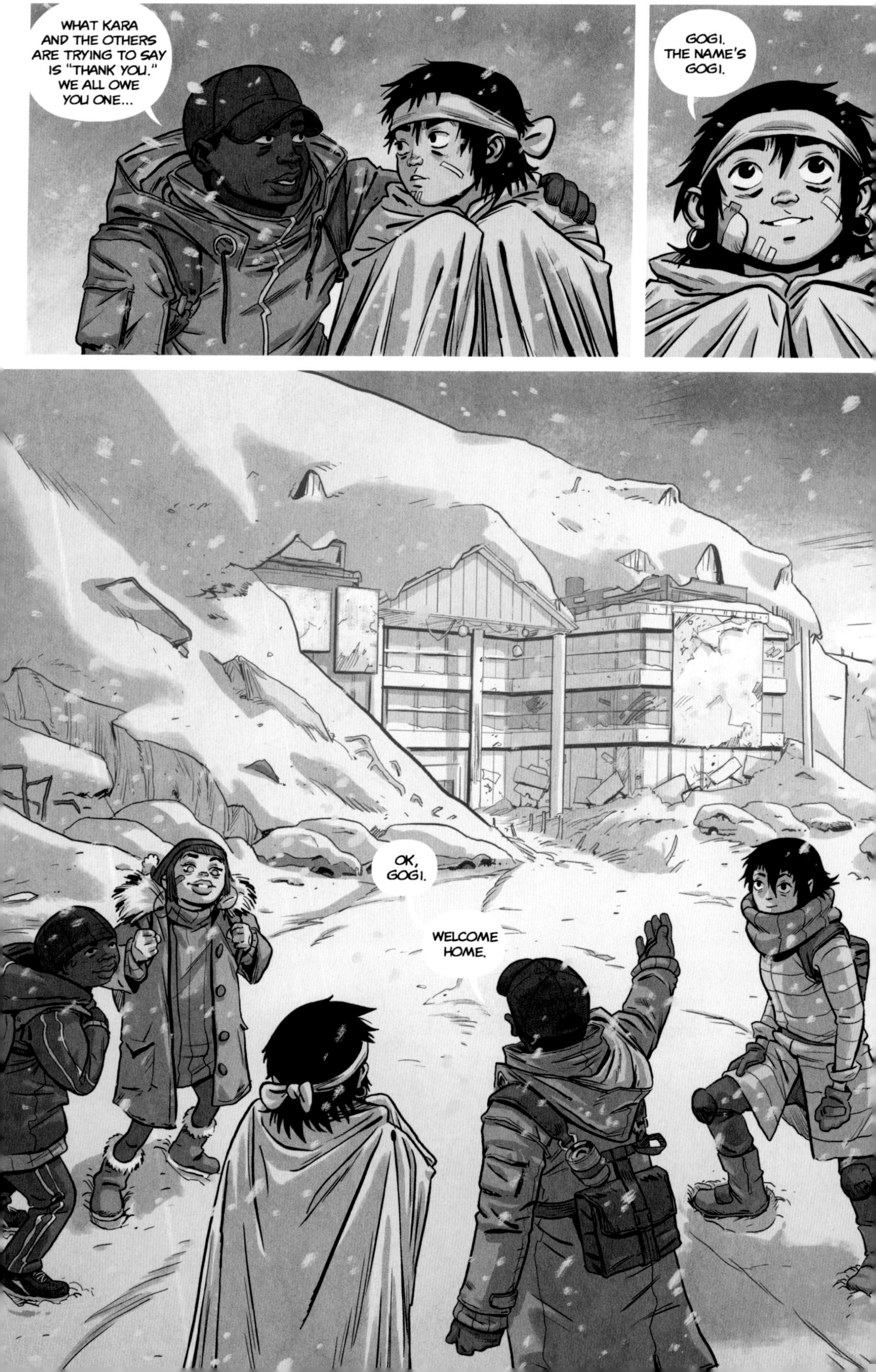
WHAT KARA AND THE OTHERS ARE TRYING TO SAY IS "THANK YOU." WE ALL OWE YOU ONE...
GOGI. THE NAME'S GOGI.
OK, GOGI.
WELCOME HOME.

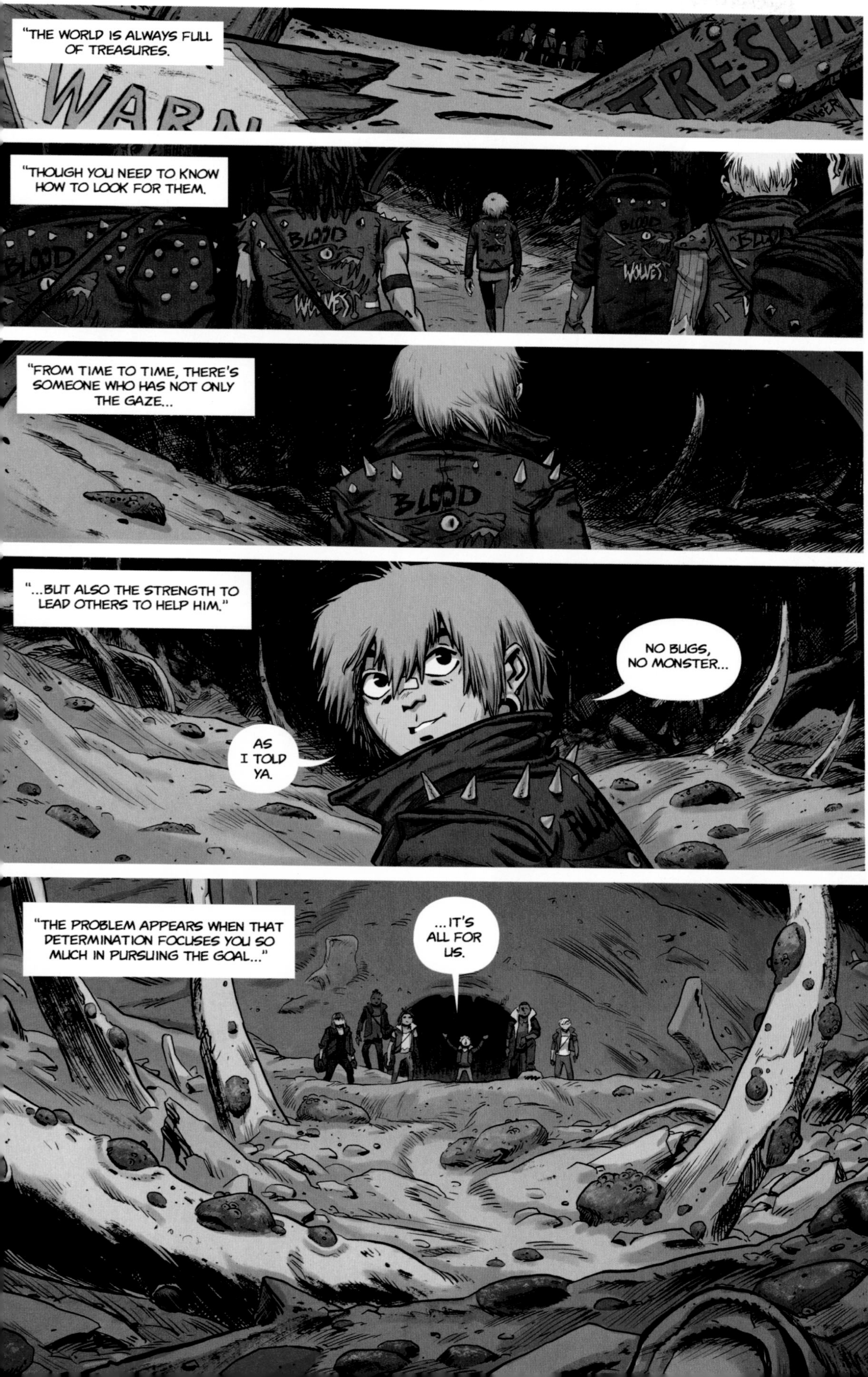
"THE WORLD IS ALWAYS FULL OF TREASURES.
WARN
TRESP
DANGER
"THOUGH YOU NEED TO KNOW HOW TO LOOK FOR THEM.
BLOOD
WOLVES
"FROM TIME TO TIME, THERE'S SOMEONE WHO HAS NOT ONLY THE GAZE...
BLOOD
"...BUT ALSO THE STRENGTH TO LEAD OTHERS TO HELP HIM."
NO BUGS, NO MONSTER...
AS I TOLD YA.
"THE PROBLEM APPEARS WHEN THAT DETERMINATION FOCUSES YOU SO MUCH IN PURSUING THE GOAL..."
...IT'S ALL FOR US.

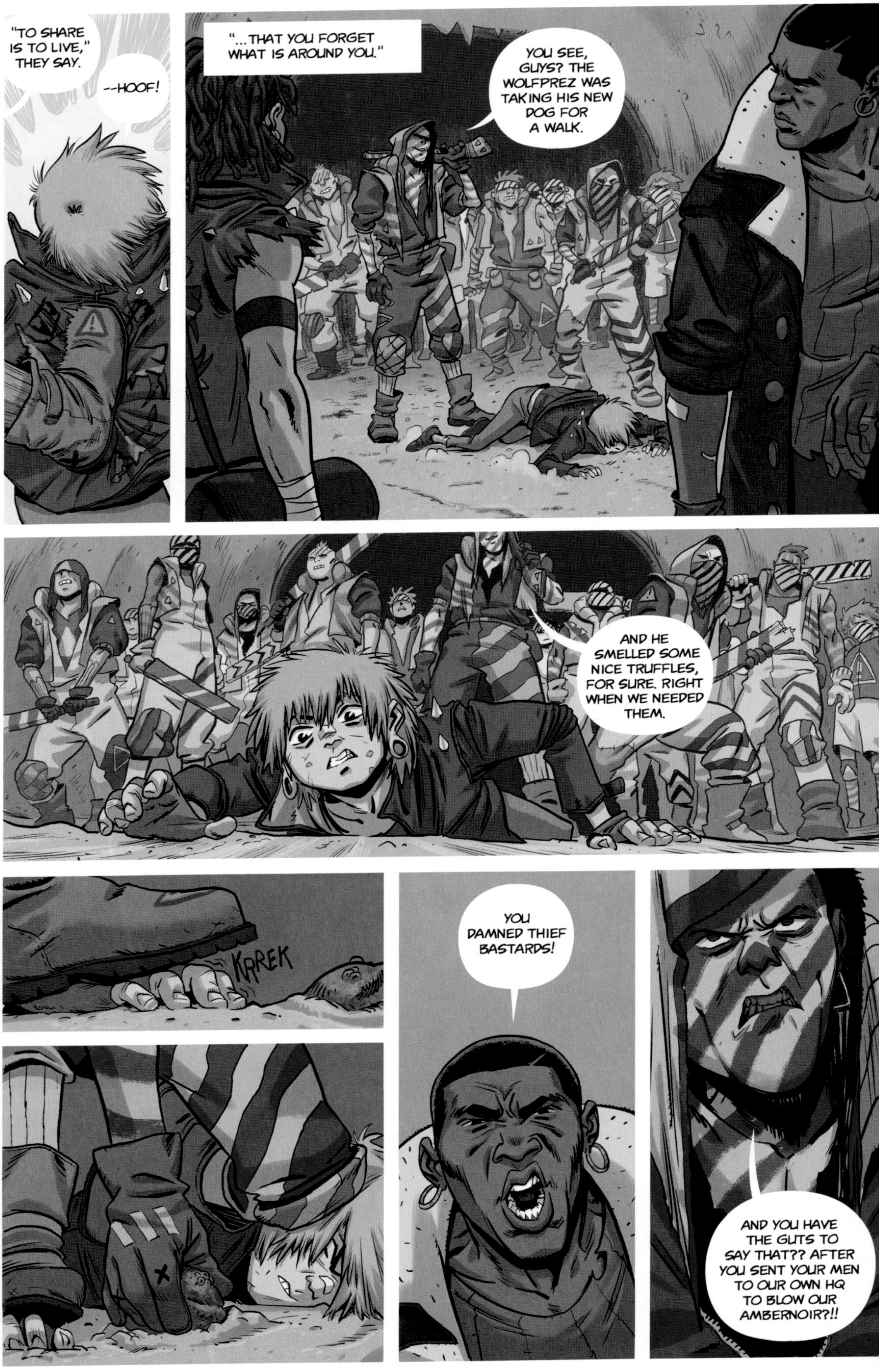
"TO SHARE IS TO LIVE," THEY SAY.
--HOOF!
"...THAT YOU FORGET WHAT IS AROUND YOU."
YOU SEE, GUYS? THE WOLFPREZ WAS TAKING HIS NEW DOG FOR A WALK.
AND HE SMELLED SOME NICE TRUFFLES, FOR SURE. RIGHT WHEN WE NEEDED THEM.
KRREK
YOU DAMNED THIEF BASTARDS!
AND YOU HAVE THE GUTS TO SAY THAT?? AFTER YOU SENT YOUR MEN TO OUR OWN HQ TO BLOW OUR AMBERNOIR?!!

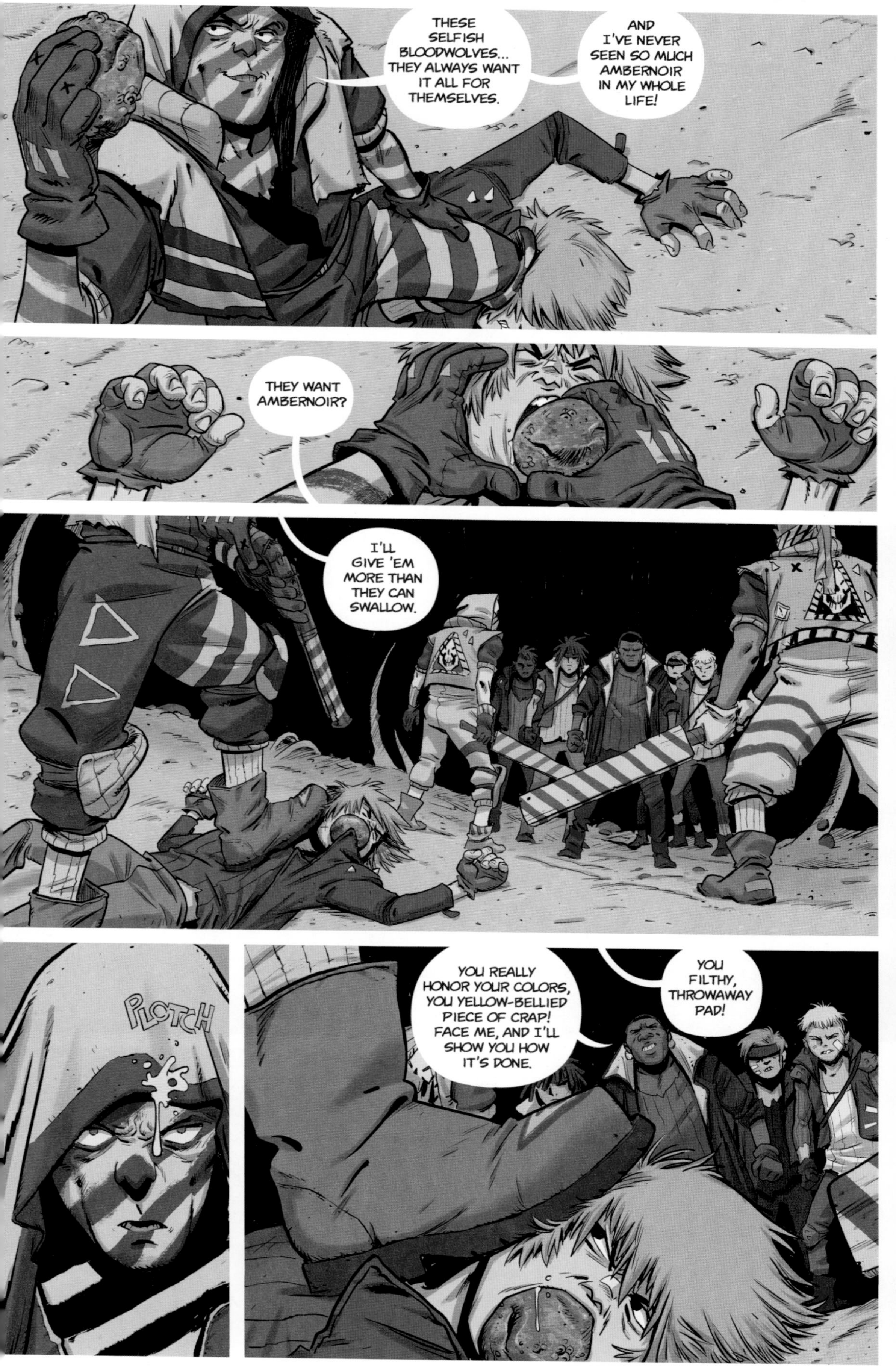
THESE SELFISH BLOODWOLVES... THEY ALWAYS WANT IT ALL FOR THEMSELVES.
AND I'VE NEVER SEEN SO MUCH AMBERNOIR IN MY WHOLE LIFE!
THEY WANT AMBERNOIR?
I'LL GIVE 'EM MORE THAN THEY CAN SWALLOW.
PLOTCH
YOU REALLY HONOR YOUR COLORS, YOU YELLOW-BELLIED PIECE OF CRAP! FACE ME, AND I'LL SHOW YOU HOW IT'S DONE.
YOU FILTHY, THROWAWAY PAD!

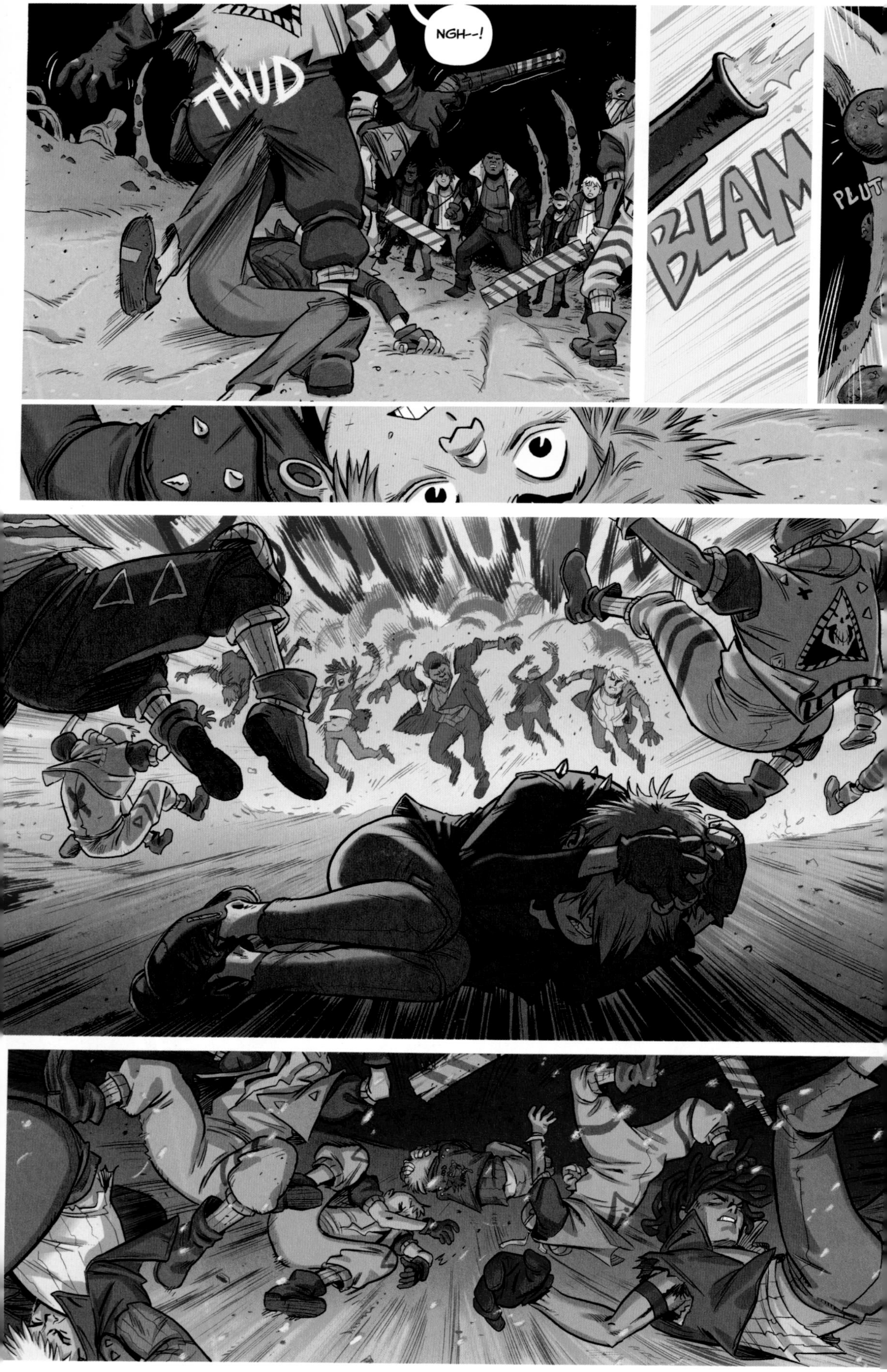
NGH--!
THUD
BLAM
PLUT

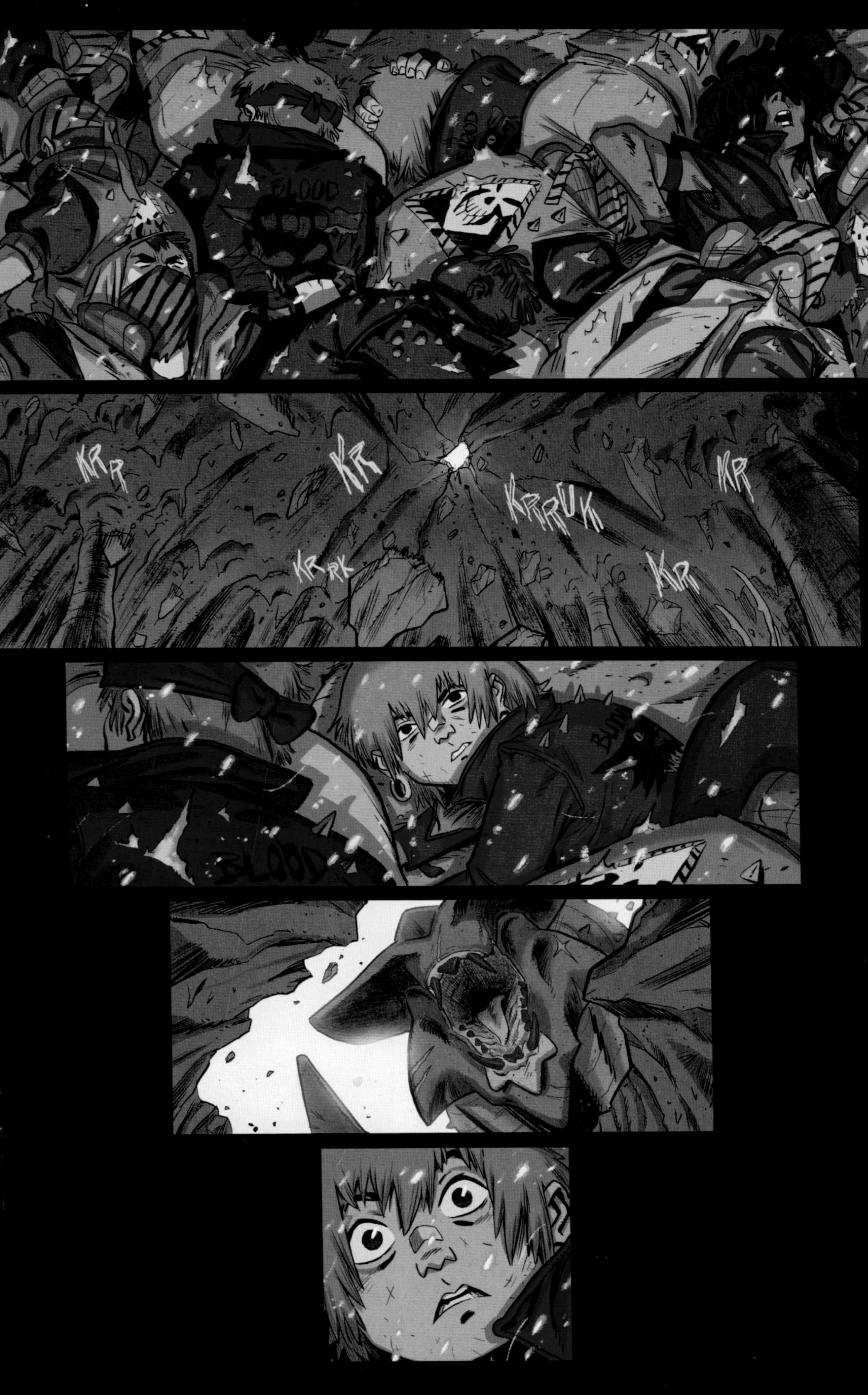
BLOOD
KRR
KR
KRRRUK
KR
KRRK
KR
BLOOD

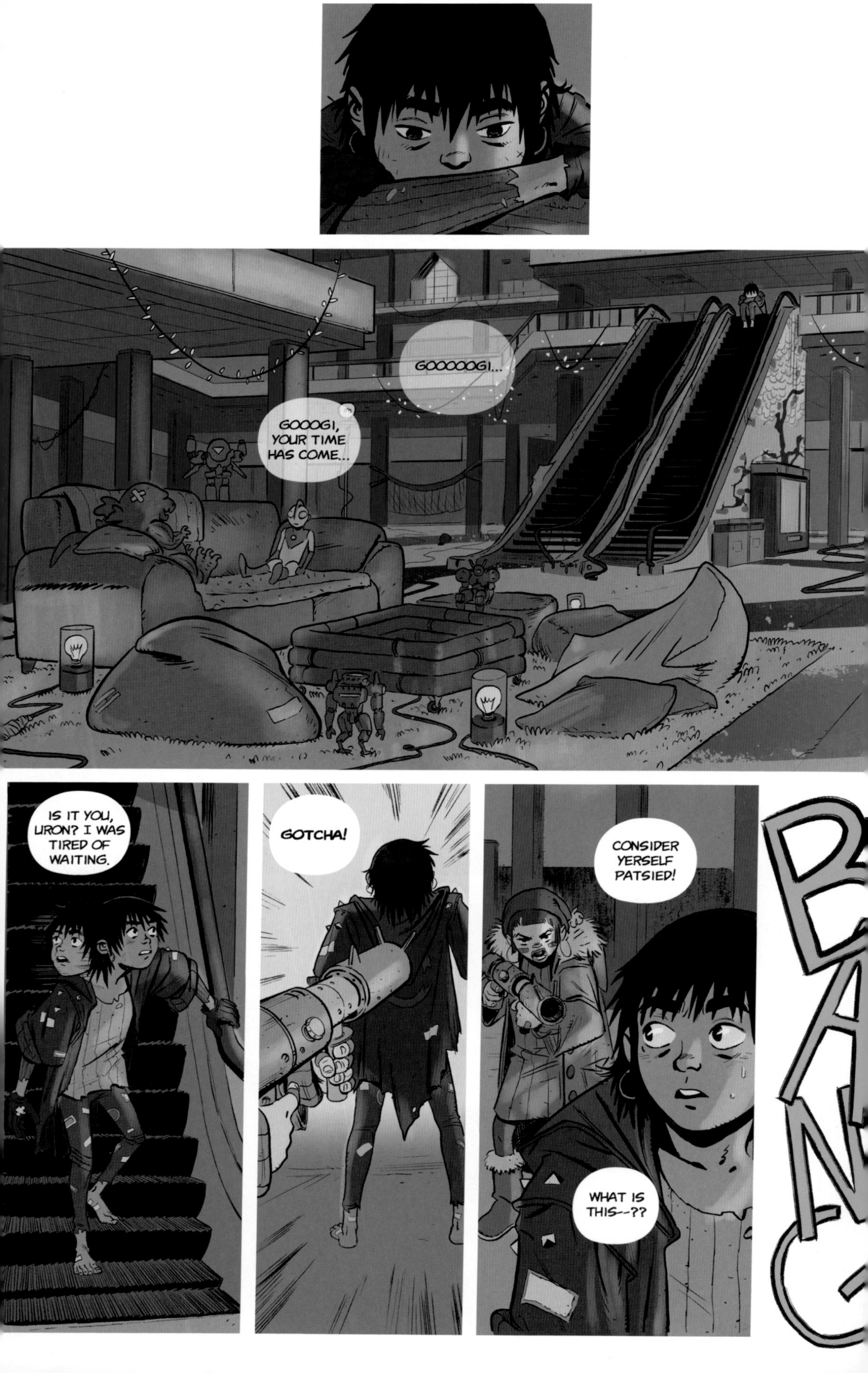
GOOOOOGI...
GOOOGI, YOUR TIME HAS COME...
IS IT YOU, URON? I WAS TIRED OF WAITING.
GOTCHA!
CONSIDER YERSELF PATSIED!
WHAT IS THIS--??
BANG

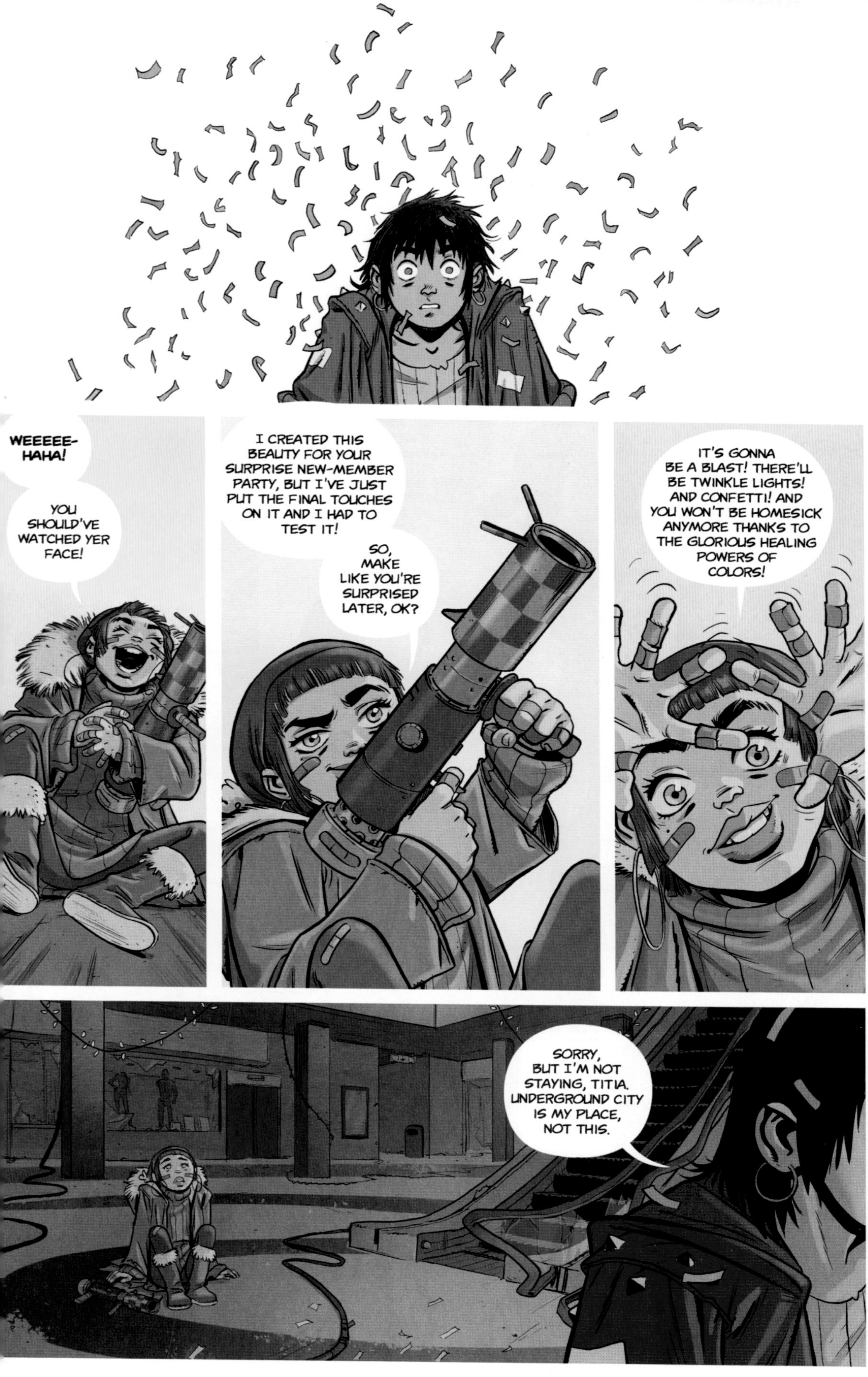
WEEEEE-HAHA!
YOU SHOULD'VE WATCHED YER FACE!
I CREATED THIS BEAUTY FOR YOUR SURPRISE NEW-MEMBER PARTY, BUT I'VE JUST PUT THE FINAL TOUCHES ON IT AND I HAD TO TEST IT!
SO, MAKE LIKE YOU'RE SURPRISED LATER, OK?
IT'S GONNA BE A BLAST! THERE'LL BE TWINKLE LIGHTS! AND CONFETTI! AND YOU WON'T BE HOMESICK ANYMORE THANKS TO THE GLORIOUS HEALING POWERS OF COLORS!
SORRY, BUT I'M NOT STAYING, TITIA. UNDERGROUND CITY IS MY PLACE, NOT THIS.

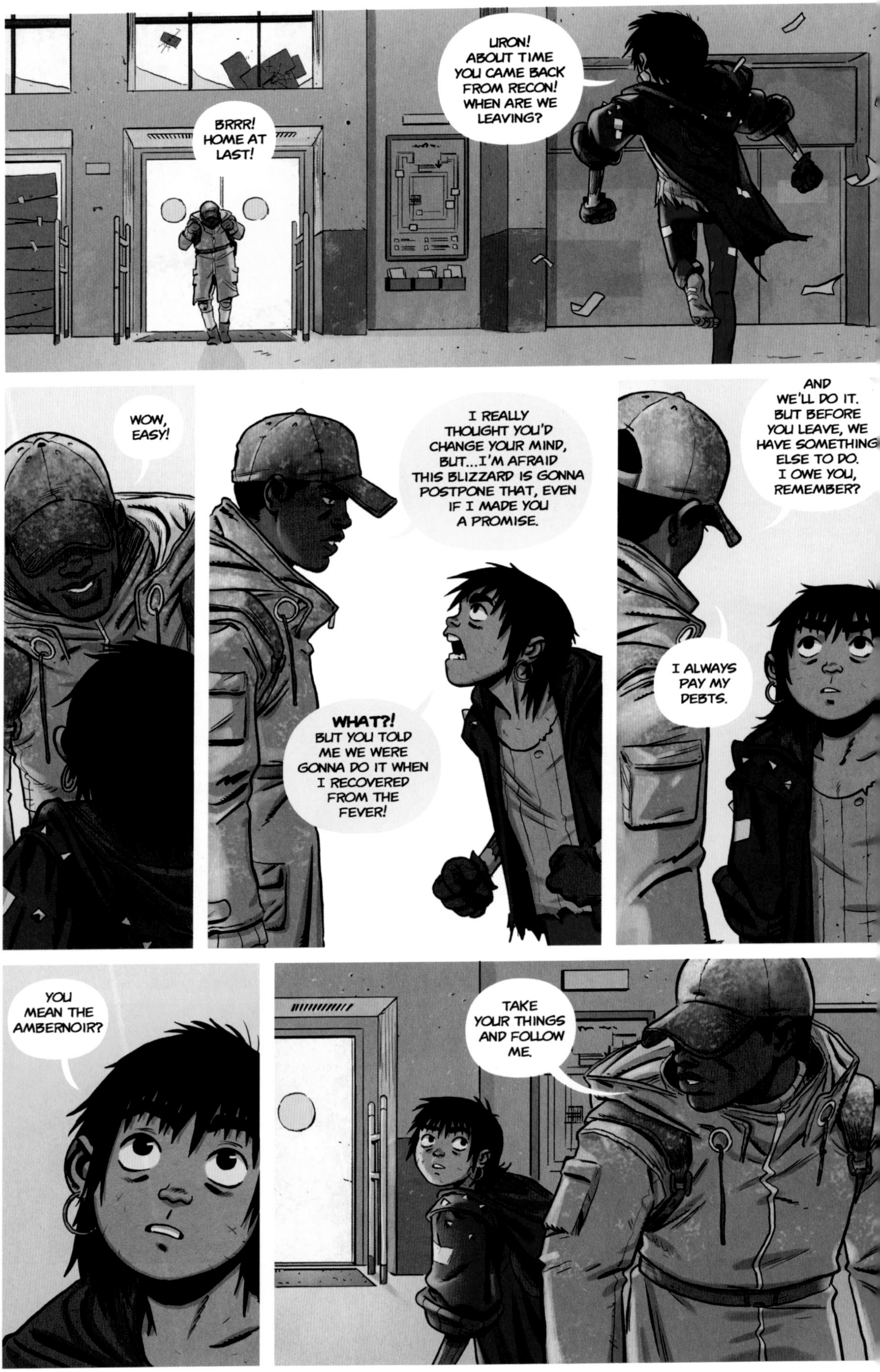
BRRR! HOME AT LAST!
URON! ABOUT TIME YOU CAME BACK FROM RECON! WHEN ARE WE LEAVING?
WOW, EASY!
I REALLY THOUGHT YOU'D CHANGE YOUR MIND, BUT...I'M AFRAID THIS BLIZZARD IS GONNA POSTPONE THAT, EVEN IF I MADE YOU A PROMISE.
WHAT?! BUT YOU TOLD ME WE WERE GONNA DO IT WHEN I RECOVERED FROM THE FEVER!
AND WE'LL DO IT. BUT BEFORE YOU LEAVE, WE HAVE SOMETHING ELSE TO DO. I OWE YOU, REMEMBER?
I ALWAYS PAY MY DEBTS.
YOU MEAN THE AMBERNOIR?
TAKE YOUR THINGS AND FOLLOW ME.

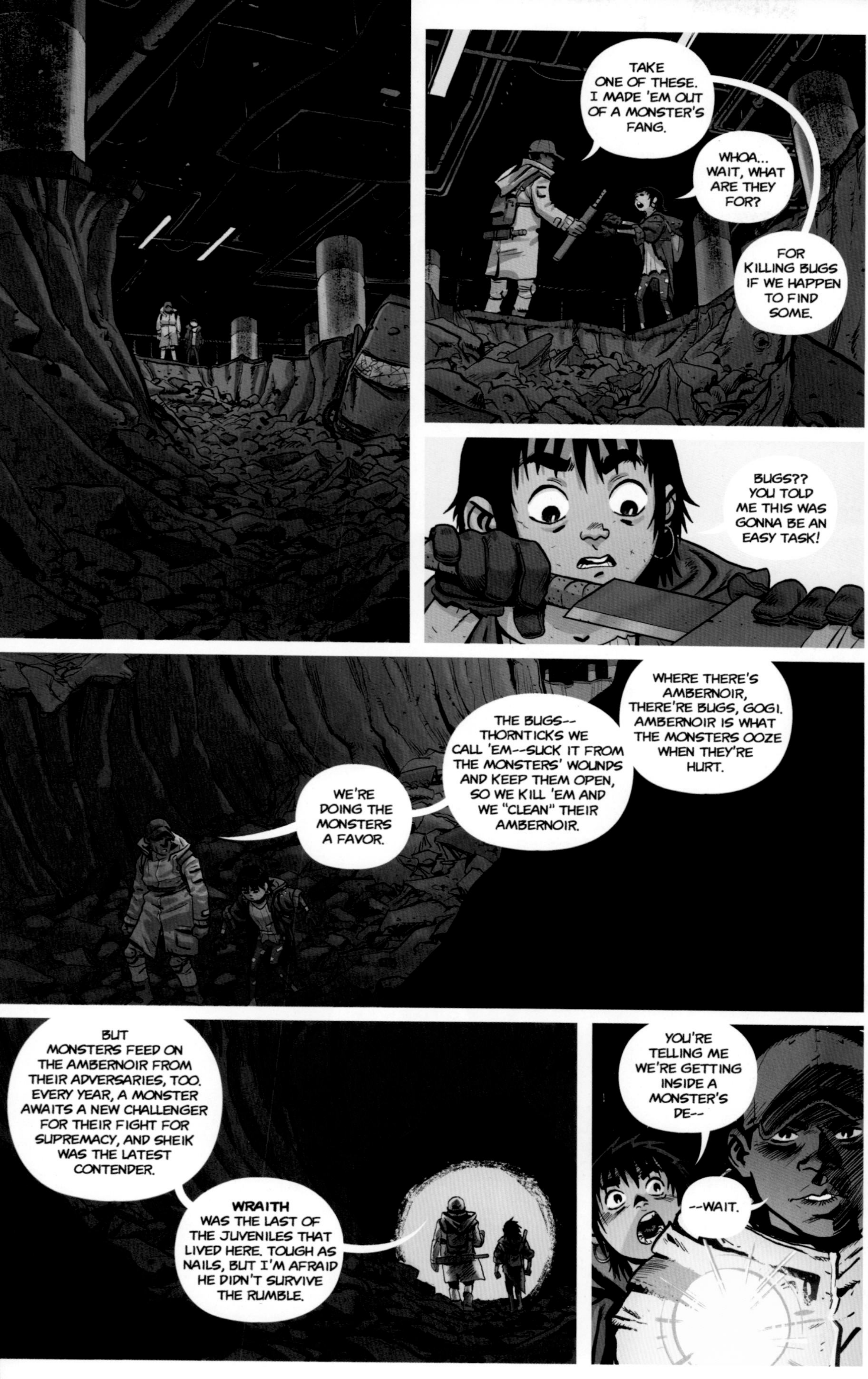
TAKE ONE OF THESE. I MADE 'EM OUT OF A MONSTER'S FANG.
WHOA... WAIT, WHAT ARE THEY FOR?
FOR KILLING BUGS IF WE HAPPEN TO FIND SOME.
BUGS?? YOU TOLD ME THIS WAS GONNA BE AN EASY TASK!
WHERE THERE'S AMBERNOIR, THERE'RE BUGS, GOGI. AMBERNOIR IS WHAT THE MONSTERS OOZE WHEN THEY'RE HURT.
THE BUGS--THORNTICKS WE CALL 'EM--SUCK IT FROM THE MONSTERS' WOUNDS AND KEEP THEM OPEN, SO WE KILL 'EM AND WE "CLEAN" THEIR AMBERNOIR.
WE'RE DOING THE MONSTERS A FAVOR.
BUT MONSTERS FEED ON THE AMBERNOIR FROM THEIR ADVERSARIES, TOO. EVERY YEAR, A MONSTER AWAITS A NEW CHALLENGER FOR THEIR FIGHT FOR SUPREMACY, AND SHEIK WAS THE LATEST CONTENDER.
WRAITH WAS THE LAST OF THE JUVENILES THAT LIVED HERE. TOUGH AS NAILS, BUT I'M AFRAID HE DIDN'T SURVIVE THE RUMBLE.
YOU'RE TELLING ME WE'RE GETTING INSIDE A MONSTER'S DE--
--WAIT.

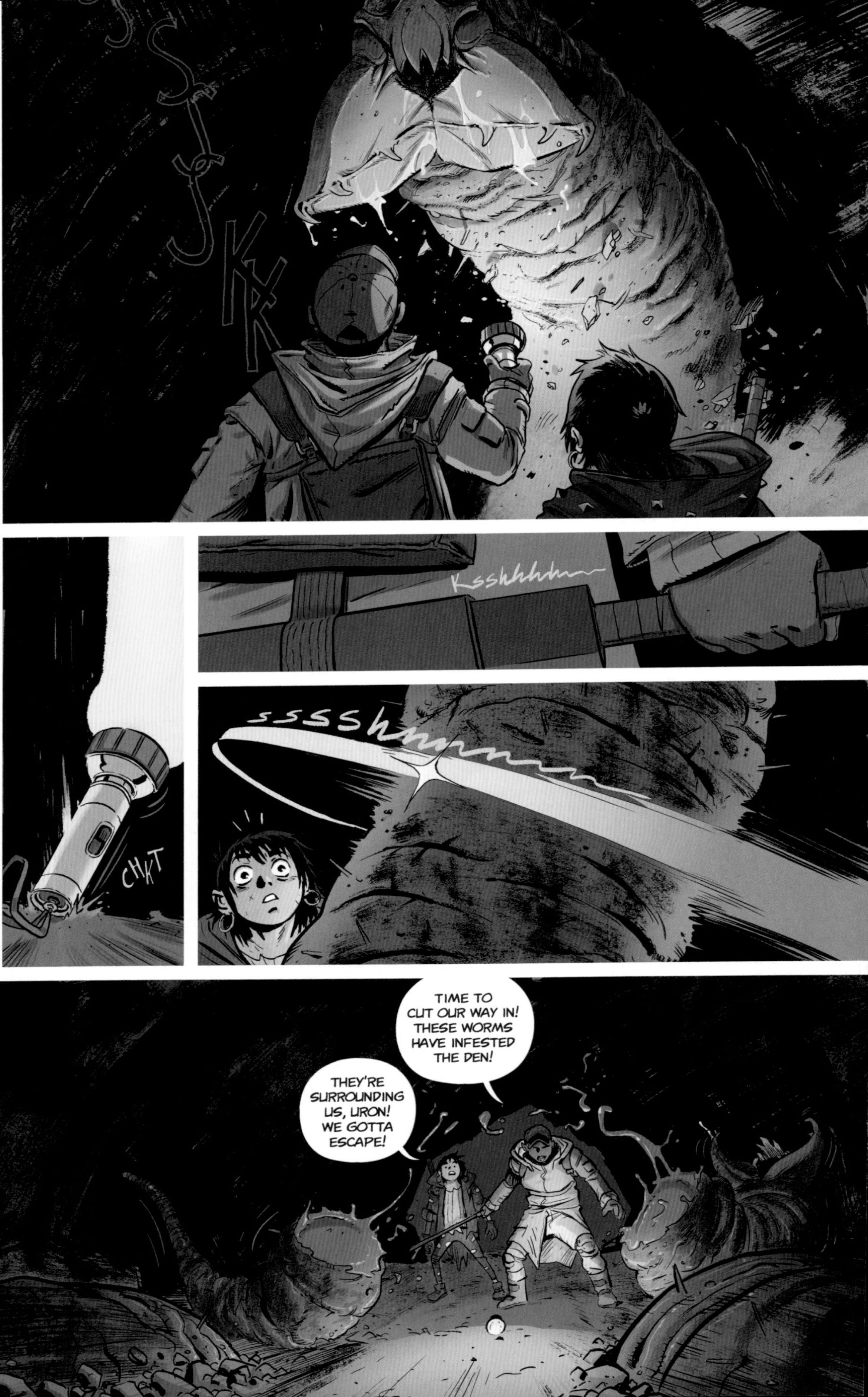
SSSSKK
Ksshhhhm
CHKT
sssShhhhmm
TIME TO CUT OUR WAY IN! THESE WORMS HAVE INFESTED THE DEN!
THEY'RE SURROUNDING US, URON! WE GOTTA ESCAPE!

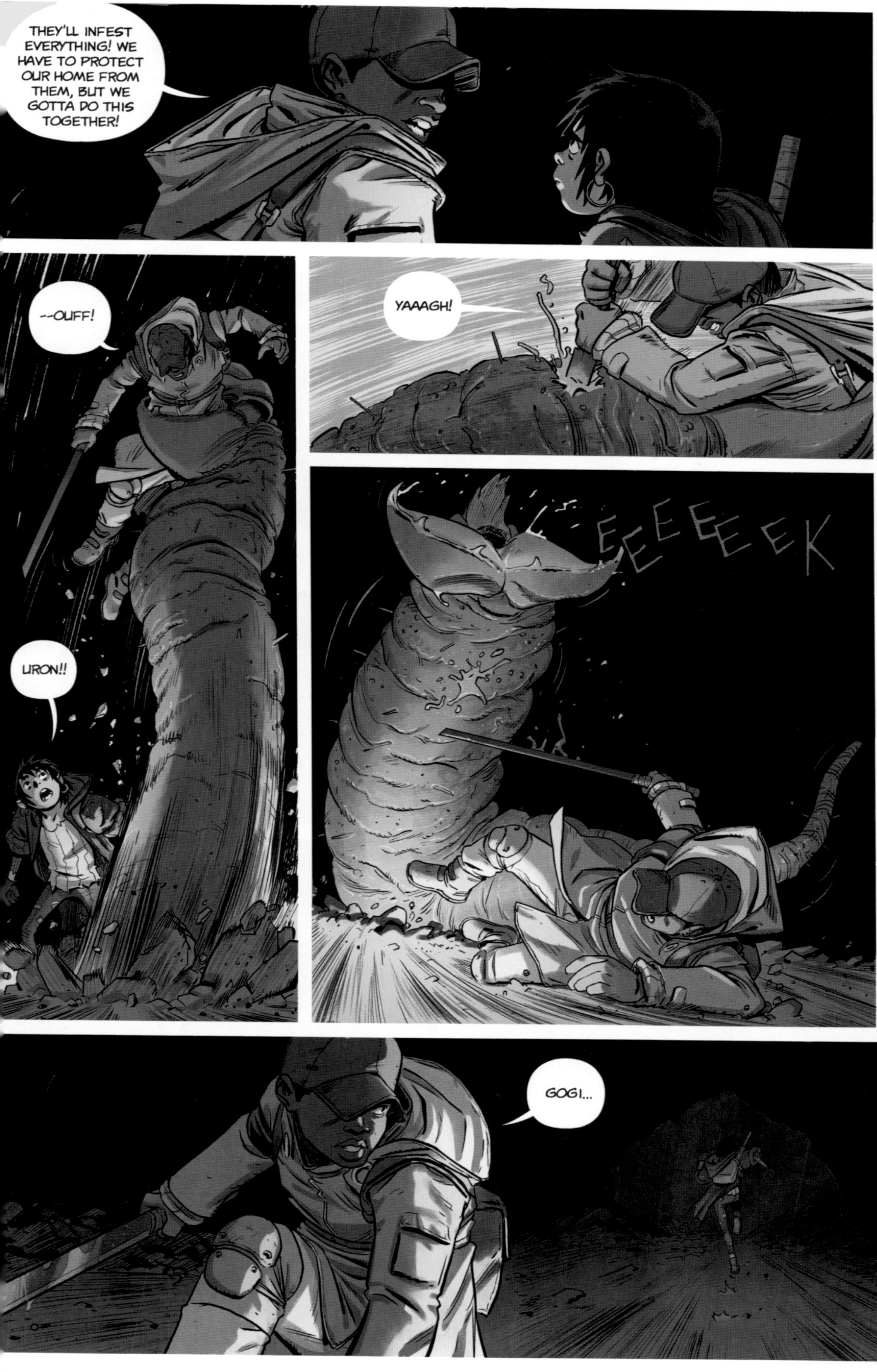
THEY'LL INFEST EVERYTHING! WE HAVE TO PROTECT OUR HOME FROM THEM, BUT WE GOTTA DO THIS TOGETHER!
--OUFF!
URON!!
YAAAGH!
EEEEEEK
GOGI...

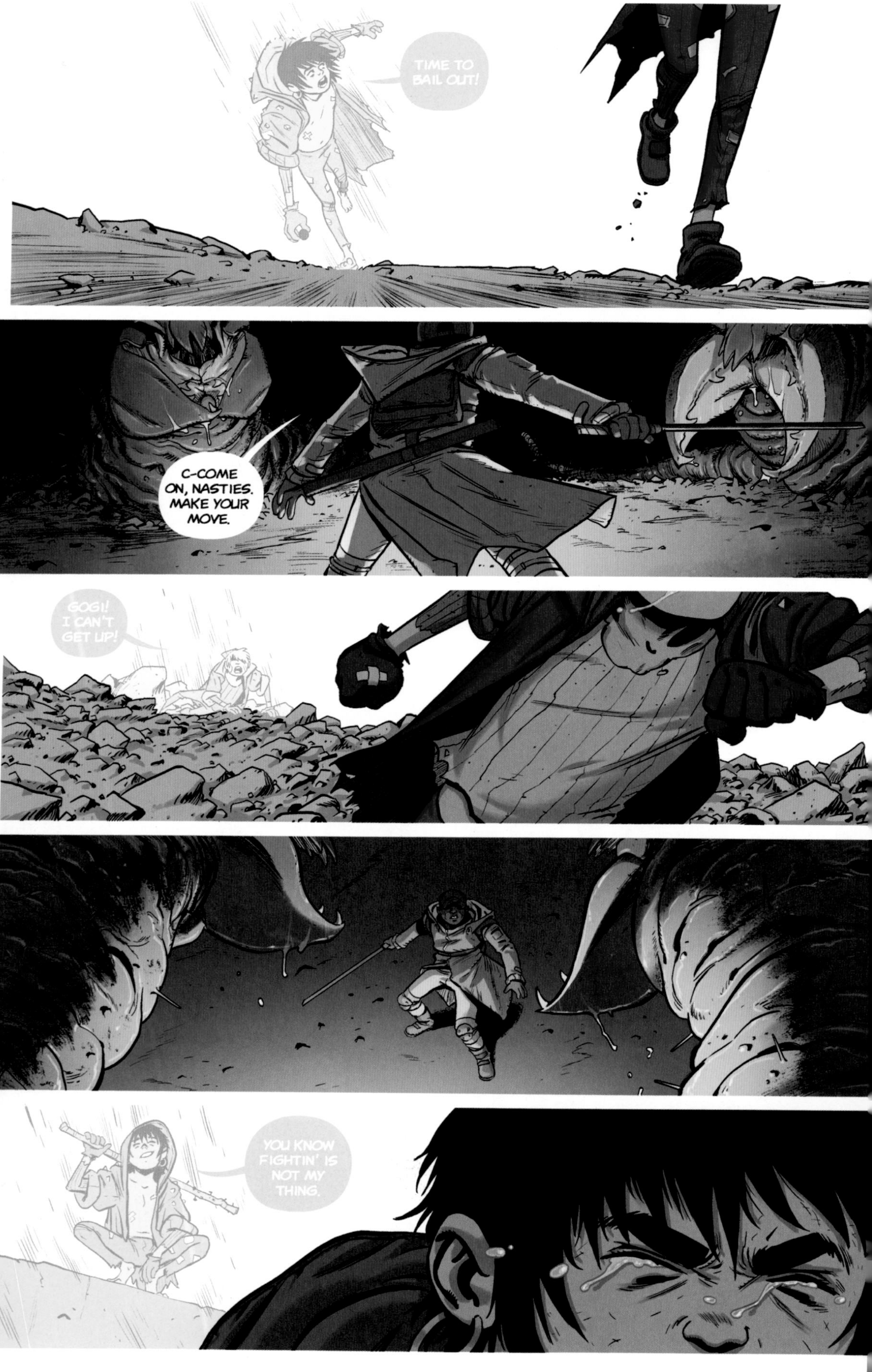
TIME TO BAIL OUT!
C-COME ON, NASTIES. MAKE YOUR MOVE.
GOGI! I CAN'T GET UP!
YOU KNOW FIGHTIN' IS NOT MY THING.

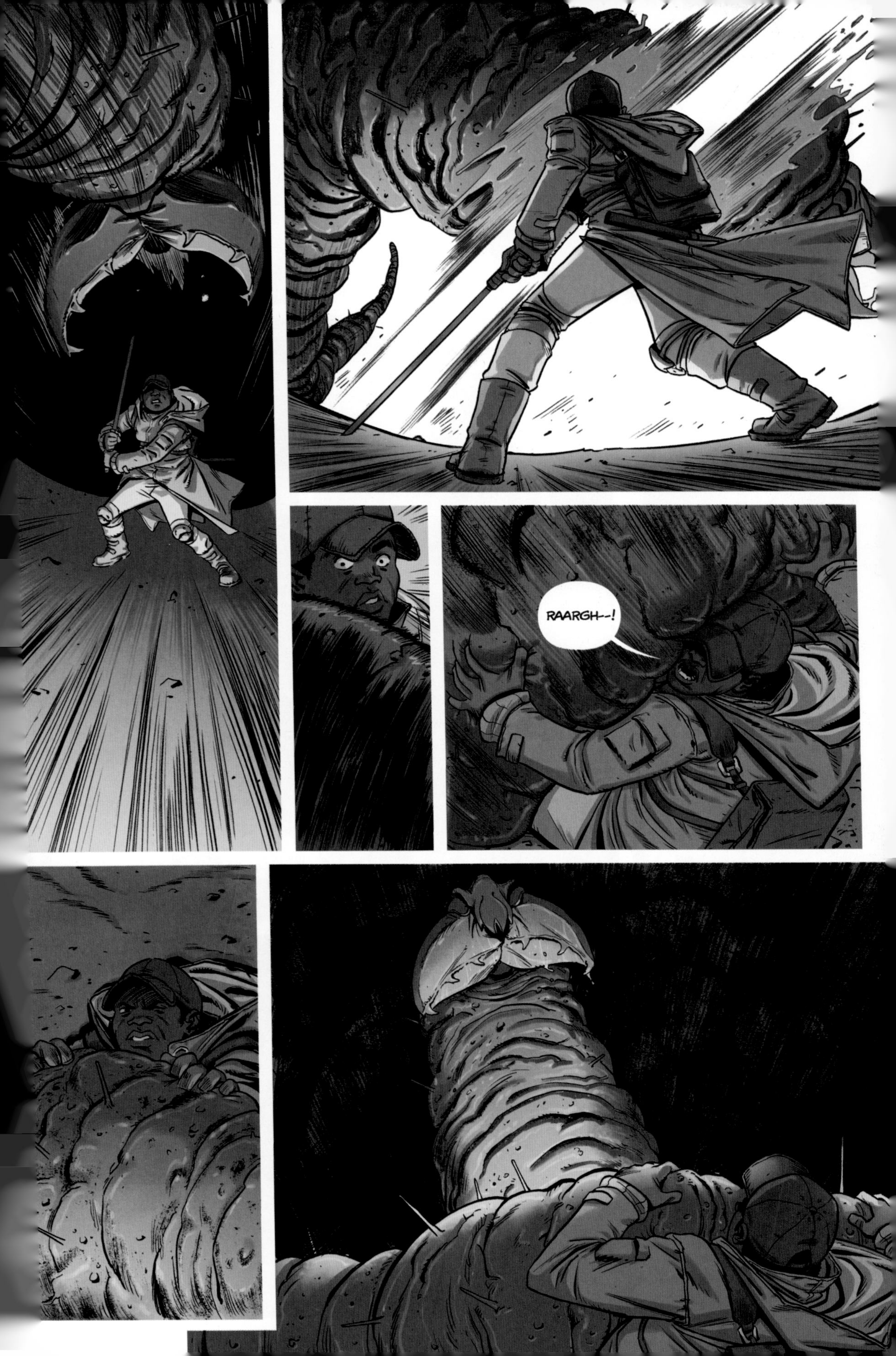
RAARGH--!

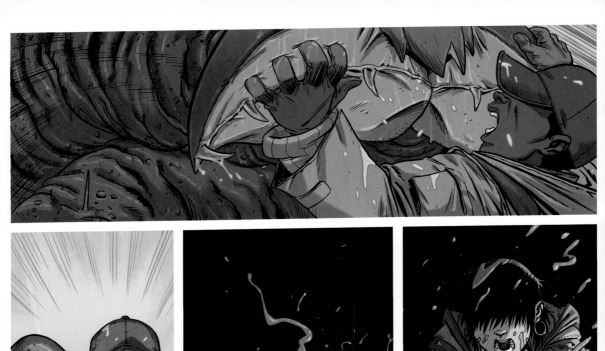

WE'LL DO THIS TOGETHER.

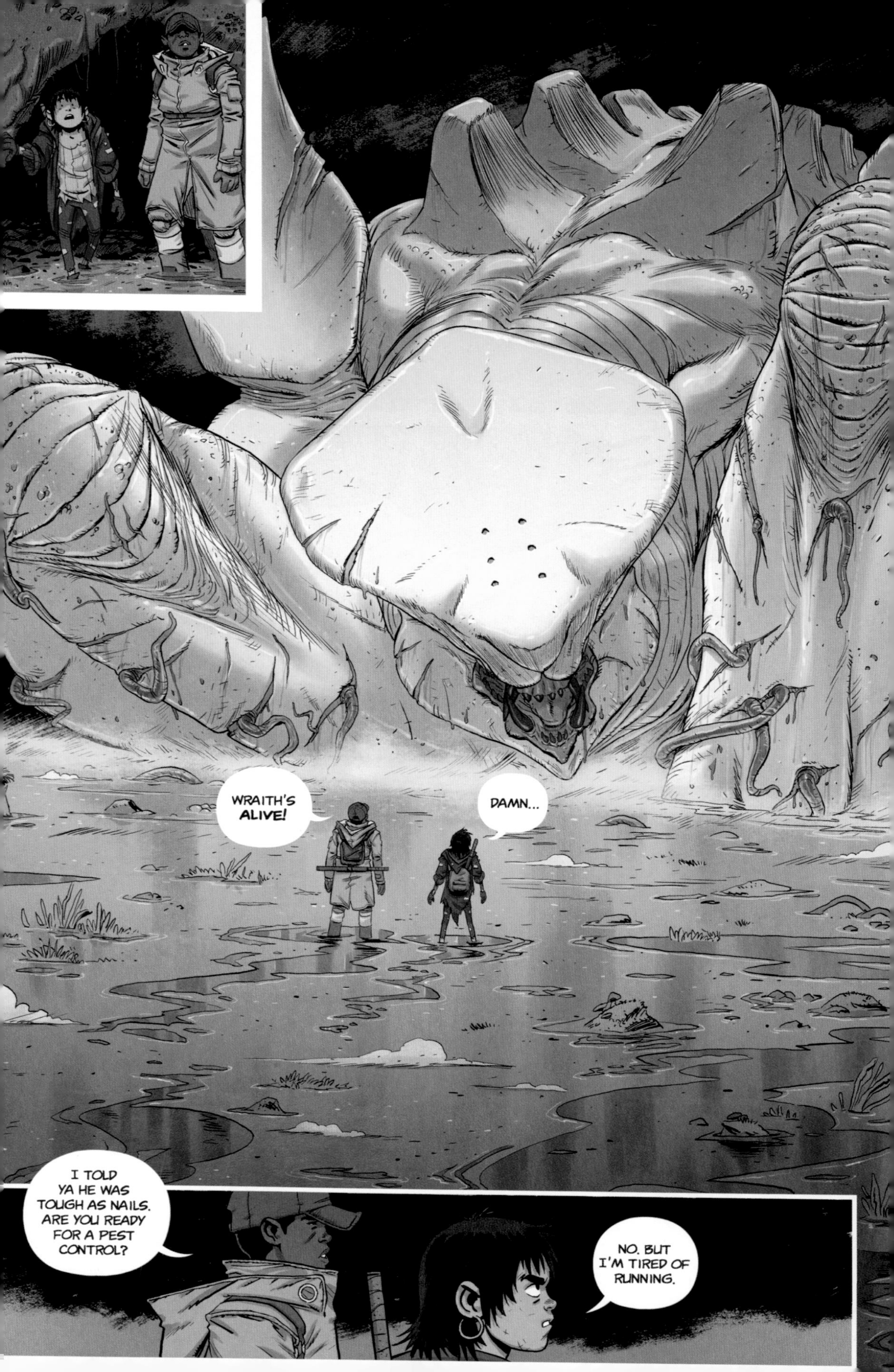
WRAITH'S ALIVE!
DAMN...
I TOLD YA HE WAS TOUGH AS NAILS. ARE YOU READY FOR A PEST CONTROL?
NO. BUT I'M TIRED OF RUNNING.

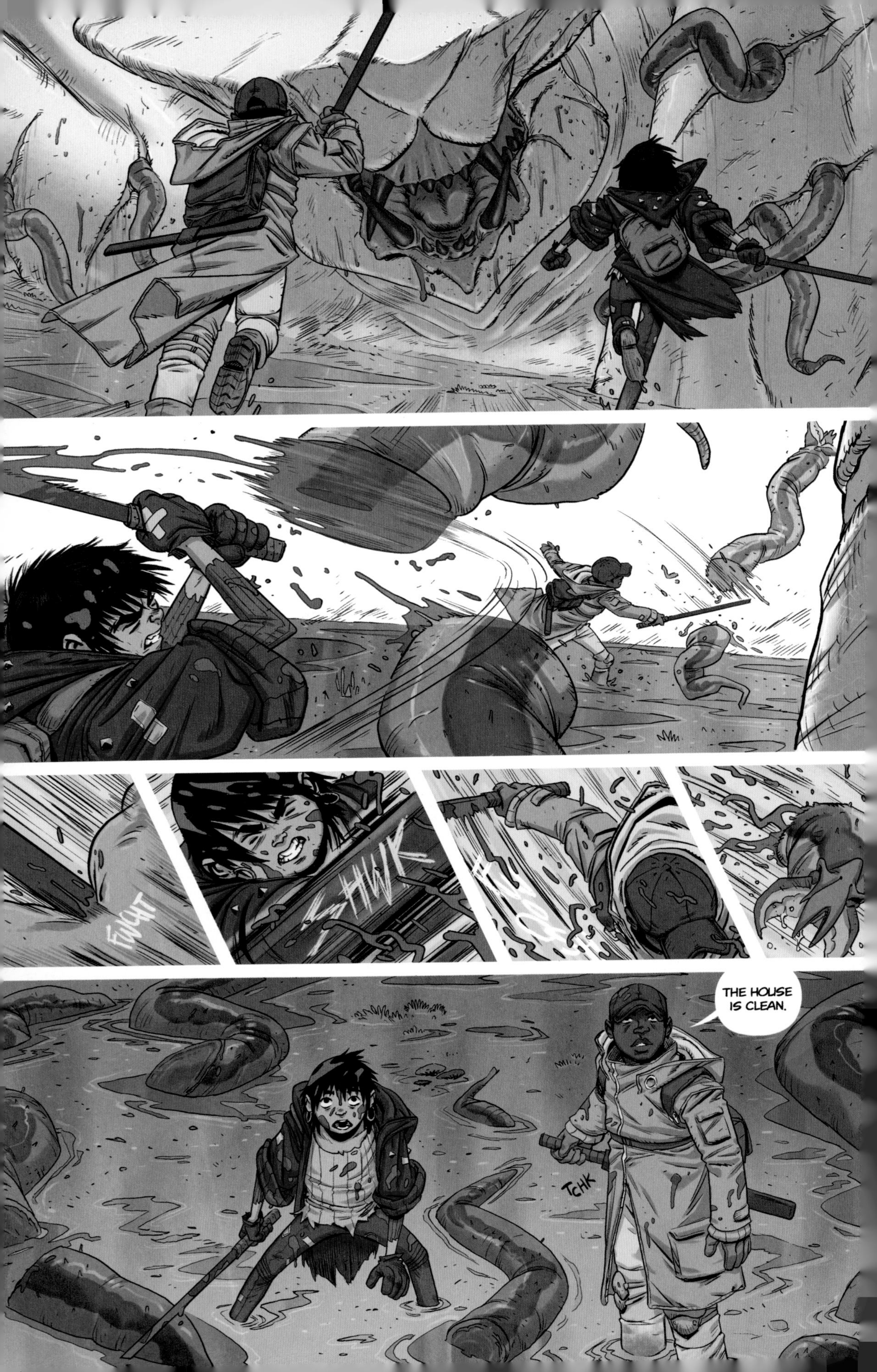
SHWK
THE HOUSE IS CLEAN.
TCHK

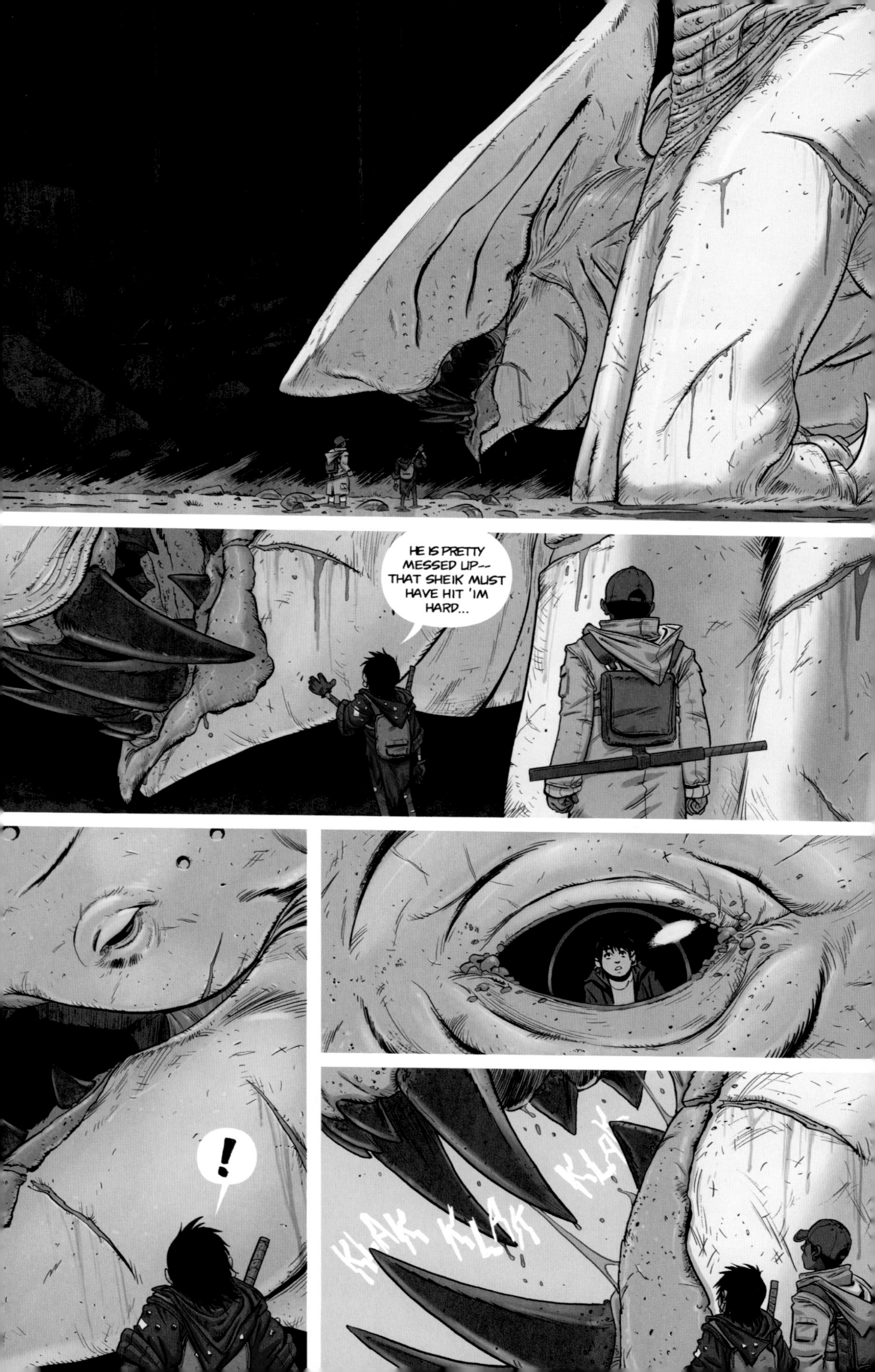
HE IS PRETTY MESSED UP-- THAT SHEIK MUST HAVE HIT 'IM HARD...
!
KLAK KLAK KLAK

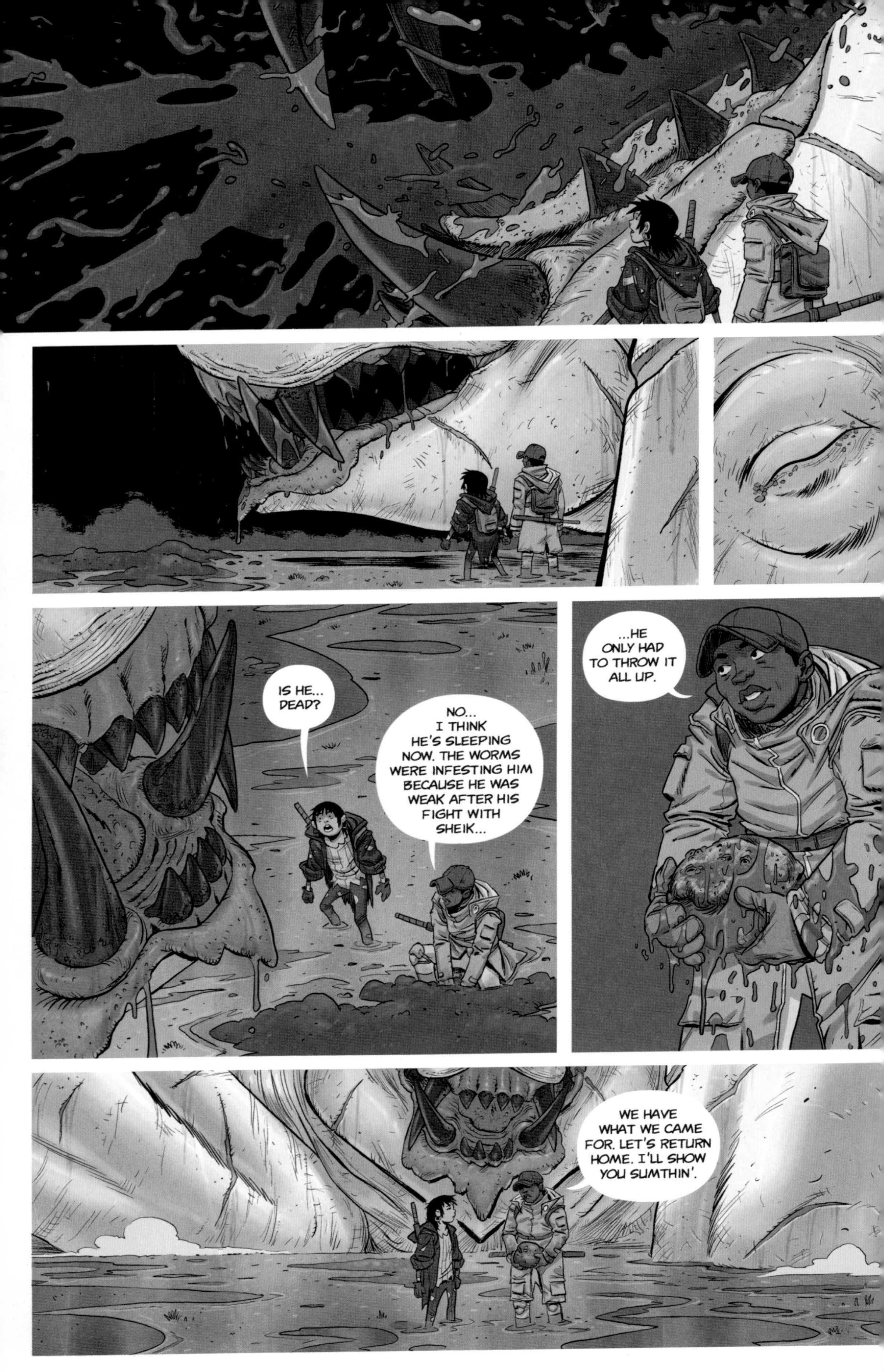
IS HE... DEAD?
NO... I THINK HE'S SLEEPING NOW. THE WORMS WERE INFESTING HIM BECAUSE HE WAS WEAK AFTER HIS FIGHT WITH SHEIK...
...HE ONLY HAD TO THROW IT ALL UP.
WE HAVE WHAT WE CAME FOR. LET'S RETURN HOME. I'LL SHOW YOU SUMTHIN'.

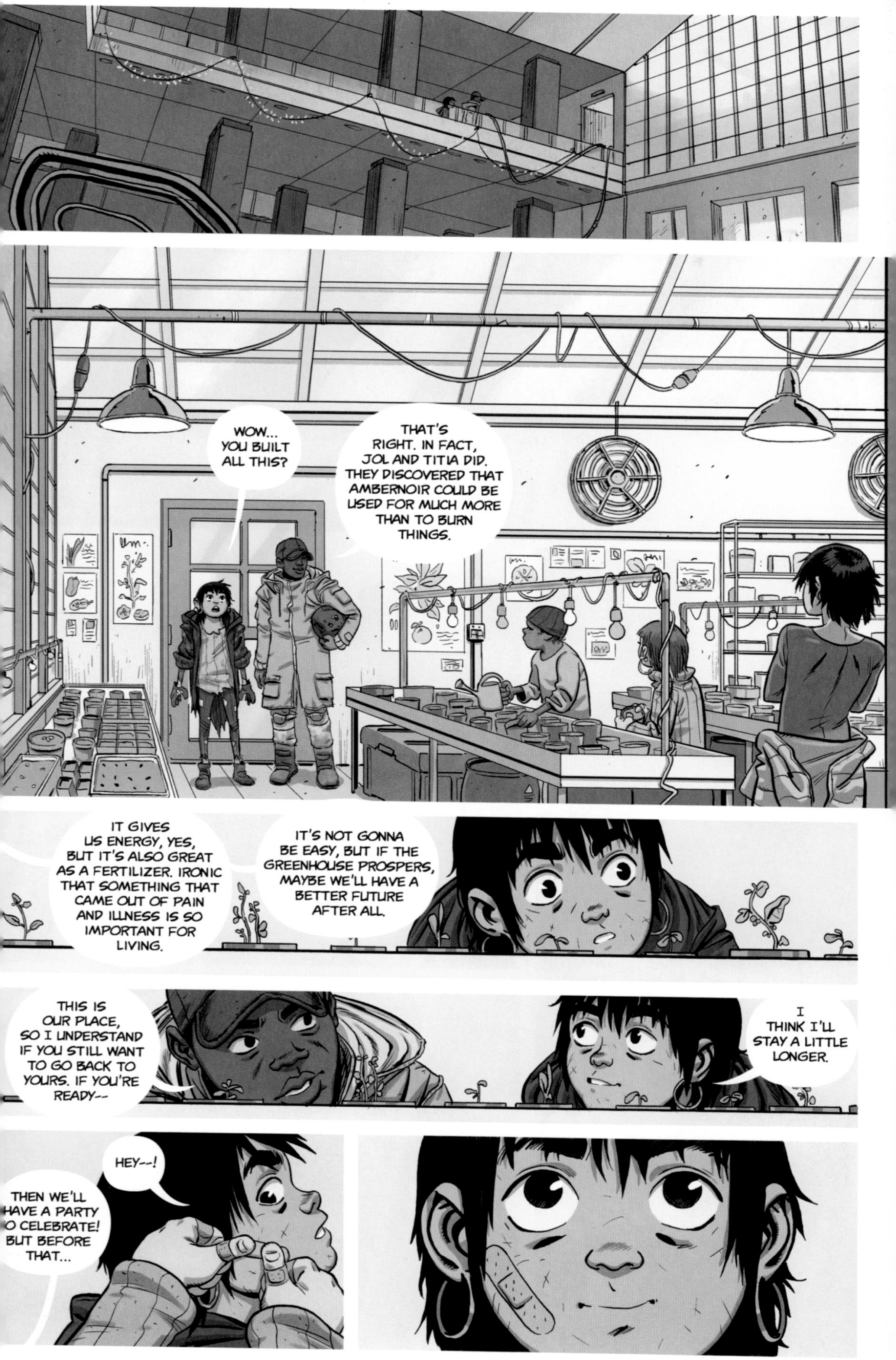
WOW... YOU BUILT ALL THIS?
THAT'S RIGHT. IN FACT, JOL AND TITIA DID. THEY DISCOVERED THAT AMBERNOIR COULD BE USED FOR MUCH MORE THAN TO BURN THINGS.
IT GIVES US ENERGY, YES, BUT IT'S ALSO GREAT AS A FERTILIZER. IRONIC THAT SOMETHING THAT CAME OUT OF PAIN AND ILLNESS IS SO IMPORTANT FOR LIVING.
IT'S NOT GONNA BE EASY, BUT IF THE GREENHOUSE PROSPERS, MAYBE WE'LL HAVE A BETTER FUTURE AFTER ALL.
THIS IS OUR PLACE, SO I UNDERSTAND IF YOU STILL WANT TO GO BACK TO YOURS. IF YOU'RE READY--
I THINK I'LL STAY A LITTLE LONGER.
HEY--!
THEN WE'LL HAVE A PARTY TO CELEBRATE! BUT BEFORE THAT...

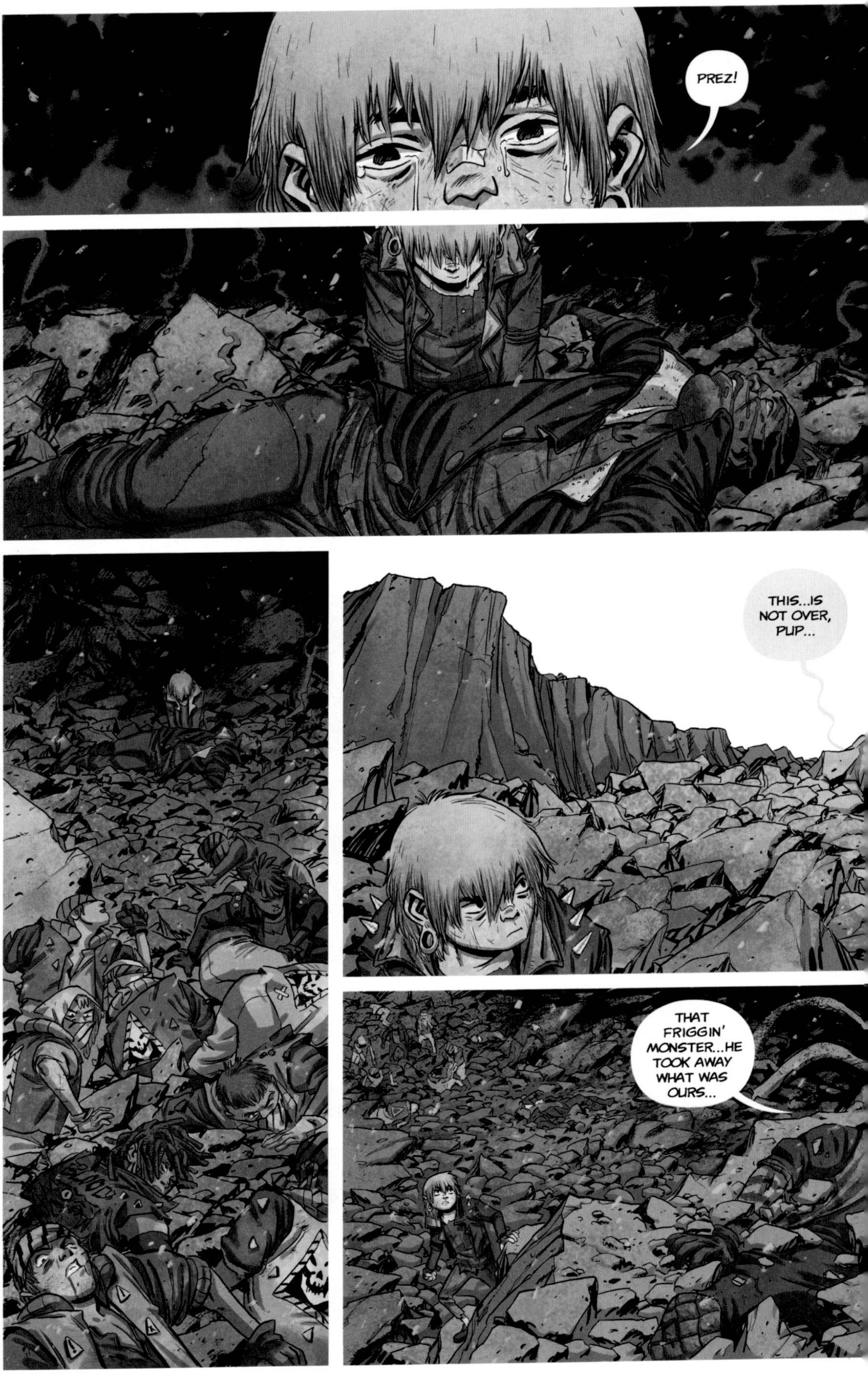
PREZ!
THIS...IS NOT OVER, PUP...
THAT FRIGGIN' MONSTER...HE TOOK AWAY WHAT WAS OURS...

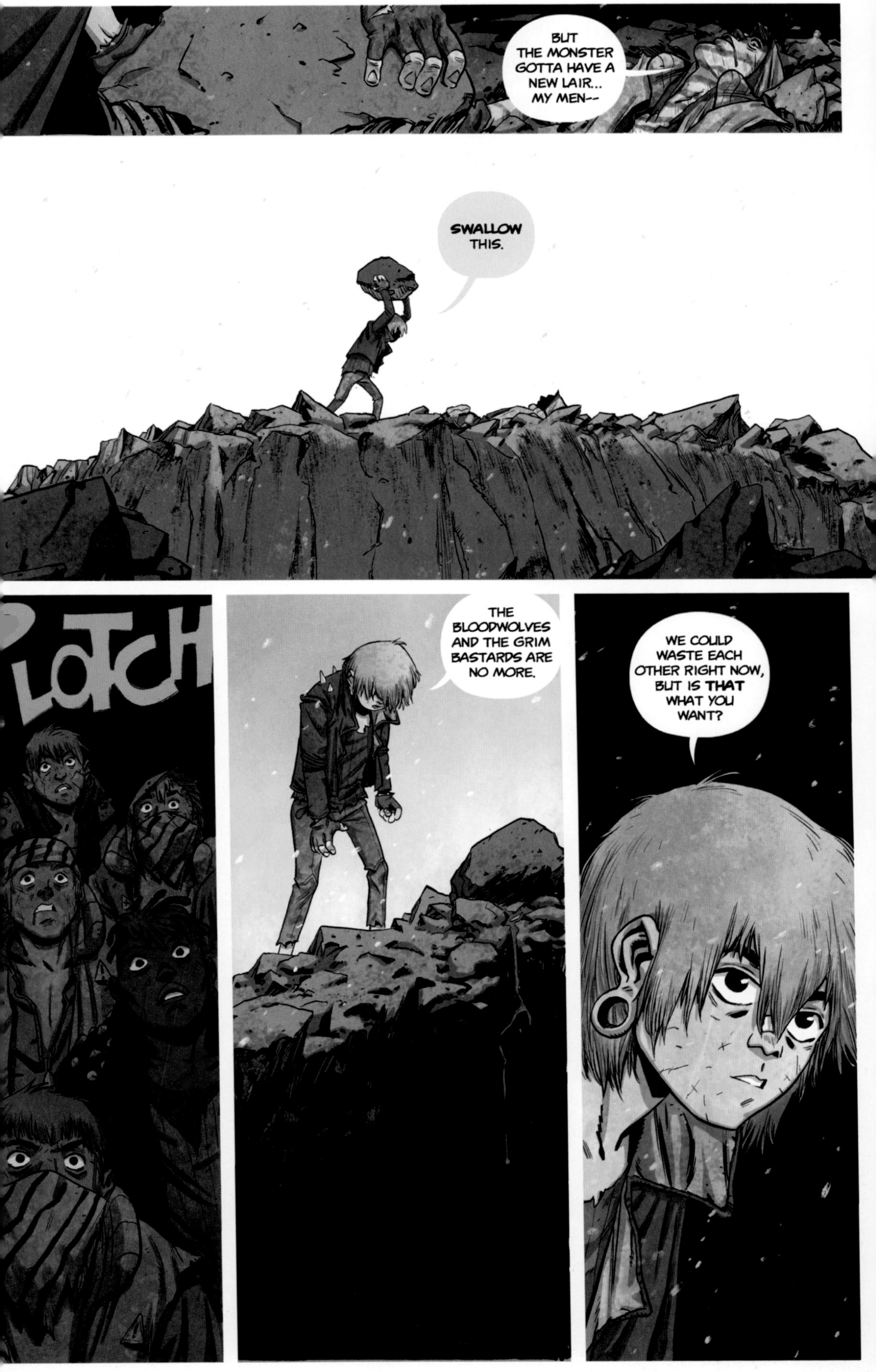
BUT THE MONSTER GOTTA HAVE A NEW LAIR... MY MEN--
SWALLOW THIS.
PLOTCH
THE BLOODWOLVES AND THE GRIM BASTARDS ARE NO MORE.
WE COULD WASTE EACH OTHER RIGHT NOW, BUT IS THAT WHAT YOU WANT?

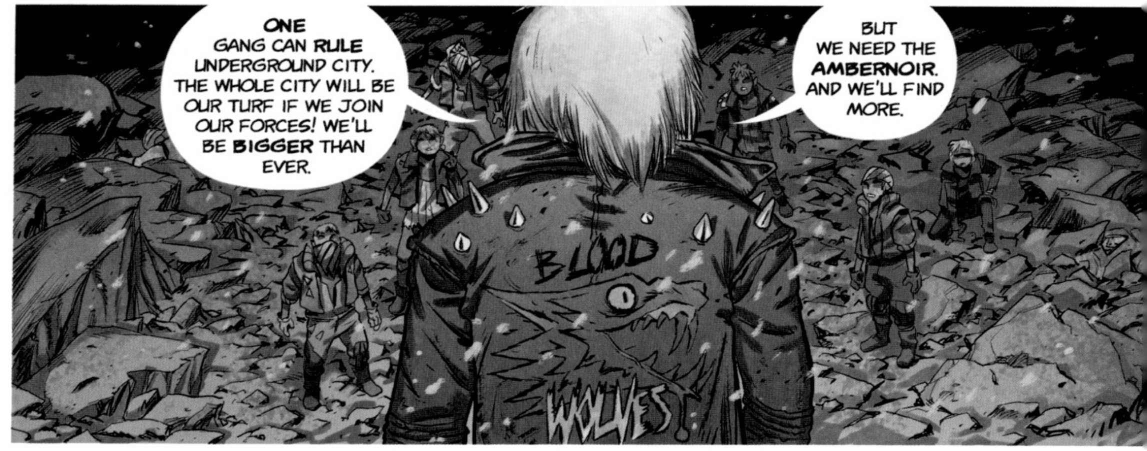
ONE GANG CAN RULE UNDERGROUND CITY. THE WHOLE CITY WILL BE OUR TURF IF WE JOIN OUR FORCES! WE'LL BE BIGGER THAN EVER.
BUT WE NEED THE AMBERNOIR. AND WE'LL FIND MORE.
BLOOD WOLVES!

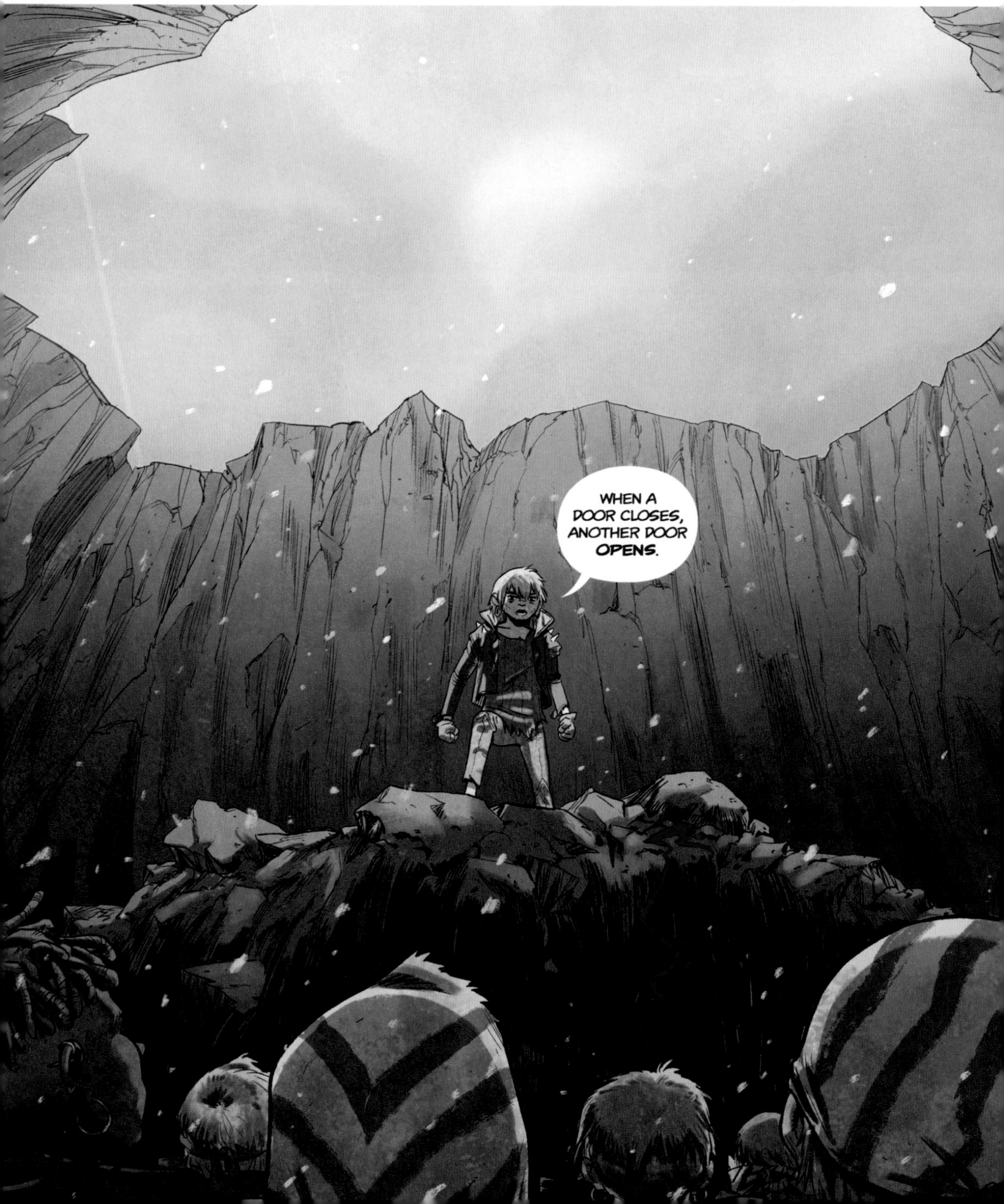
WHEN A DOOR CLOSES, ANOTHER DOOR OPENS.

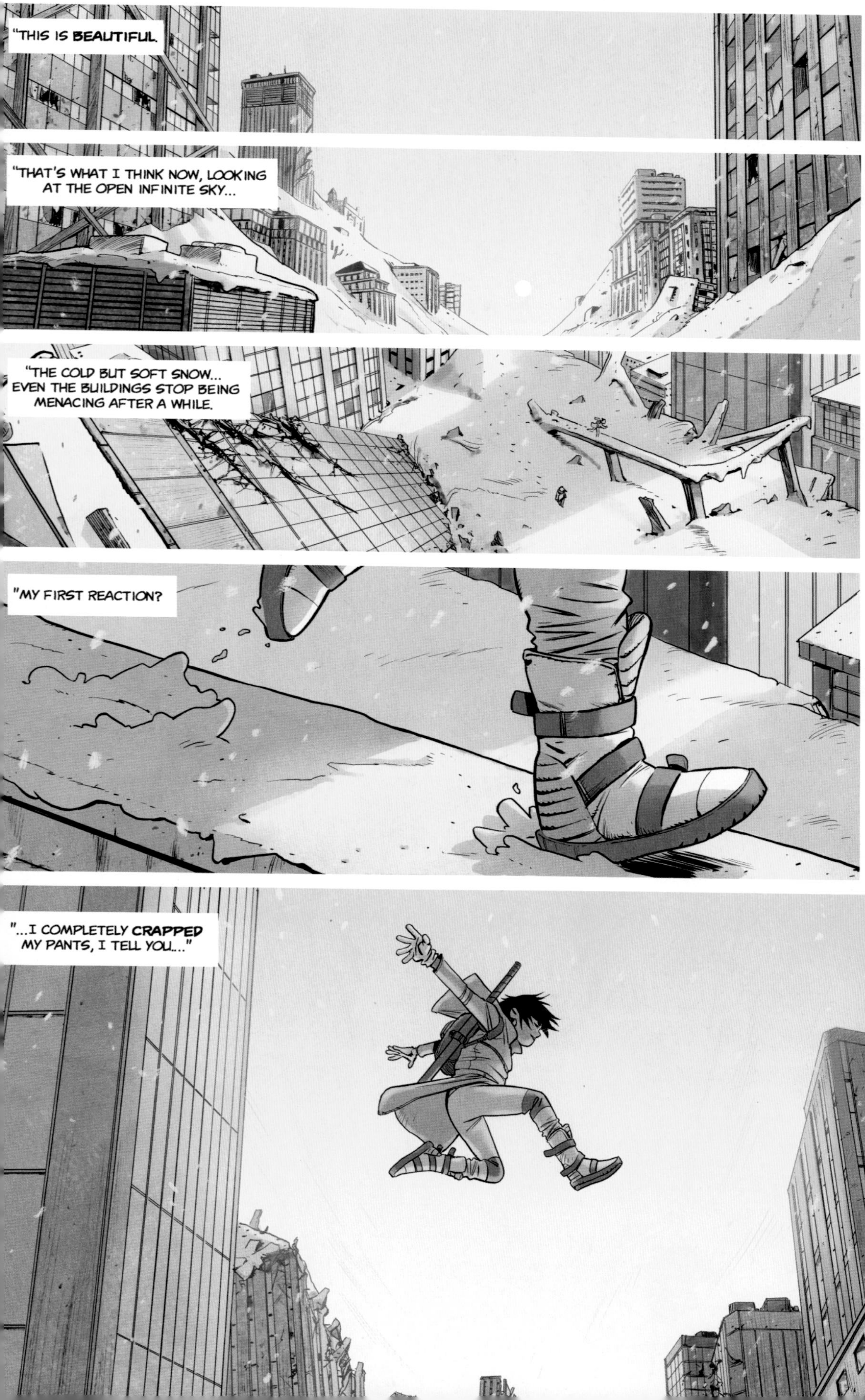
"THIS IS BEAUTIFUL.
"THAT'S WHAT I THINK NOW, LOOKING AT THE OPEN INFINITE SKY...
"THE COLD BUT SOFT SNOW... EVEN THE BUILDINGS STOP BEING MENACING AFTER A WHILE.
"MY FIRST REACTION?
"...I COMPLETELY CRAPPED MY PANTS, I TELL YOU..."

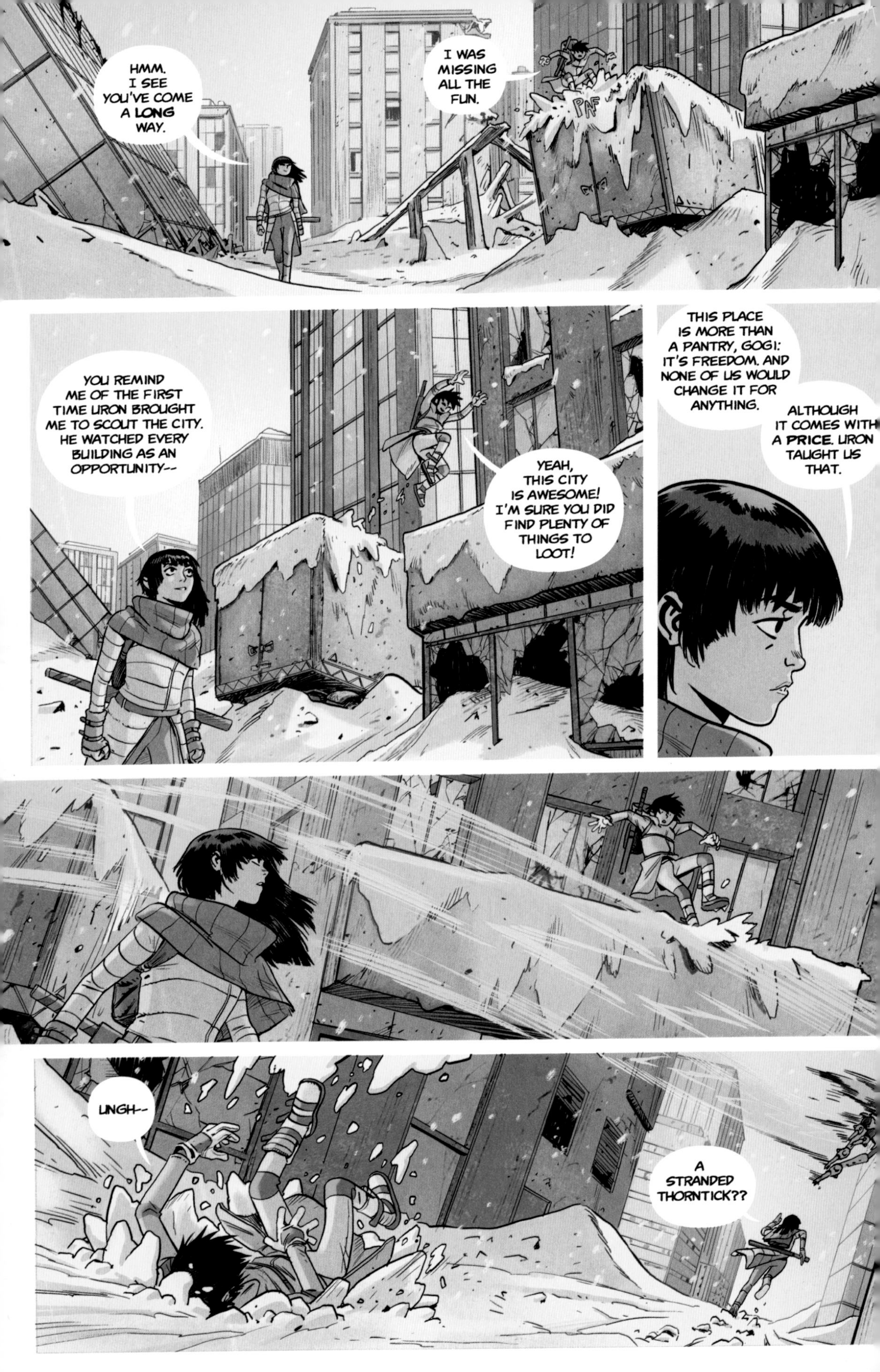
HMM. I SEE YOU'VE COME A LONG WAY.
I WAS MISSING ALL THE FUN.
PAF
YOU REMIND ME OF THE FIRST TIME URON BROUGHT ME TO SCOUT THE CITY. HE WATCHED EVERY BUILDING AS AN OPPORTUNITY--
YEAH, THIS CITY IS AWESOME! I'M SURE YOU DID FIND PLENTY OF THINGS TO LOOT!
THIS PLACE IS MORE THAN A PANTRY, GOGI: IT'S FREEDOM. AND NONE OF US WOULD CHANGE IT FOR ANYTHING.
ALTHOUGH IT COMES WITH A PRICE. URON TAUGHT US THAT.
UNGH--
A STRANDED THORNTICK??

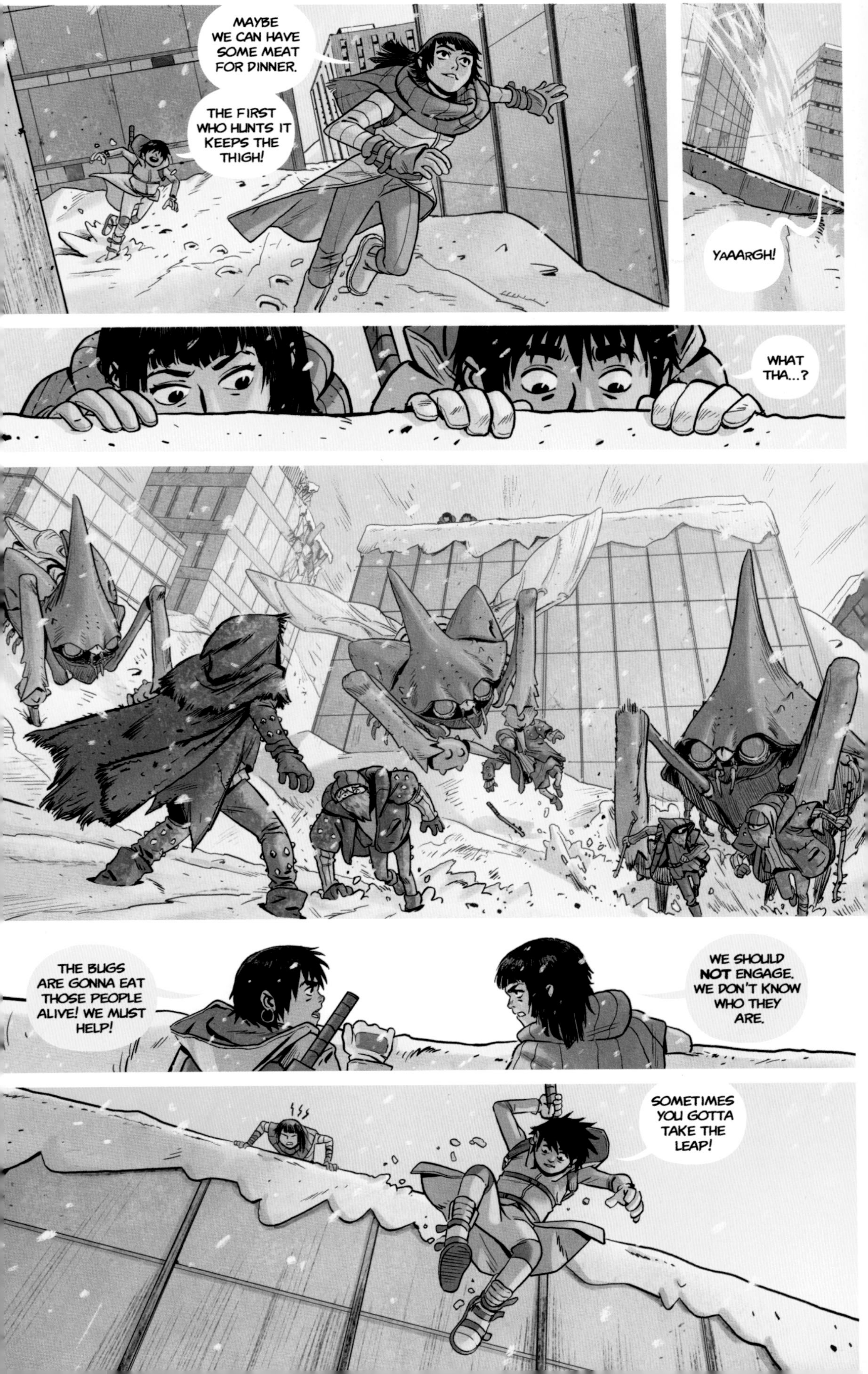
MAYBE WE CAN HAVE SOME MEAT FOR DINNER.
THE FIRST WHO HUNTS IT KEEPS THE THIGH!
YAAARGH!
WHAT THA...?
THE BUGS ARE GONNA EAT THOSE PEOPLE ALIVE! WE MUST HELP!
WE SHOULD **NOT** ENGAGE. WE DON'T KNOW WHO THEY ARE.
SOMETIMES YOU GOTTA TAKE THE LEAP!

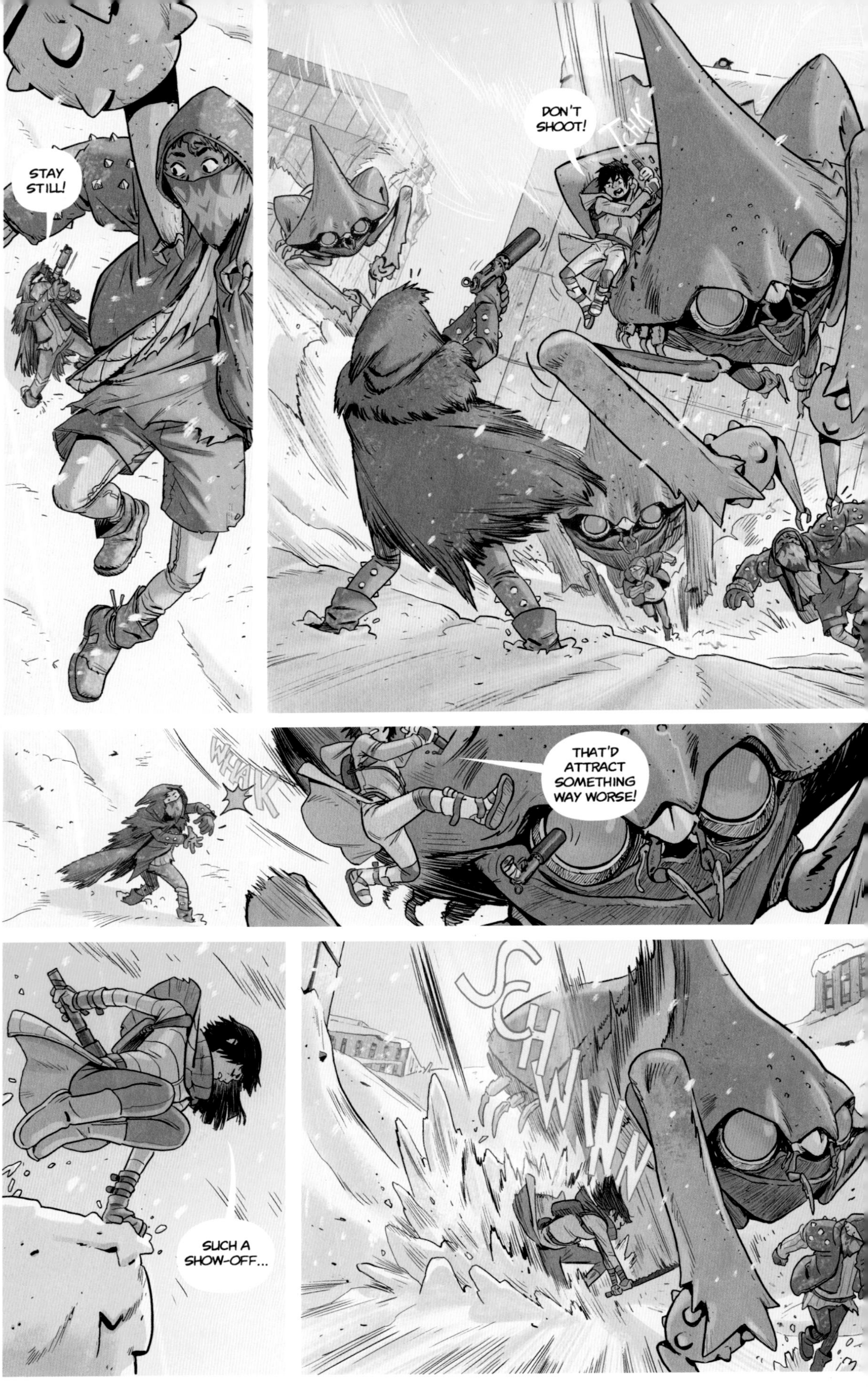
STAY STILL!
DON'T SHOOT!
TCHK
WHAK
THAT'D ATTRACT SOMETHING WAY WORSE!
SUCH A SHOW-OFF...
SCHWINNN

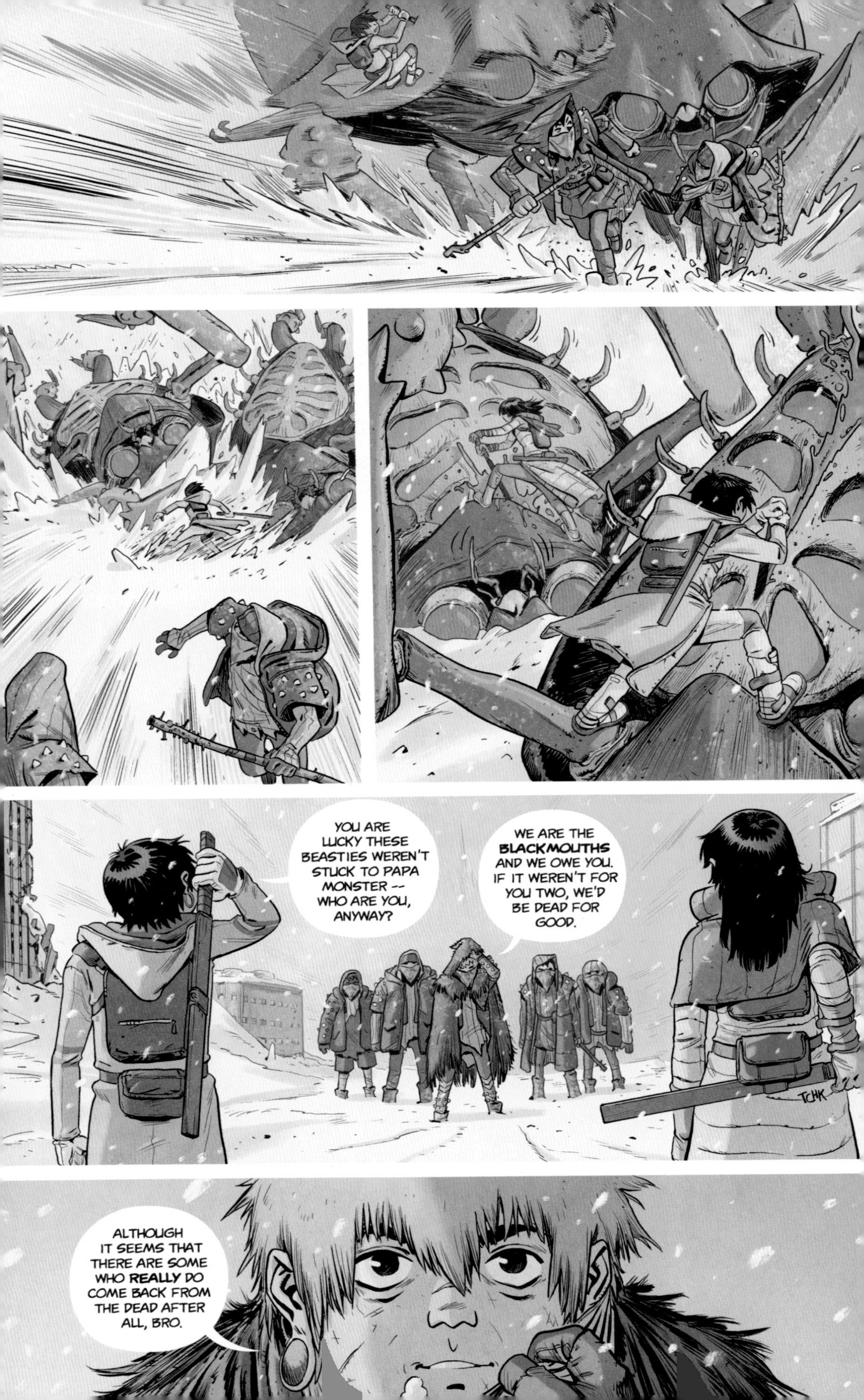
YOU ARE LUCKY THESE BEASTIES WEREN'T STUCK TO PAPA MONSTER -- WHO ARE YOU, ANYWAY?
WE ARE THE **BLACKMOUTHS** AND WE OWE YOU. IF IT WEREN'T FOR YOU TWO, WE'D BE DEAD FOR GOOD.
TCHK
ALTHOUGH IT SEEMS THAT THERE ARE SOME WHO **REALLY** DO COME BACK FROM THE DEAD AFTER ALL, BRO.

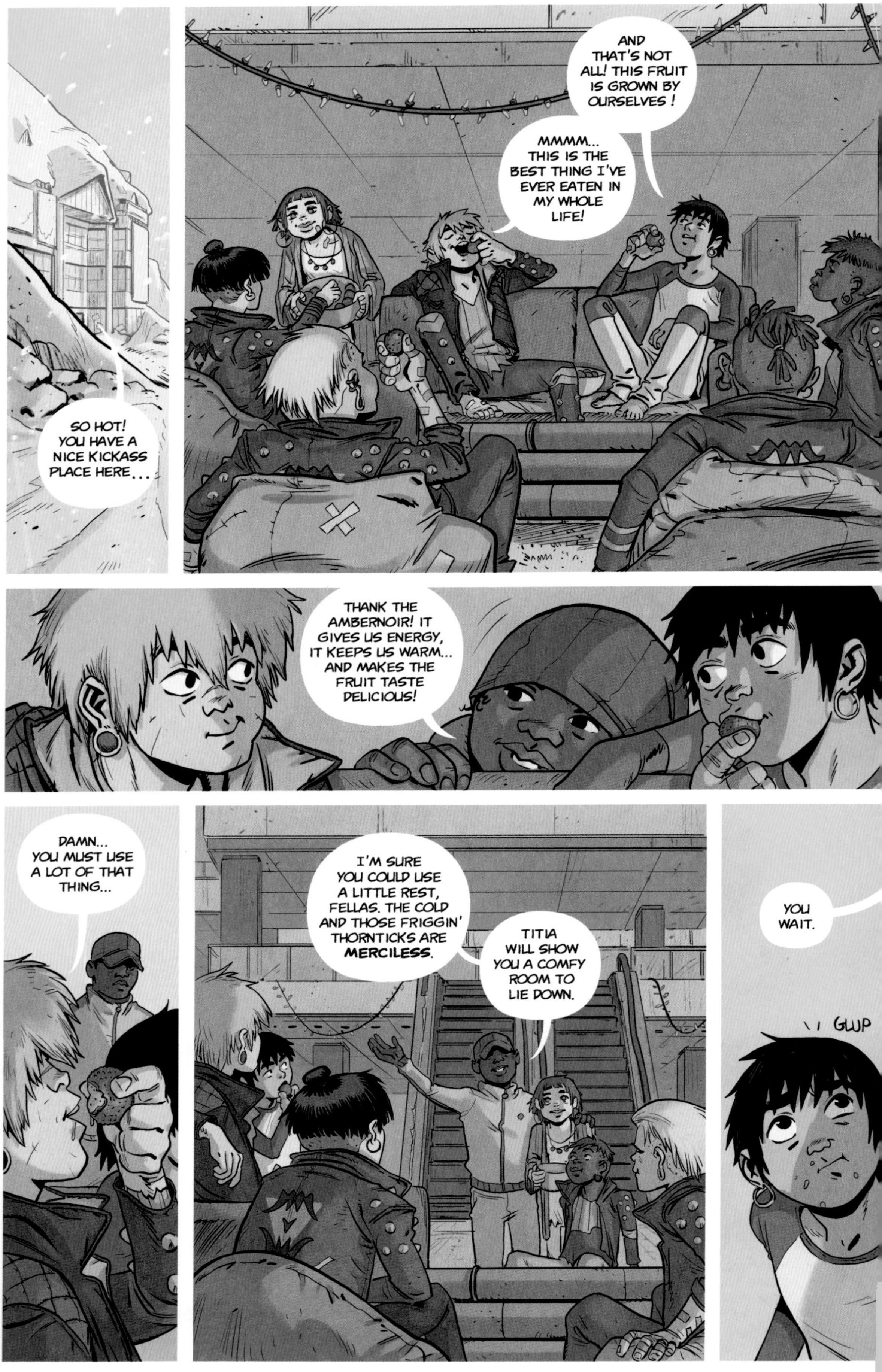
SO HOT! YOU HAVE A NICE KICKASS PLACE HERE...
MMMM... THIS IS THE BEST THING I'VE EVER EATEN IN MY WHOLE LIFE!
AND THAT'S NOT ALL! THIS FRUIT IS GROWN BY OURSELVES !
THANK THE AMBERNOIR! IT GIVES US ENERGY, IT KEEPS US WARM... AND MAKES THE FRUIT TASTE DELICIOUS!
DAMN... YOU MUST USE A LOT OF THAT THING...
I'M SURE YOU COULD USE A LITTLE REST, FELLAS. THE COLD AND THOSE FRIGGIN' THORNTICKS ARE **MERCILESS**.
TITIA WILL SHOW YOU A COMFY ROOM TO LIE DOWN.
YOU WAIT.
GLUP

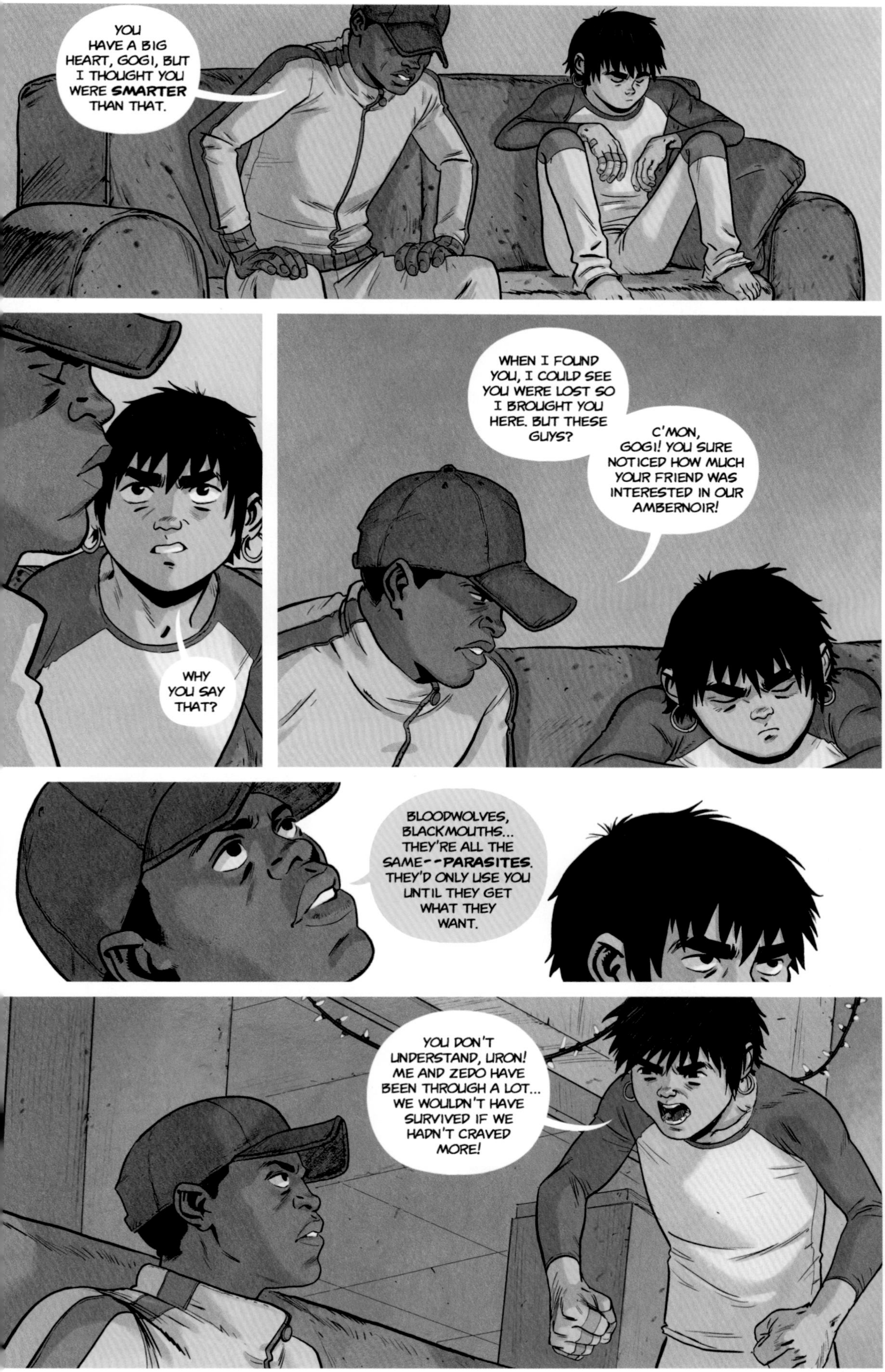
YOU HAVE A BIG HEART, GOGI, BUT I THOUGHT YOU WERE SMARTER THAN THAT.
WHY YOU SAY THAT?
WHEN I FOUND YOU, I COULD SEE YOU WERE LOST SO I BROUGHT YOU HERE. BUT THESE GUYS?
C'MON, GOGI! YOU SURE NOTICED HOW MUCH YOUR FRIEND WAS INTERESTED IN OUR AMBERNOIR!
BLOODWOLVES, BLACKMOUTHS... THEY'RE ALL THE SAME--PARASITES. THEY'D ONLY USE YOU UNTIL THEY GET WHAT THEY WANT.
YOU DON'T UNDERSTAND, URON! ME AND ZEDO HAVE BEEN THROUGH A LOT... WE WOULDN'T HAVE SURVIVED IF WE HADN'T CRAVED MORE!

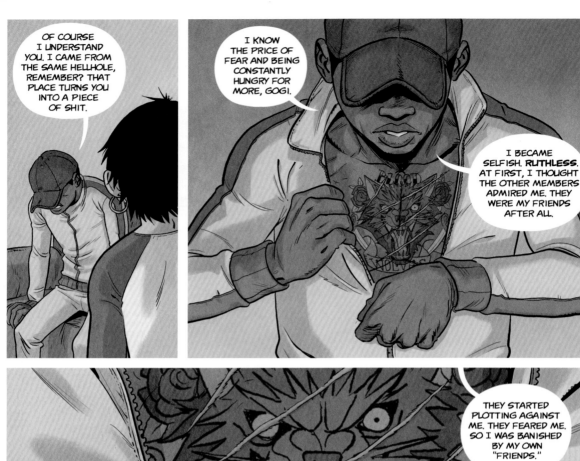

OF COURSE I UNDERSTAND YOU. I CAME FROM THE SAME HELLHOLE, REMEMBER? THAT PLACE TURNS YOU INTO A PIECE OF SHIT.

I KNOW THE PRICE OF FEAR AND BEING CONSTANTLY HUNGRY FOR MORE, GOGI.

I BECAME SELFISH. **RUTHLESS.** AT FIRST, I THOUGHT THE OTHER MEMBERS ADMIRED ME. THEY WERE MY FRIENDS AFTER ALL.

THEY STARTED PLOTTING AGAINST ME. THEY FEARED ME. SO I WAS BANISHED BY MY OWN "FRIENDS."

AMBITION IS A **MONSTER** THAT GROWS UNTIL IT DEVOURS YOU, GOGI. AND ZEDO IS **VERY** AMBITIOUS.

YOU ALWAYS TALK ABOUT FAMILY, BUT YOU DON'T SEEM TO GET THAT ZEDO **IS** MY FAMILY!

AND I'M NOT GONNA ABANDON HIM AGAIN!

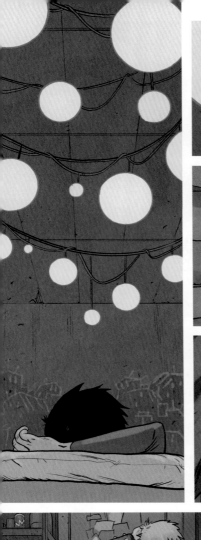

HEY... I WAS WONDERING IF YOU WERE AWAKE.

HUH?

KNOCK

KNOCK

I COULDN'T SLEEP THE FIRST DAY OUT HERE, NEITHER-- WHAT'S UP?

LOOK, MAN, I WANTED TO THANK YOU AGAIN FOR WHAT YOU DID FOR ME AND MY MEN.

WOW. YOU GIVING ME THANKS INSTEAD OF MAKING EXCUSES? MAYBE THE THORNTICKS DID BITE YOU ON THE BRAIN OR SUMTHIN'.

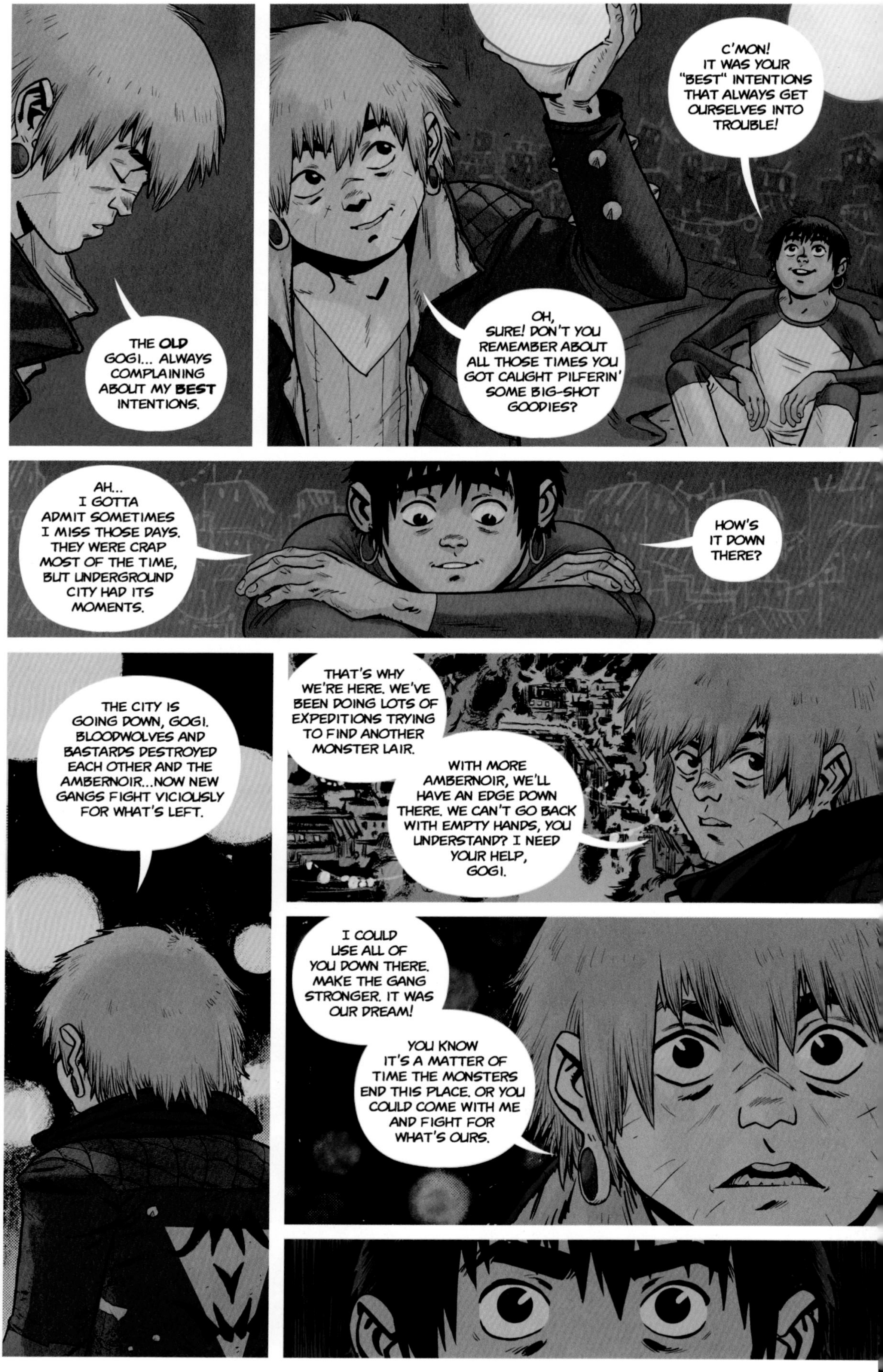
THE **OLD** GOGI... ALWAYS COMPLAINING ABOUT MY **BEST** INTENTIONS.
OH, SURE! DON'T YOU REMEMBER ABOUT ALL THOSE TIMES YOU GOT CAUGHT PILFERIN' SOME BIG-SHOT GOODIES?
C'MON! IT WAS YOUR "BEST" INTENTIONS THAT ALWAYS GET OURSELVES INTO TROUBLE!
AH... I GOTTA ADMIT SOMETIMES I MISS THOSE DAYS. THEY WERE CRAP MOST OF THE TIME, BUT UNDERGROUND CITY HAD ITS MOMENTS.
HOW'S IT DOWN THERE?
THE CITY IS GOING DOWN, GOGI. BLOODWOLVES AND BASTARDS DESTROYED EACH OTHER AND THE AMBERNOIR...NOW NEW GANGS FIGHT VICIOUSLY FOR WHAT'S LEFT.
THAT'S WHY WE'RE HERE. WE'VE BEEN DOING LOTS OF EXPEDITIONS TRYING TO FIND ANOTHER MONSTER LAIR.
WITH MORE AMBERNOIR, WE'LL HAVE AN EDGE DOWN THERE. WE CAN'T GO BACK WITH EMPTY HANDS, YOU UNDERSTAND? I NEED YOUR HELP, GOGI.
I COULD USE ALL OF YOU DOWN THERE. MAKE THE GANG STRONGER. IT WAS OUR DREAM!
YOU KNOW IT'S A MATTER OF TIME THE MONSTERS END THIS PLACE. OR YOU COULD COME WITH ME AND FIGHT FOR WHAT'S OURS.

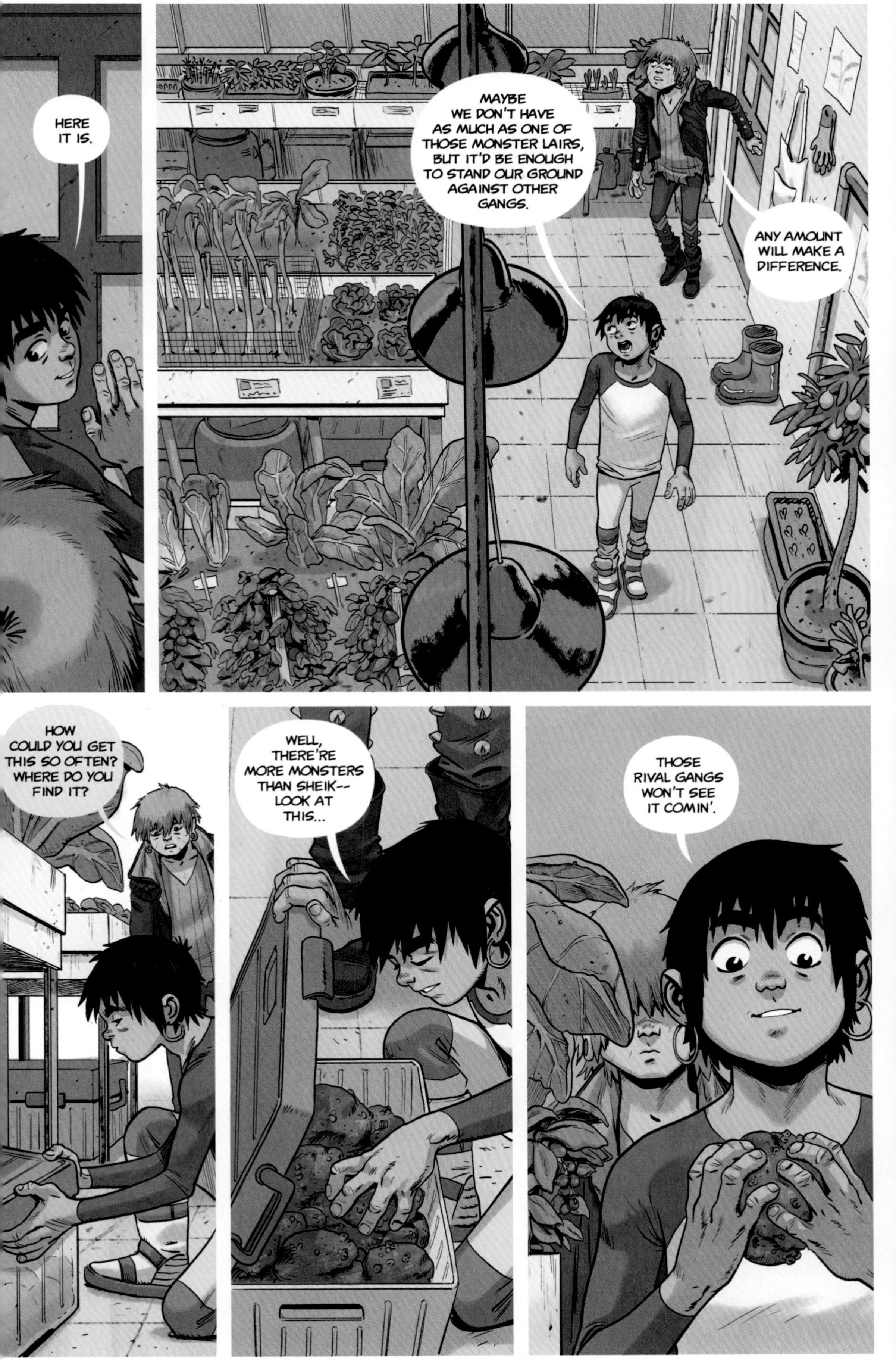
HERE IT IS.
MAYBE WE DON'T HAVE AS MUCH AS ONE OF THOSE MONSTER LAIRS, BUT IT'D BE ENOUGH TO STAND OUR GROUND AGAINST OTHER GANGS.
ANY AMOUNT WILL MAKE A DIFFERENCE.
HOW COULD YOU GET THIS SO OFTEN? WHERE DO YOU FIND IT?
WELL, THERE'RE MORE MONSTERS THAN SHEIK-- LOOK AT THIS...
THOSE RIVAL GANGS WON'T SEE IT COMIN'.

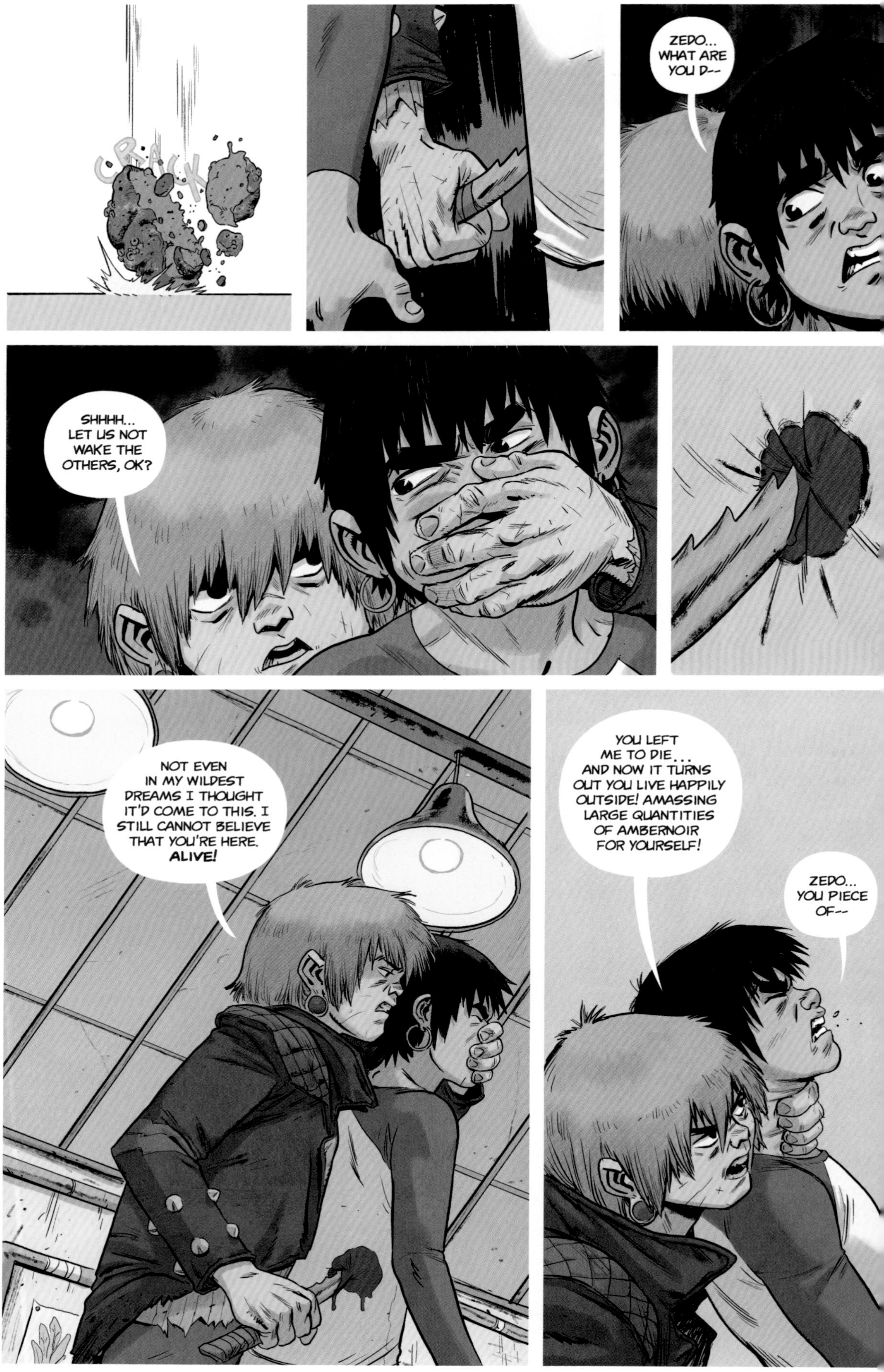
CRACK
ZEDO... WHAT ARE YOU D--
SHHHH... LET US NOT WAKE THE OTHERS, OK?
NOT EVEN IN MY WILDEST DREAMS I THOUGHT IT'D COME TO THIS. I STILL CANNOT BELIEVE THAT YOU'RE HERE. ALIVE!
YOU LEFT ME TO DIE... AND NOW IT TURNS OUT YOU LIVE HAPPILY OUTSIDE! AMASSING LARGE QUANTITIES OF AMBERNOIR FOR YOURSELF!
ZEDO... YOU PIECE OF--

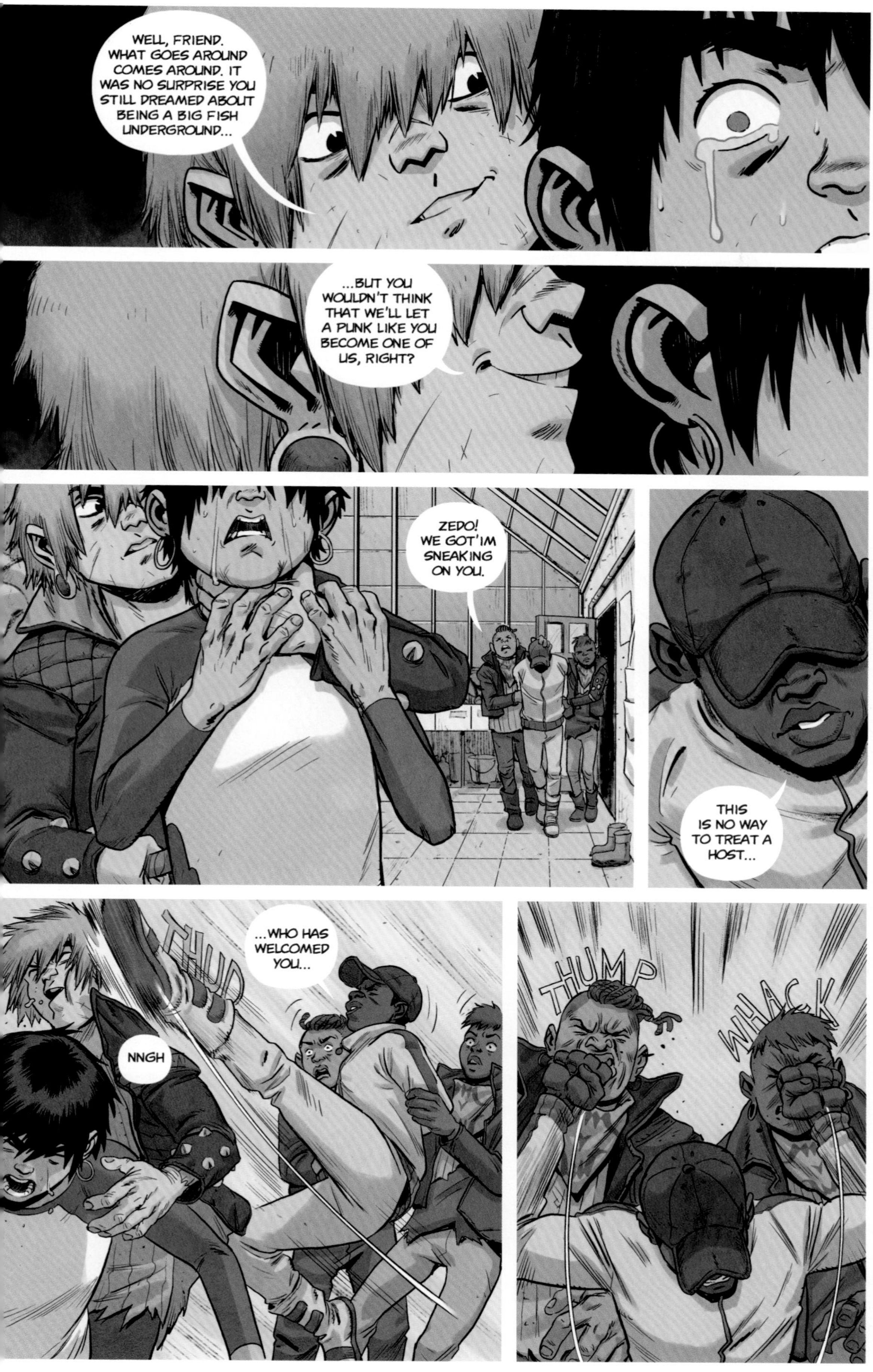
WELL, FRIEND. WHAT GOES AROUND COMES AROUND. IT WAS NO SURPRISE YOU STILL DREAMED ABOUT BEING A BIG FISH UNDERGROUND...
...BUT YOU WOULDN'T THINK THAT WE'LL LET A PUNK LIKE YOU BECOME ONE OF US, RIGHT?
ZEDO! WE GOT'IM SNEAKING ON YOU.
THIS IS NO WAY TO TREAT A HOST...
THUD
...WHO HAS WELCOMED YOU...
NNGH
THUMP
WHACK

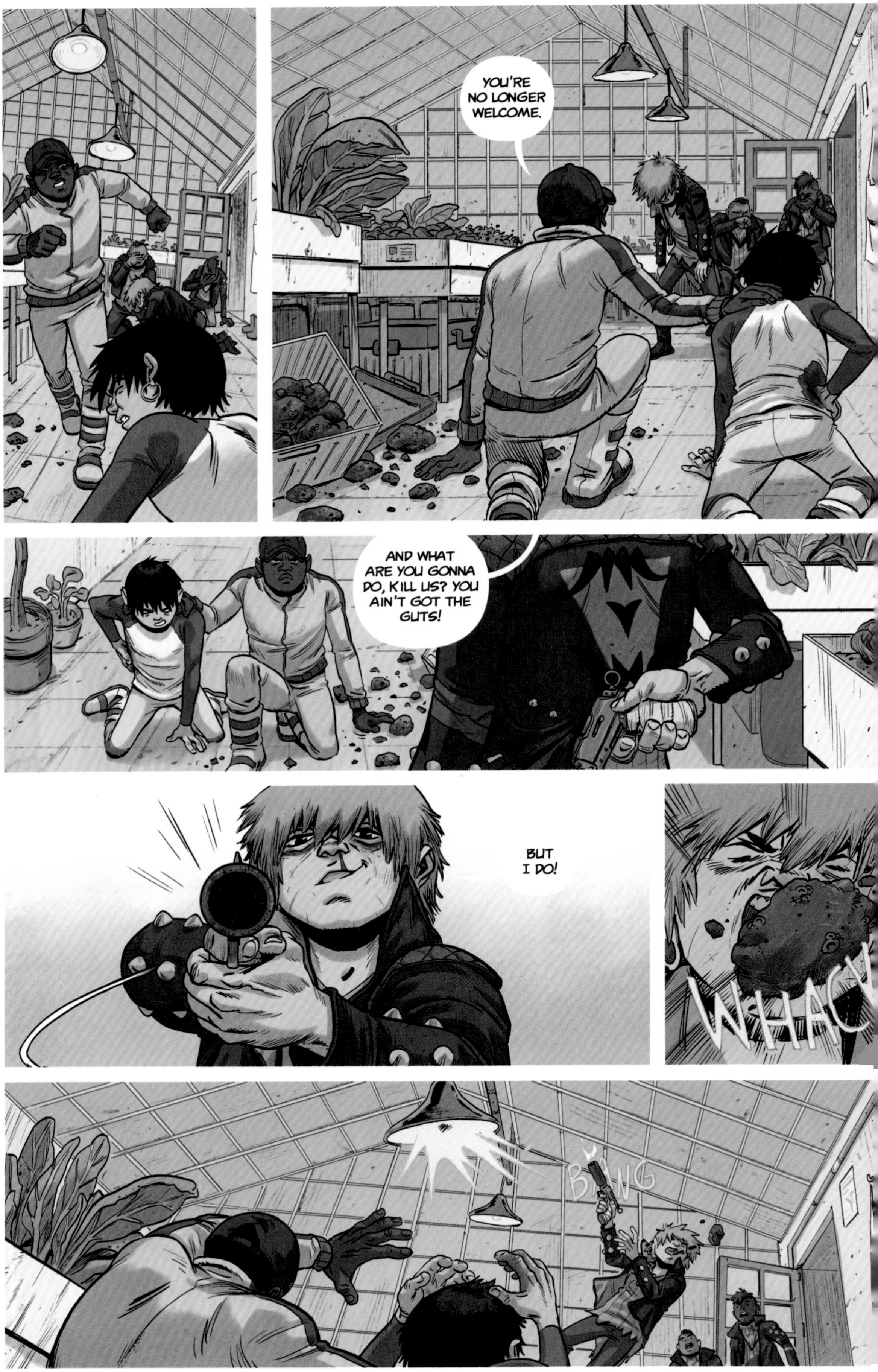
YOU'RE NO LONGER WELCOME.
AND WHAT ARE YOU GONNA DO, KILL US? YOU AIN'T GOT THE GUTS!
BUT I DO!
WHAC
BANG

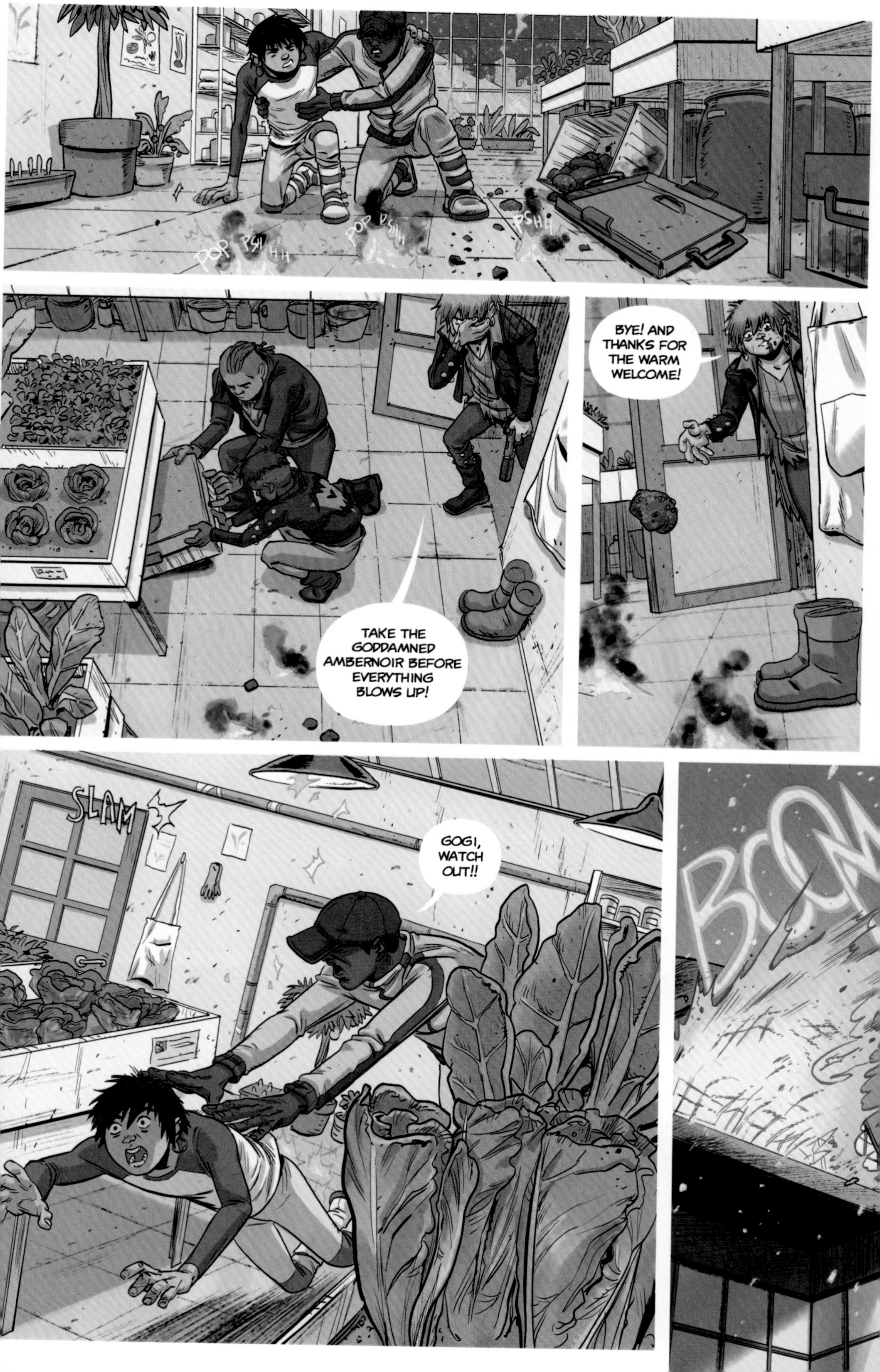
POP PSHHH
POP PSHH
PSHH
TAKE THE GODDAMNED AMBERNOIR BEFORE EVERYTHING BLOWS UP!
BYE! AND THANKS FOR THE WARM WELCOME!
SLAM
GOGI, WATCH OUT!!

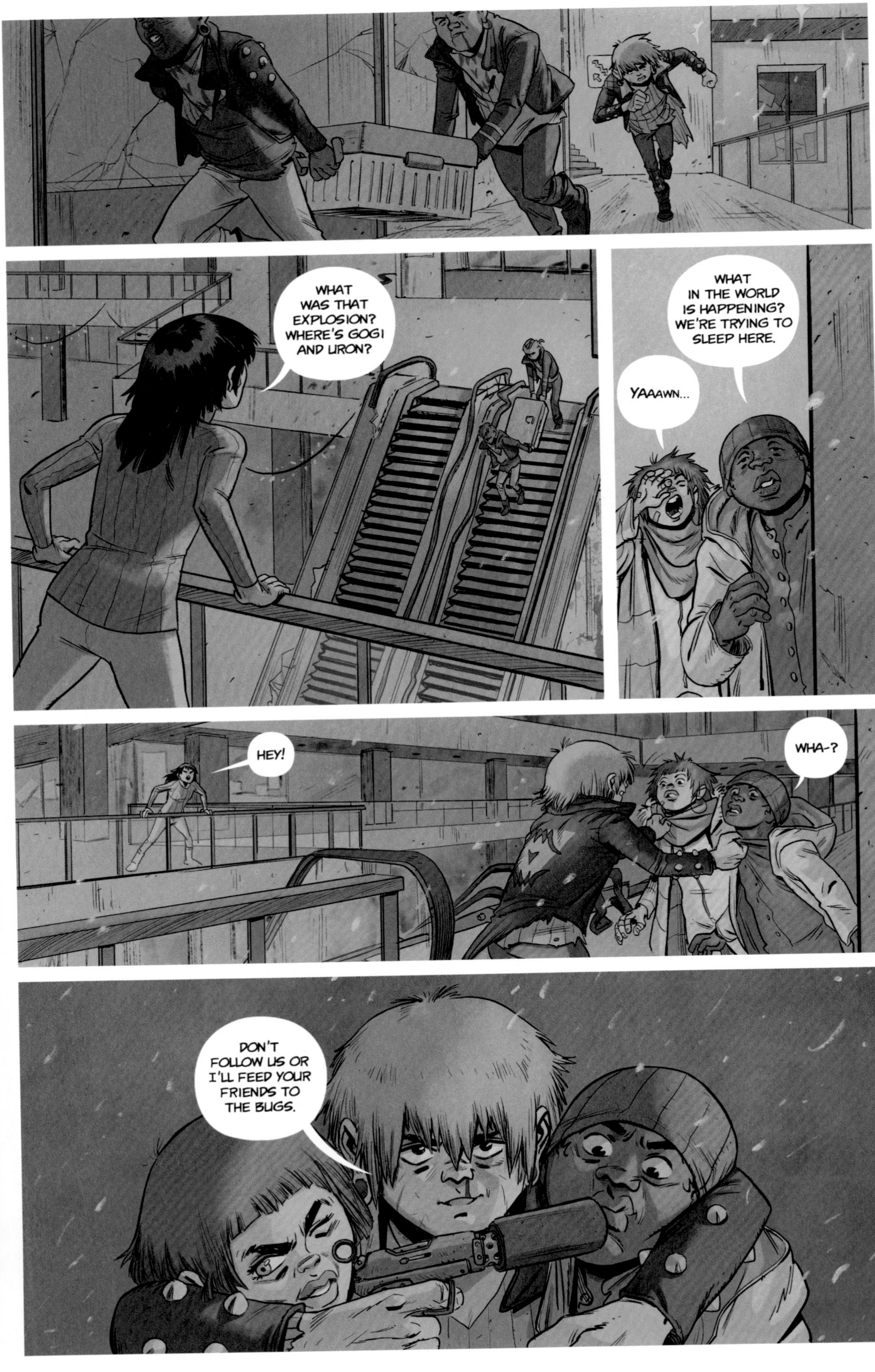
WHAT WAS THAT EXPLOSION? WHERE'S GOGI AND URON?
WHAT IN THE WORLD IS HAPPENING? WE'RE TRYING TO SLEEP HERE.
YAAAWN...
HEY!
WHA-?
DON'T FOLLOW US OR I'LL FEED YOUR FRIENDS TO THE BUGS.

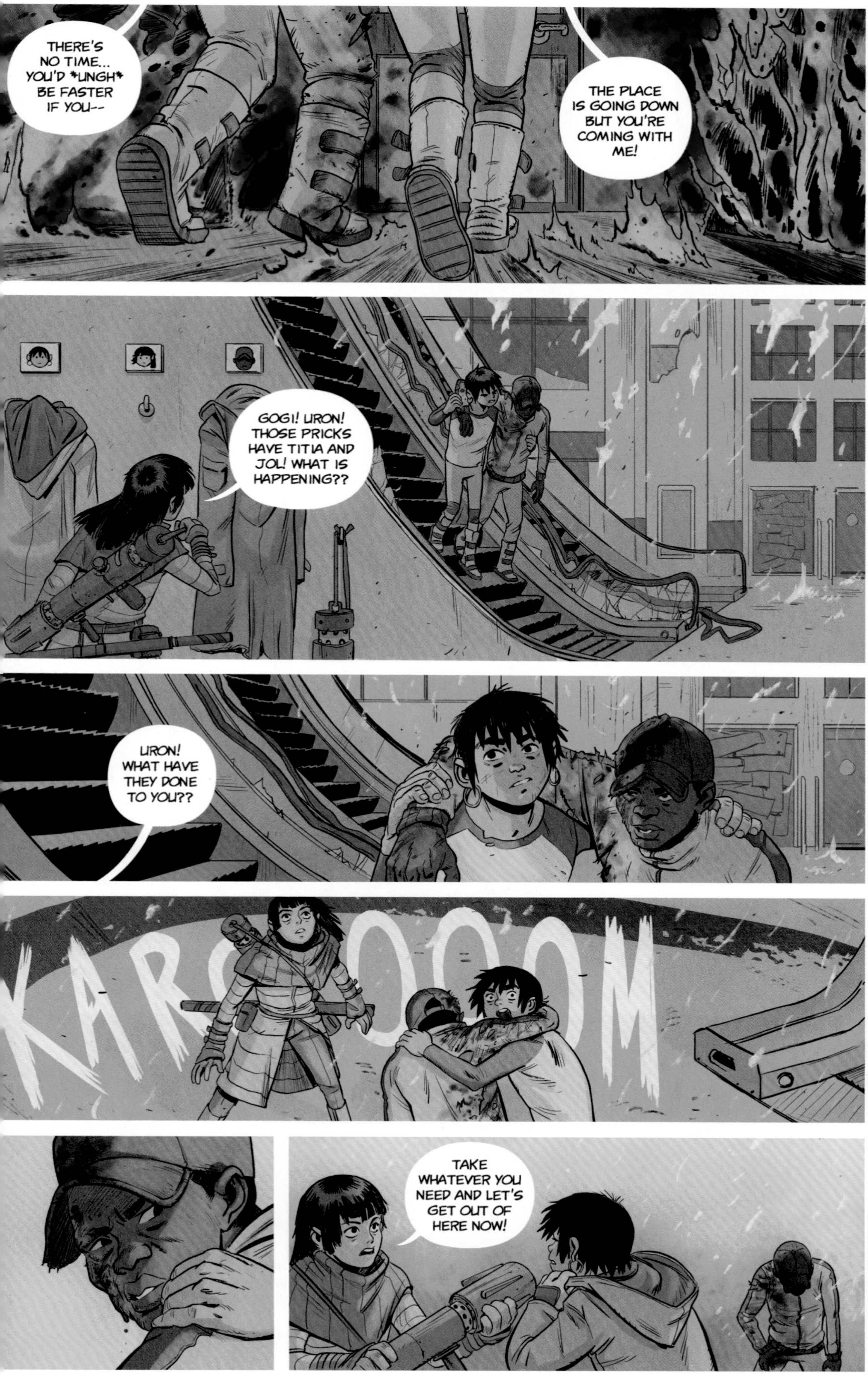
THERE'S NO TIME... YOU'D *UNGH* BE FASTER IF YOU--
THE PLACE IS GOING DOWN BUT YOU'RE COMING WITH ME!
GOGI! URON! THOSE PRICKS HAVE TITIA AND JOL! WHAT IS HAPPENING??
URON! WHAT HAVE THEY DONE TO YOU??
KAROOOOM
TAKE WHATEVER YOU NEED AND LET'S GET OUT OF HERE NOW!

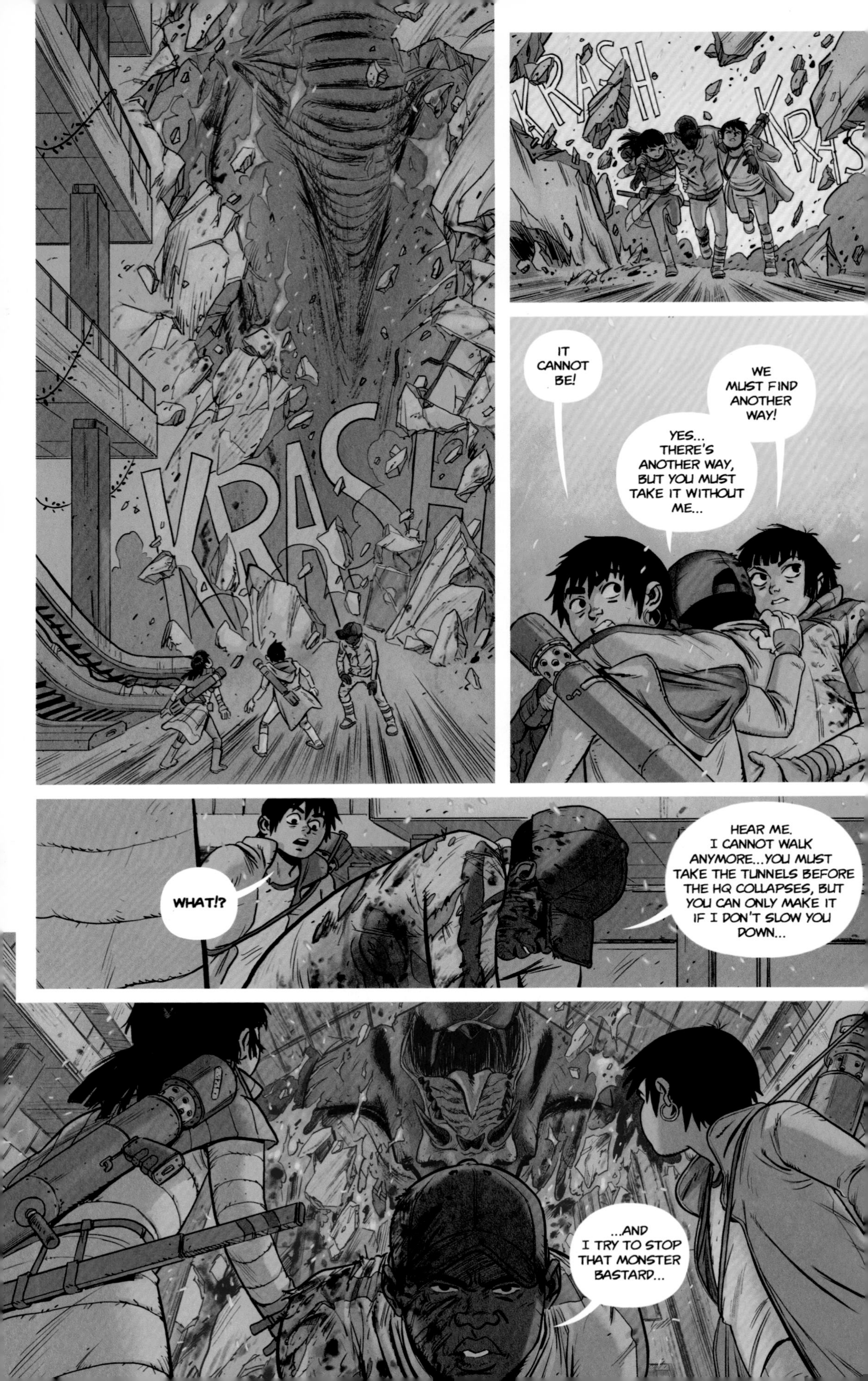
KRASH
KRASH
KRASH
IT CANNOT BE!
WE MUST FIND ANOTHER WAY!
YES... THERE'S ANOTHER WAY, BUT YOU MUST TAKE IT WITHOUT ME...
WHAT!?
HEAR ME. I CANNOT WALK ANYMORE...YOU MUST TAKE THE TUNNELS BEFORE THE HQ COLLAPSES, BUT YOU CAN ONLY MAKE IT IF I DON'T SLOW YOU DOWN...
...AND I TRY TO STOP THAT MONSTER BASTARD...

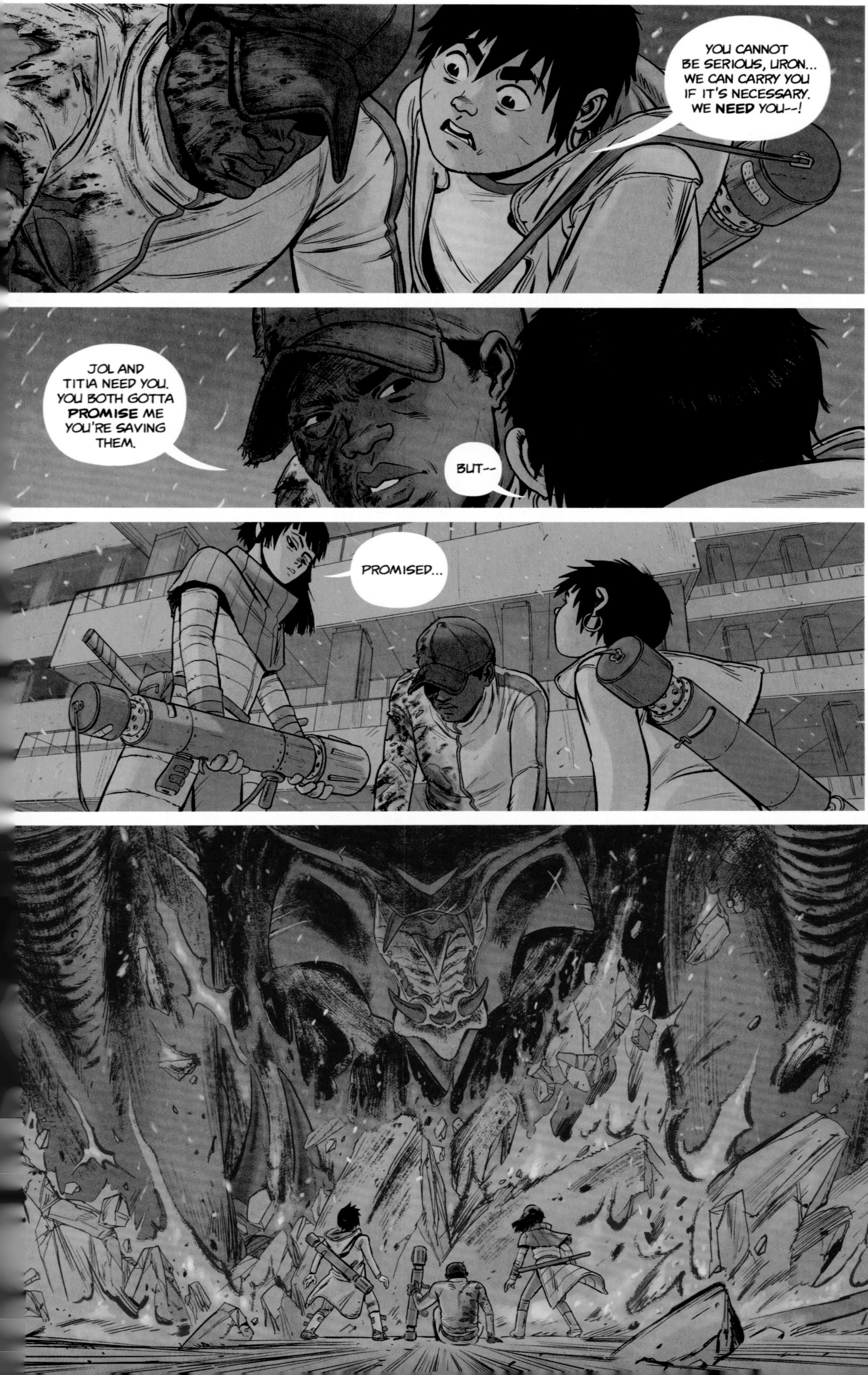
YOU CANNOT BE SERIOUS, URON... WE CAN CARRY YOU IF IT'S NECESSARY. WE **NEED** YOU--!
JOL AND TITIA NEED YOU. YOU BOTH GOTTA **PROMISE** ME YOU'RE SAVING THEM.
BUT--
PROMISED...

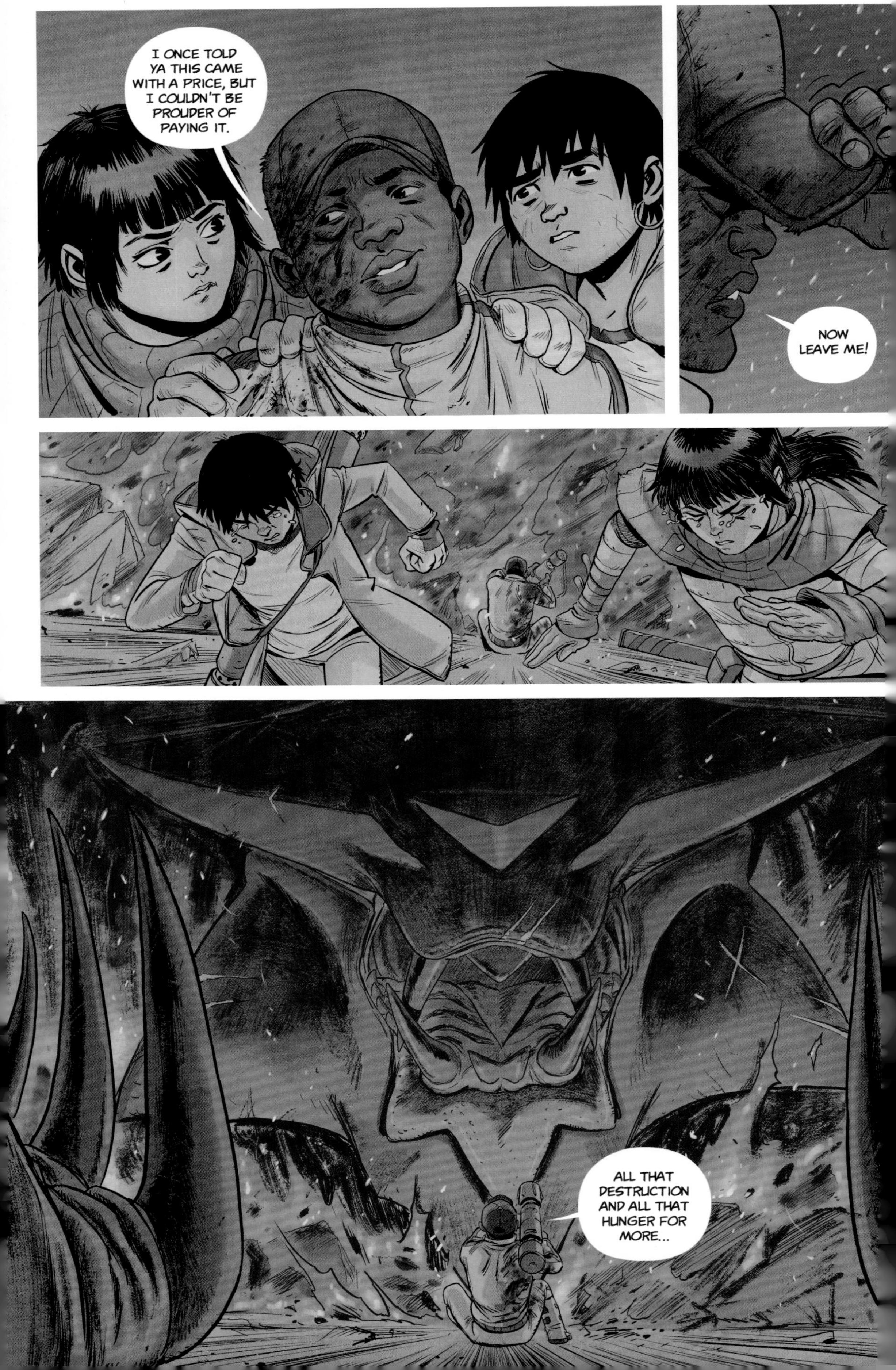
I ONCE TOLD YA THIS CAME WITH A PRICE, BUT I COULDN'T BE PROUDER OF PAYING IT.
NOW LEAVE ME!
ALL THAT DESTRUCTION AND ALL THAT HUNGER FOR MORE...

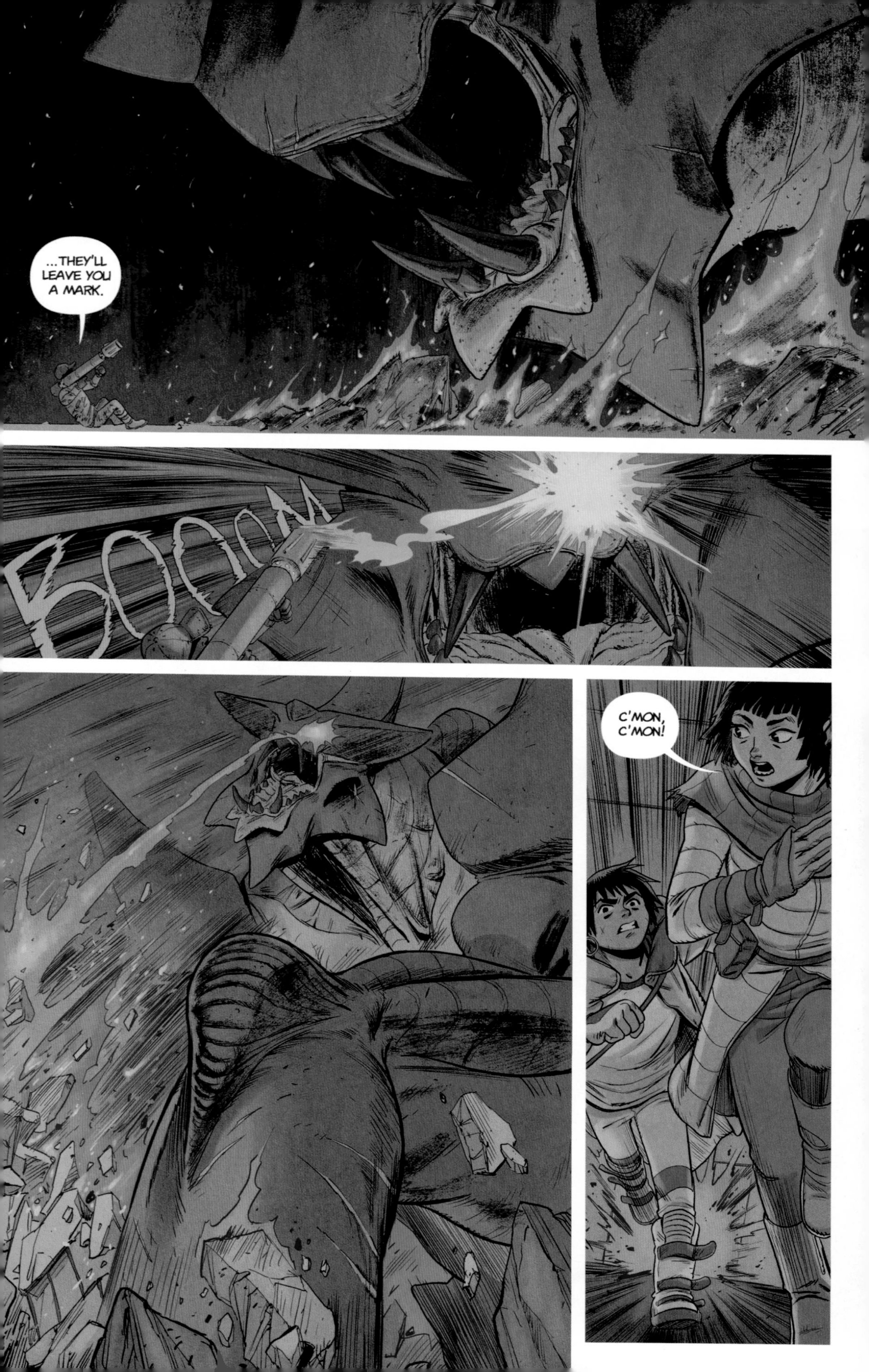
...THEY'LL LEAVE YOU A MARK.
BOOOM
C'MON, C'MON!

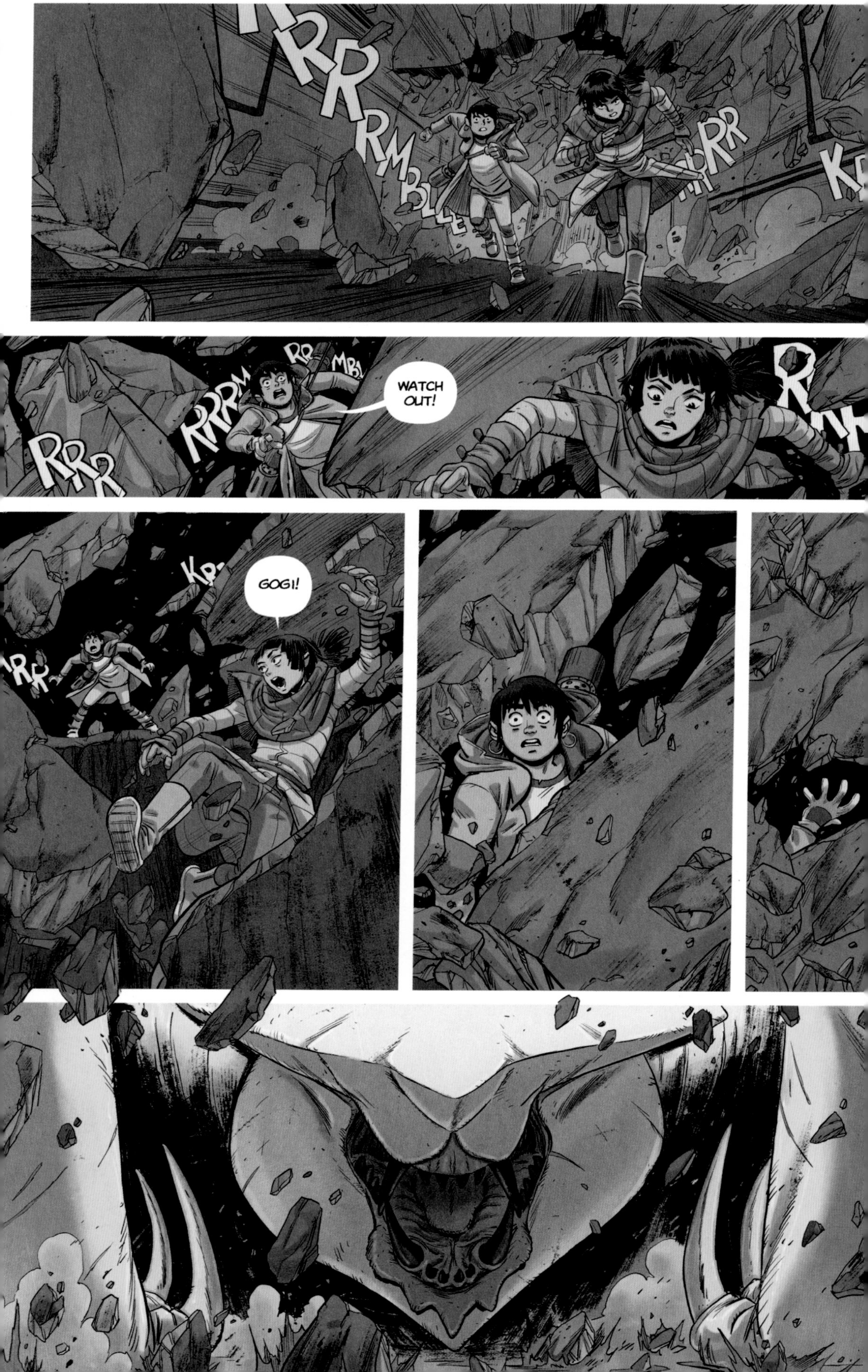
WATCH OUT!
GOGI!

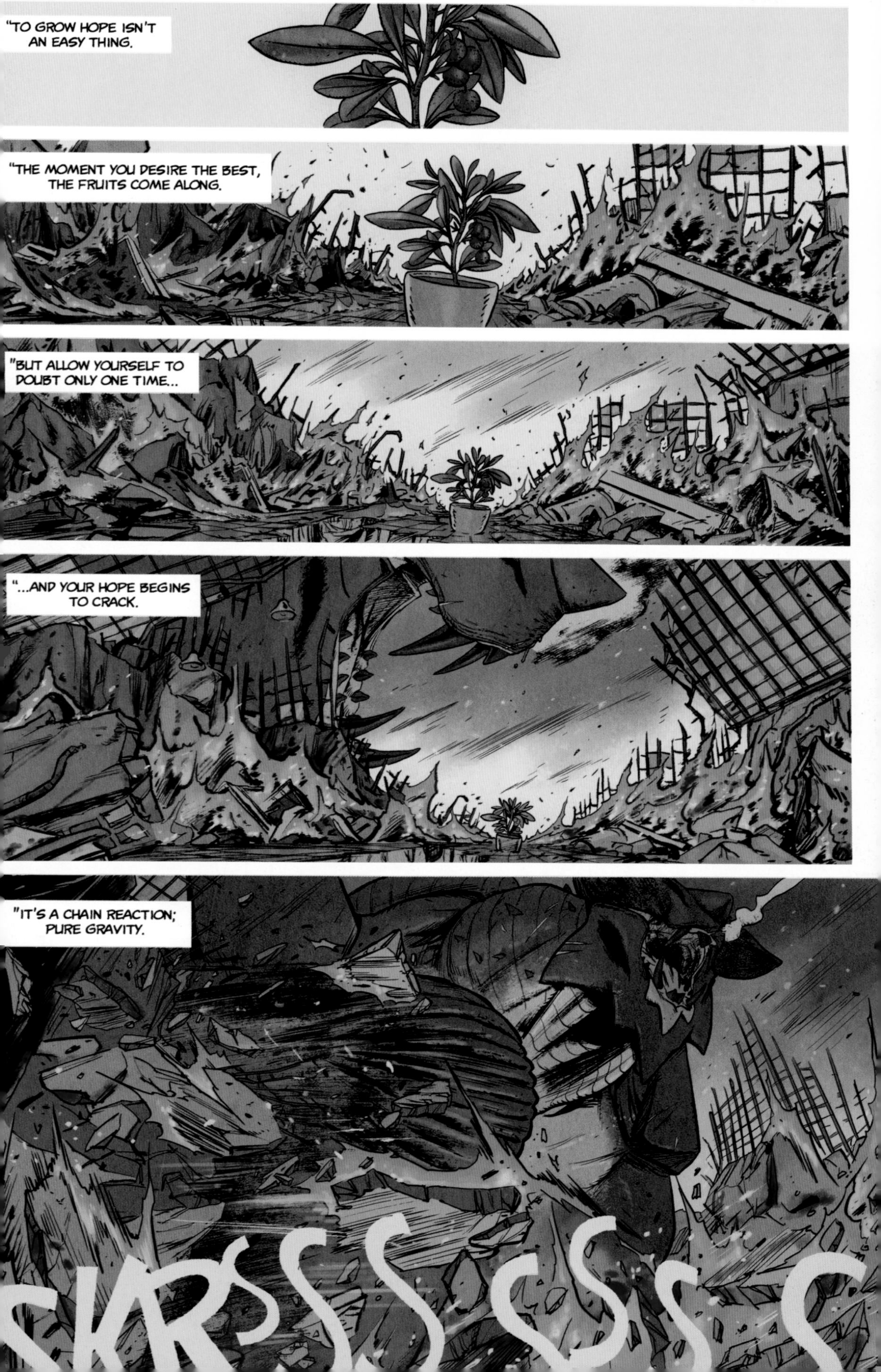
"TO GROW HOPE ISN'T AN EASY THING.
"THE MOMENT YOU DESIRE THE BEST, THE FRUITS COME ALONG.
"BUT ALLOW YOURSELF TO DOUBT ONLY ONE TIME...
"...AND YOUR HOPE BEGINS TO CRACK.
"IT'S A CHAIN REACTION; PURE GRAVITY.
SKRSSSSSSC

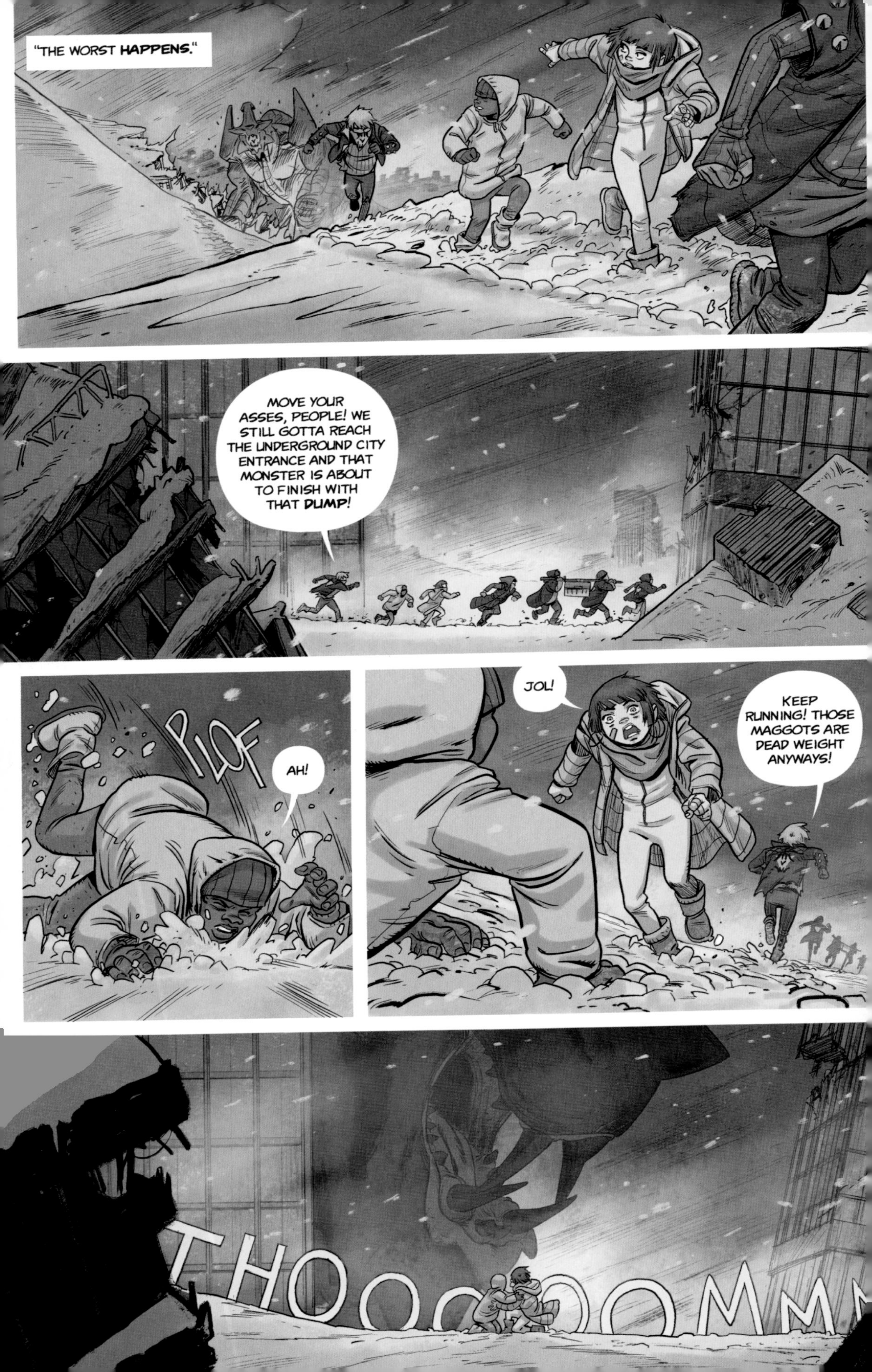
"THE WORST HAPPENS."
MOVE YOUR ASSES, PEOPLE! WE STILL GOTTA REACH THE UNDERGROUND CITY ENTRANCE AND THAT MONSTER IS ABOUT TO FINISH WITH THAT DUMP!
PLOF
AH!
JOL!
KEEP RUNNING! THOSE MAGGOTS ARE DEAD WEIGHT ANYWAYS!
THOOOOOMMM

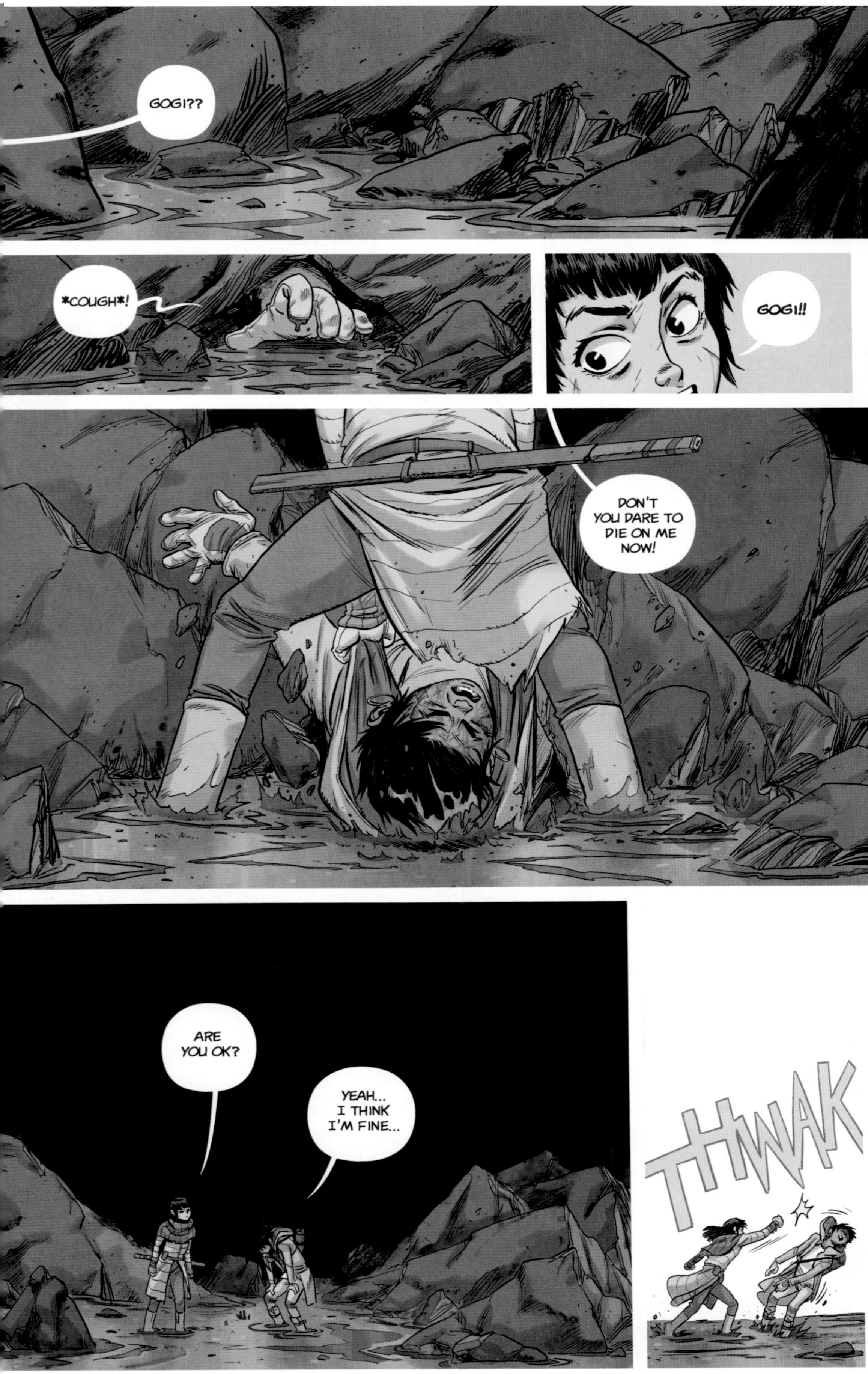
GOGI??
COUGH!
GOGI!!
DON'T YOU DARE TO DIE ON ME NOW!
ARE YOU OK?
YEAH... I THINK I'M FINE...
THWAK

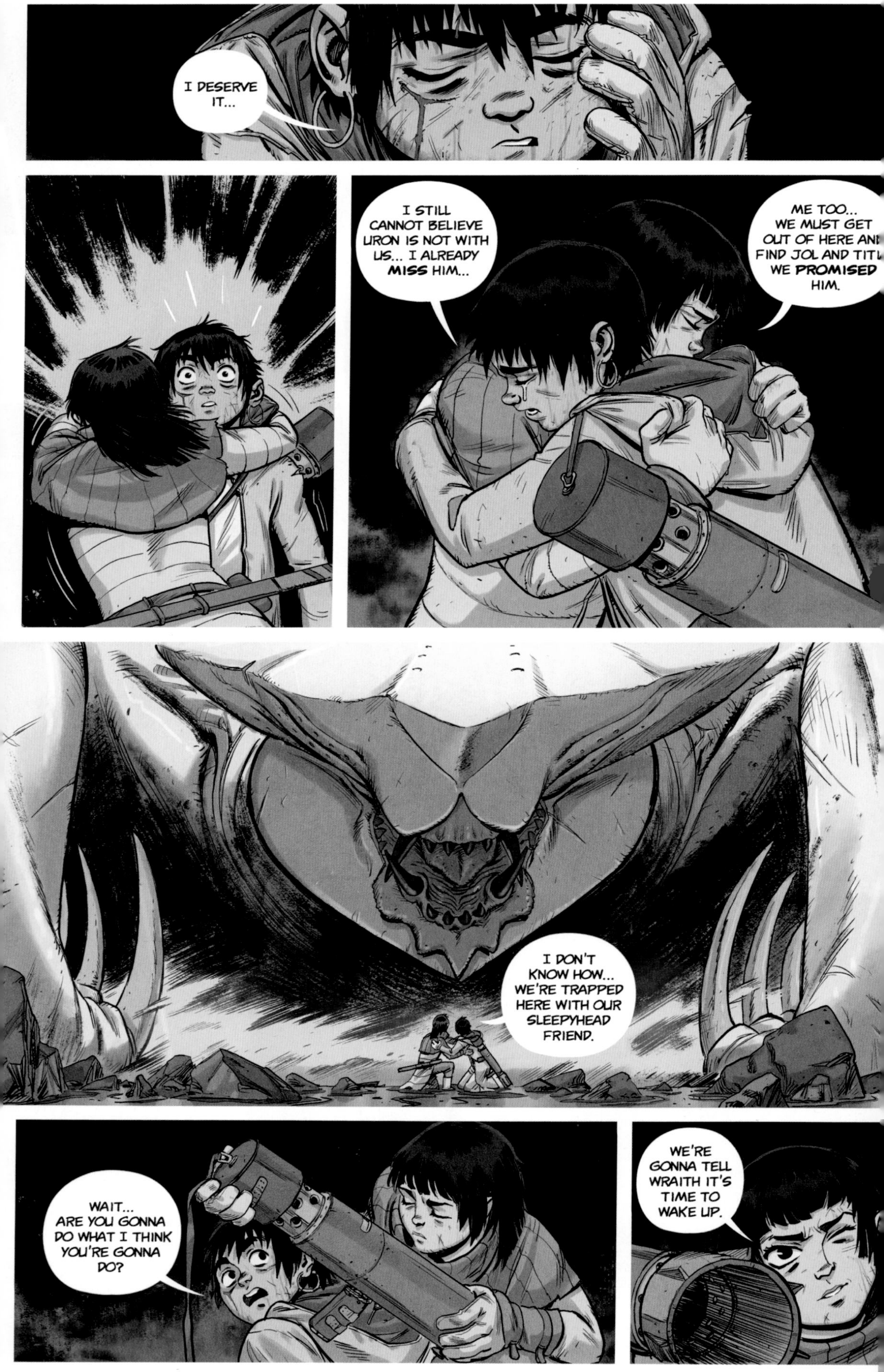
I DESERVE IT...
I STILL CANNOT BELIEVE URON IS NOT WITH US... I ALREADY **MISS** HIM...
ME TOO... WE MUST GET OUT OF HERE AN FIND JOL AND TIT WE **PROMISED** HIM.
I DON'T KNOW HOW... WE'RE TRAPPED HERE WITH OUR SLEEPYHEAD FRIEND.
WAIT... ARE YOU GONNA DO WHAT I THINK YOU'RE GONNA DO?
WE'RE GONNA TELL WRAITH IT'S TIME TO WAKE UP.

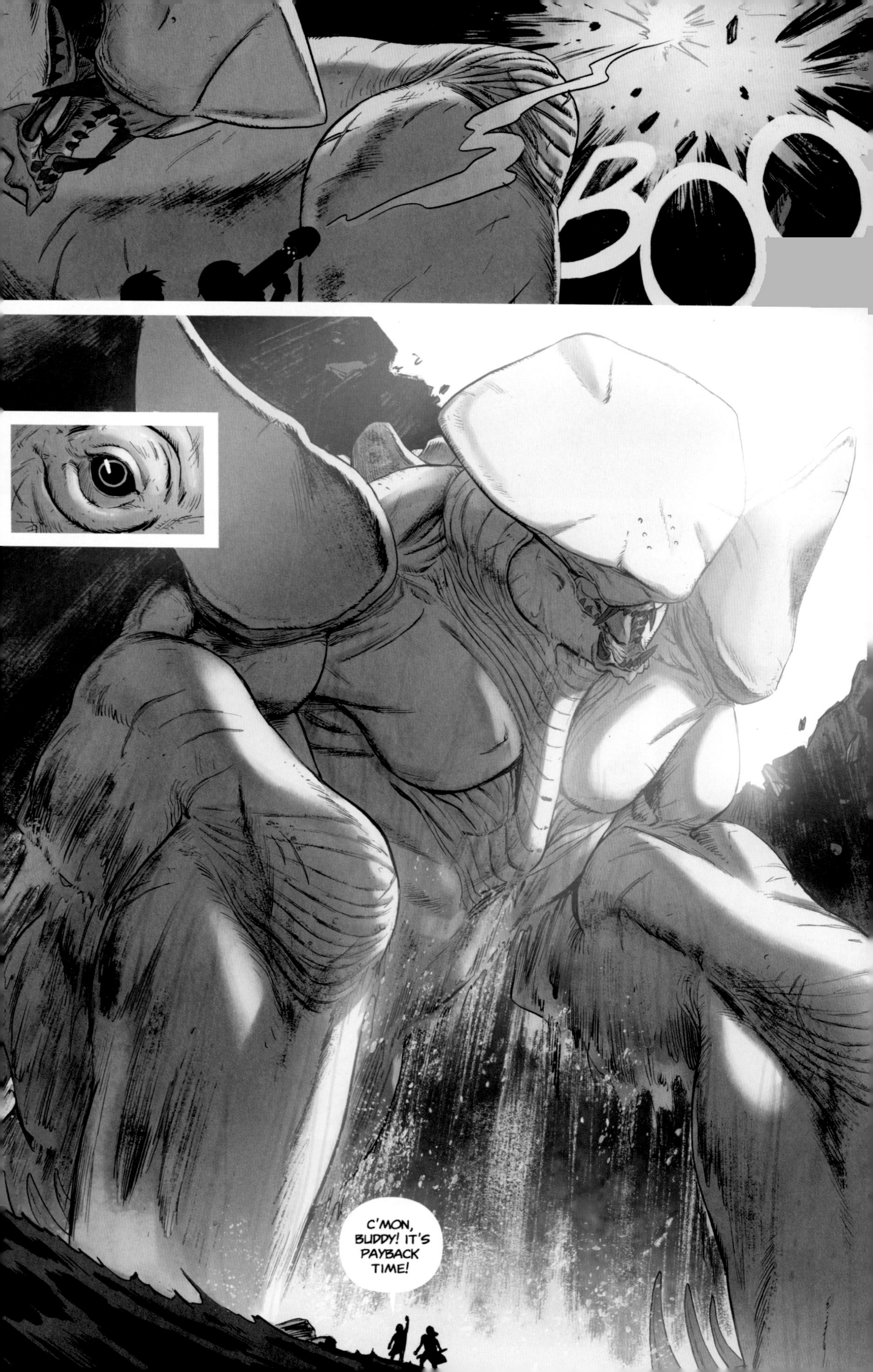
BOOM
C'MON, BUDDY! IT'S PAYBACK TIME!

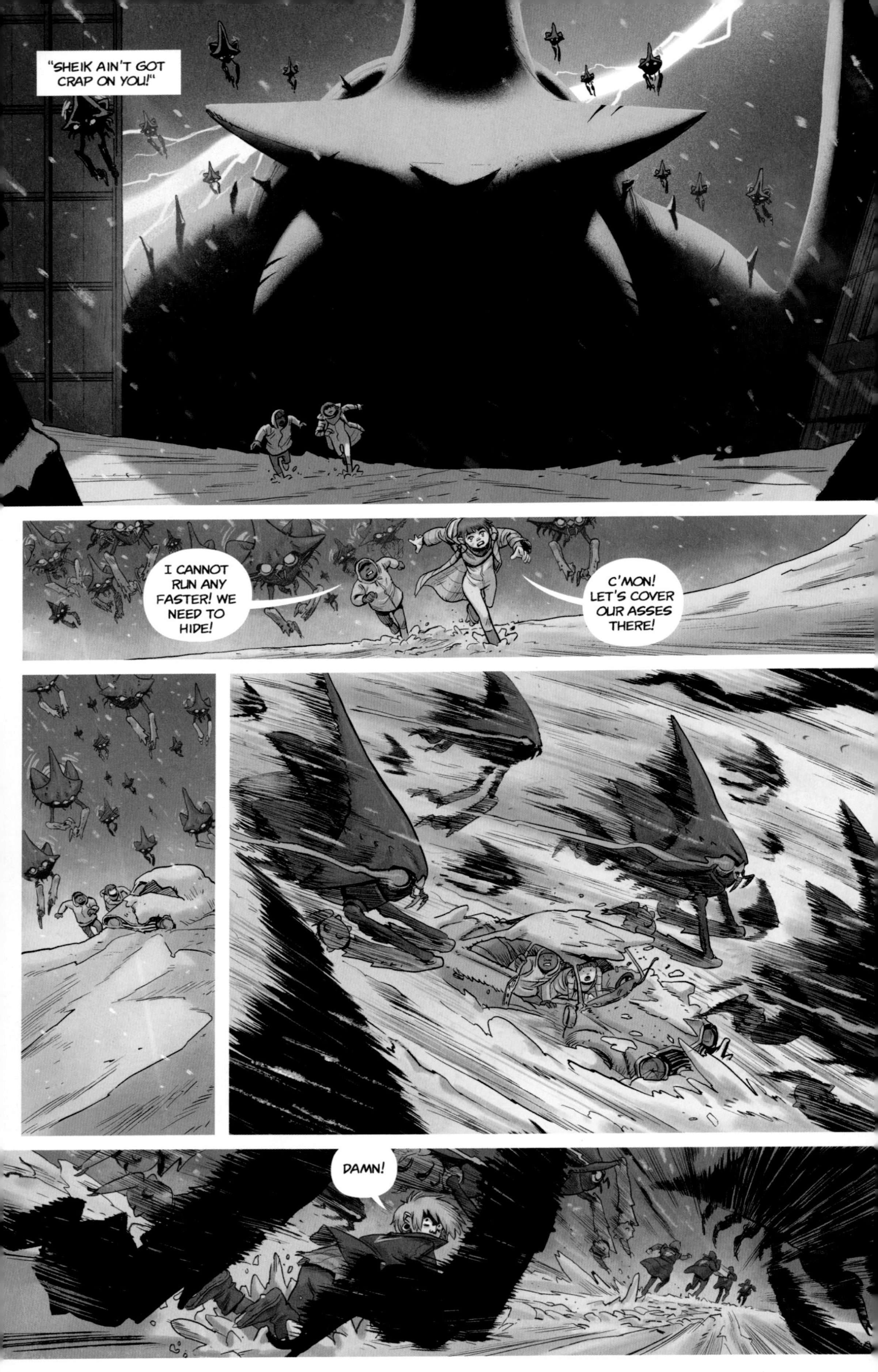
"SHEIK AIN'T GOT CRAP ON YOU!"
I CANNOT RUN ANY FASTER! WE NEED TO HIDE!
C'MON! LET'S COVER OUR ASSES THERE!
DAMN!

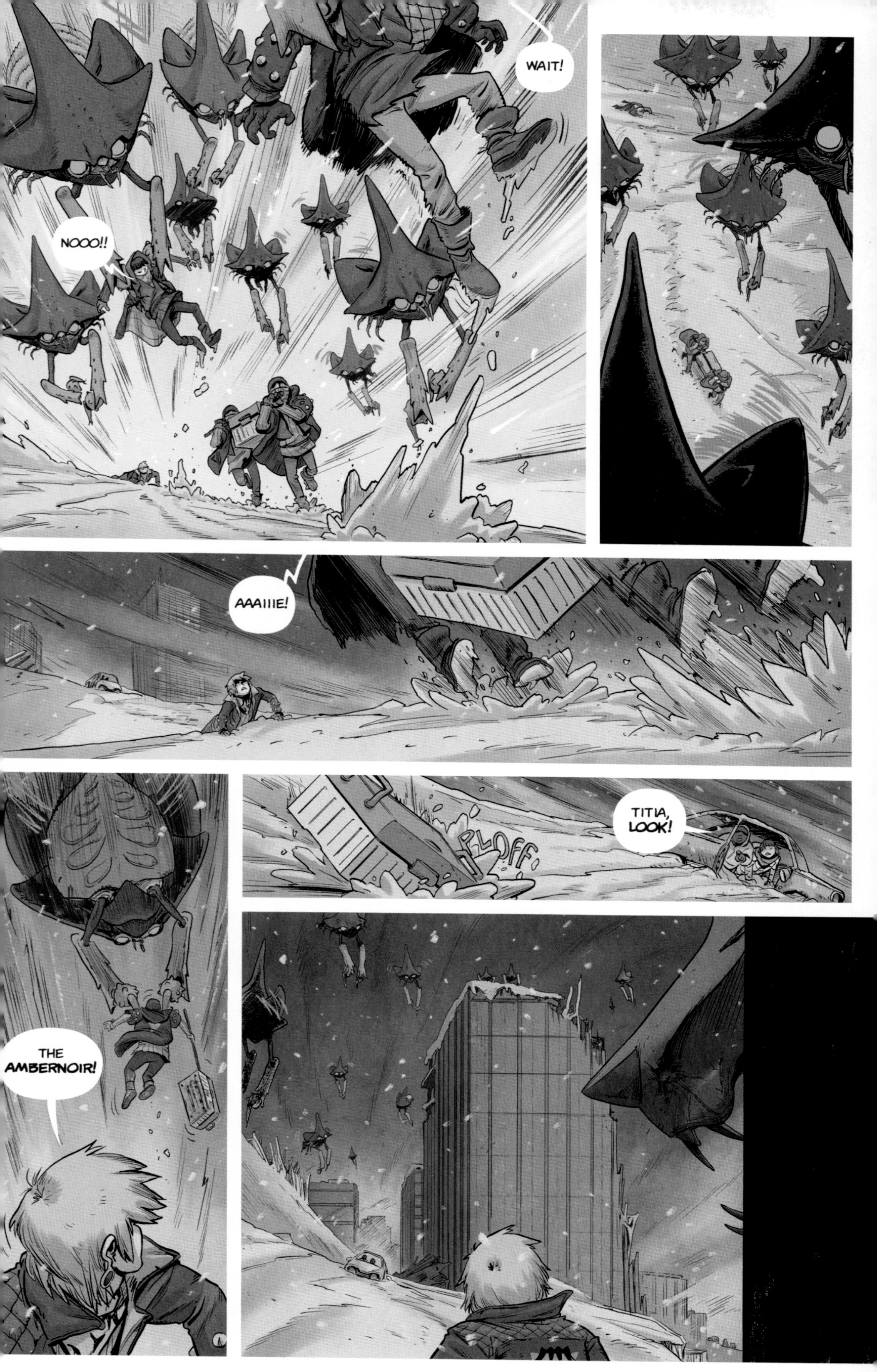
WAIT!
NOOO!!
AAAIIIE!
PLOFF
TITIA, LOOK!
THE AMBERNOIR!

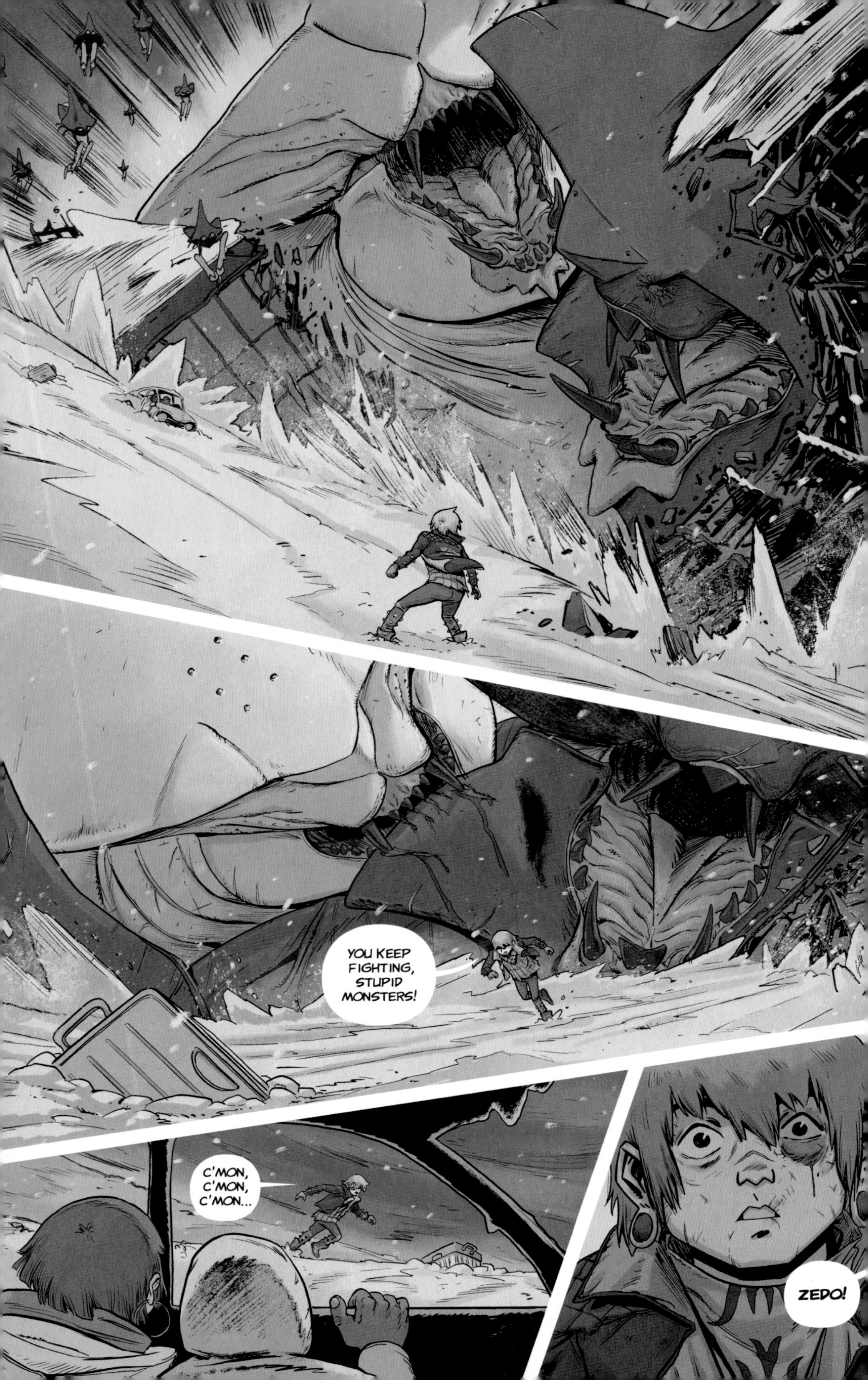
YOU KEEP FIGHTING, STUPID MONSTERS!
C'MON, C'MON, C'MON...
ZEDO!

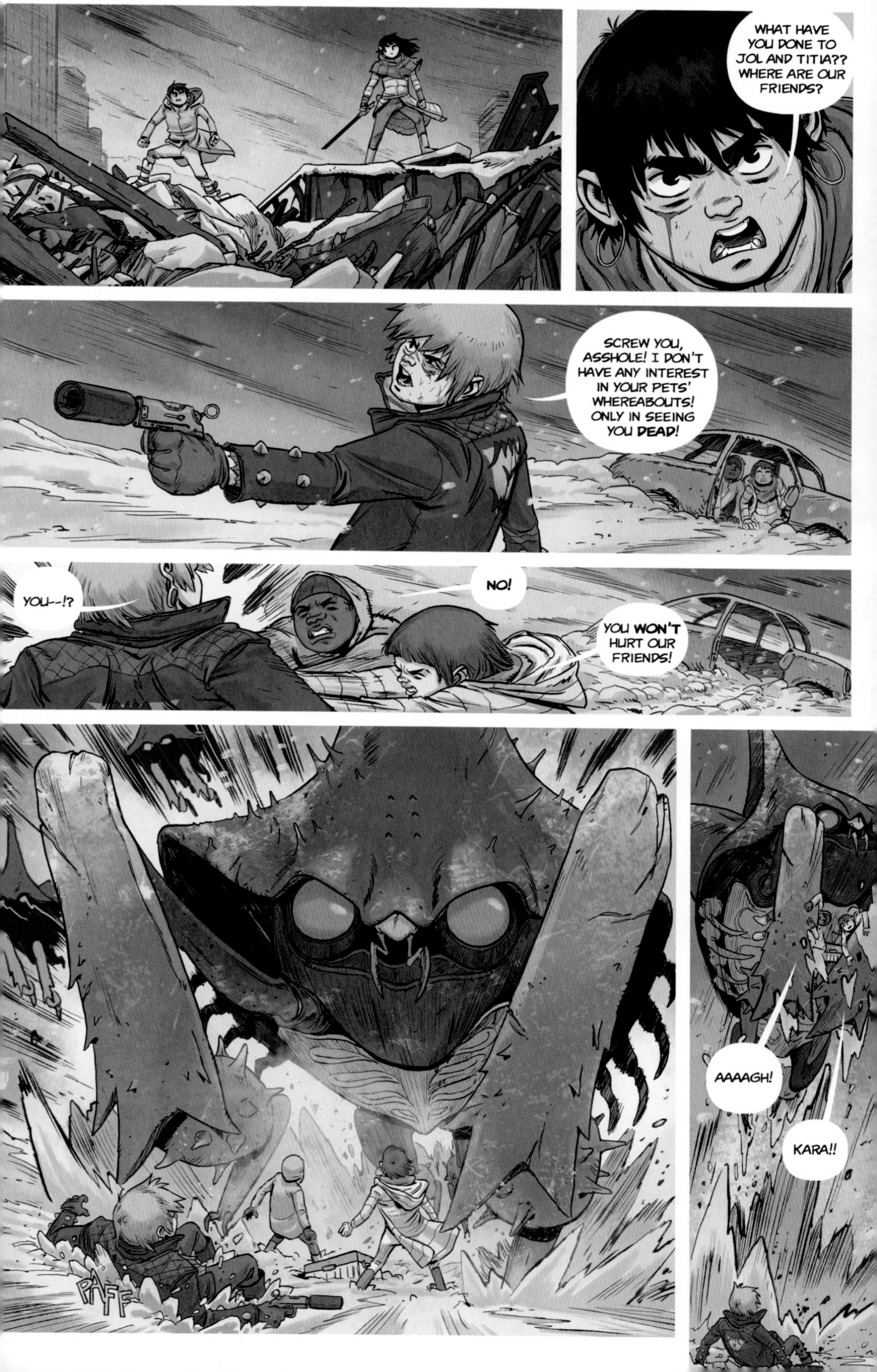
WHAT HAVE YOU DONE TO JOL AND TITIA?? WHERE ARE OUR FRIENDS?
SCREW YOU, ASSHOLE! I DON'T HAVE ANY INTEREST IN YOUR PETS' WHEREABOUTS! ONLY IN SEEING YOU **DEAD**!
YOU--!?
NO!
YOU **WON'T** HURT OUR FRIENDS!
PAFF
AAAAGH!
KARA!!

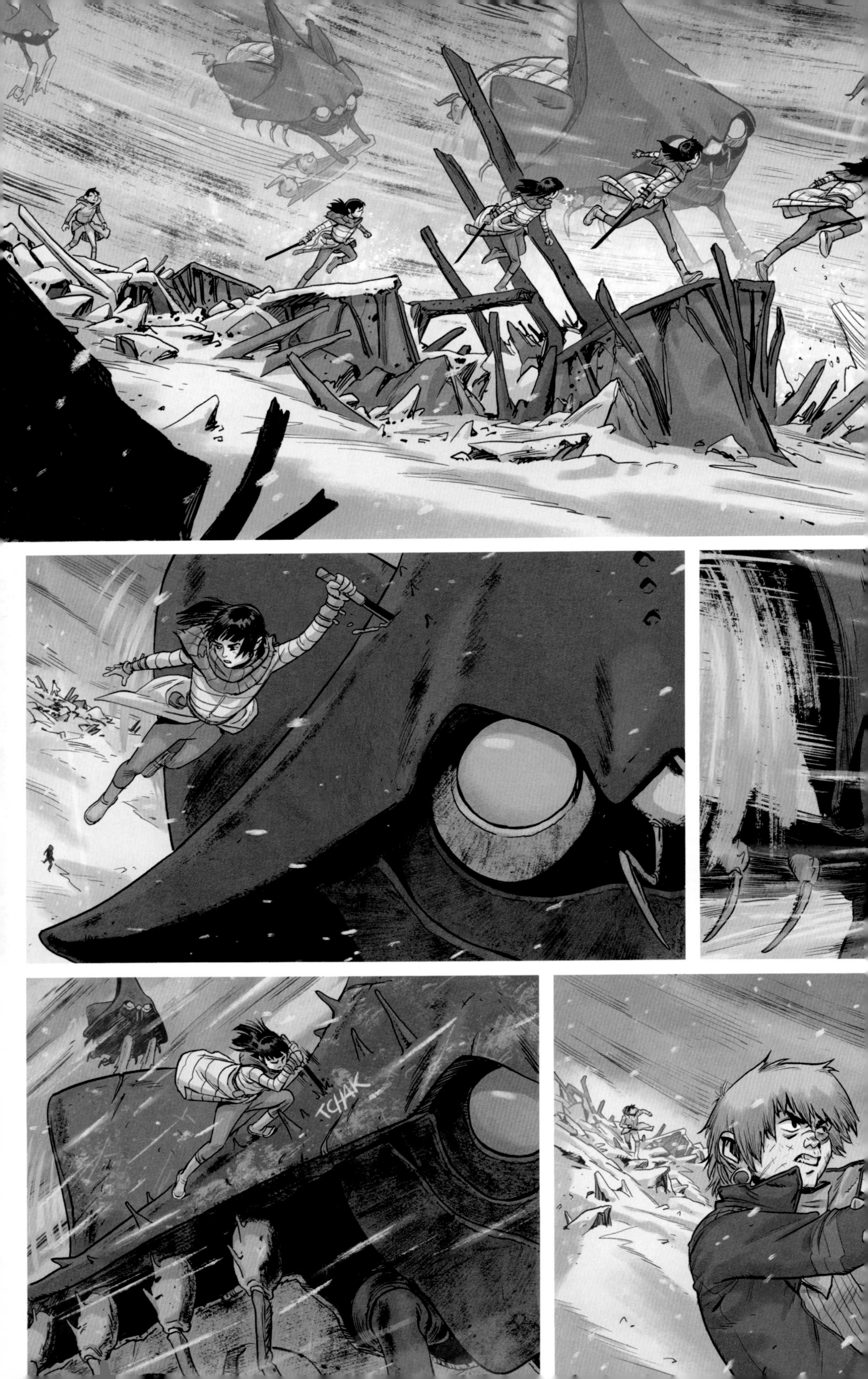
TCHAK

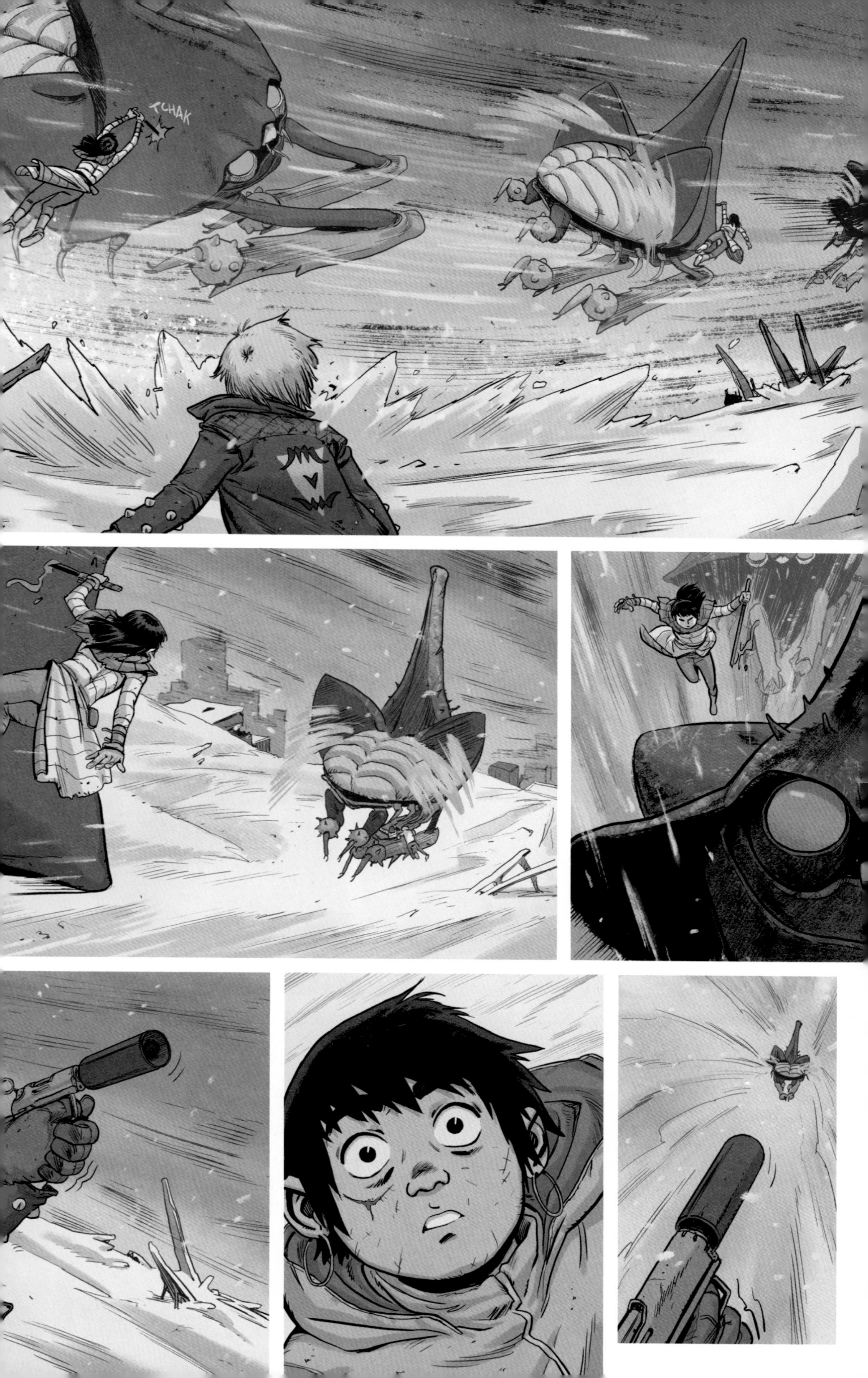
TCHAK

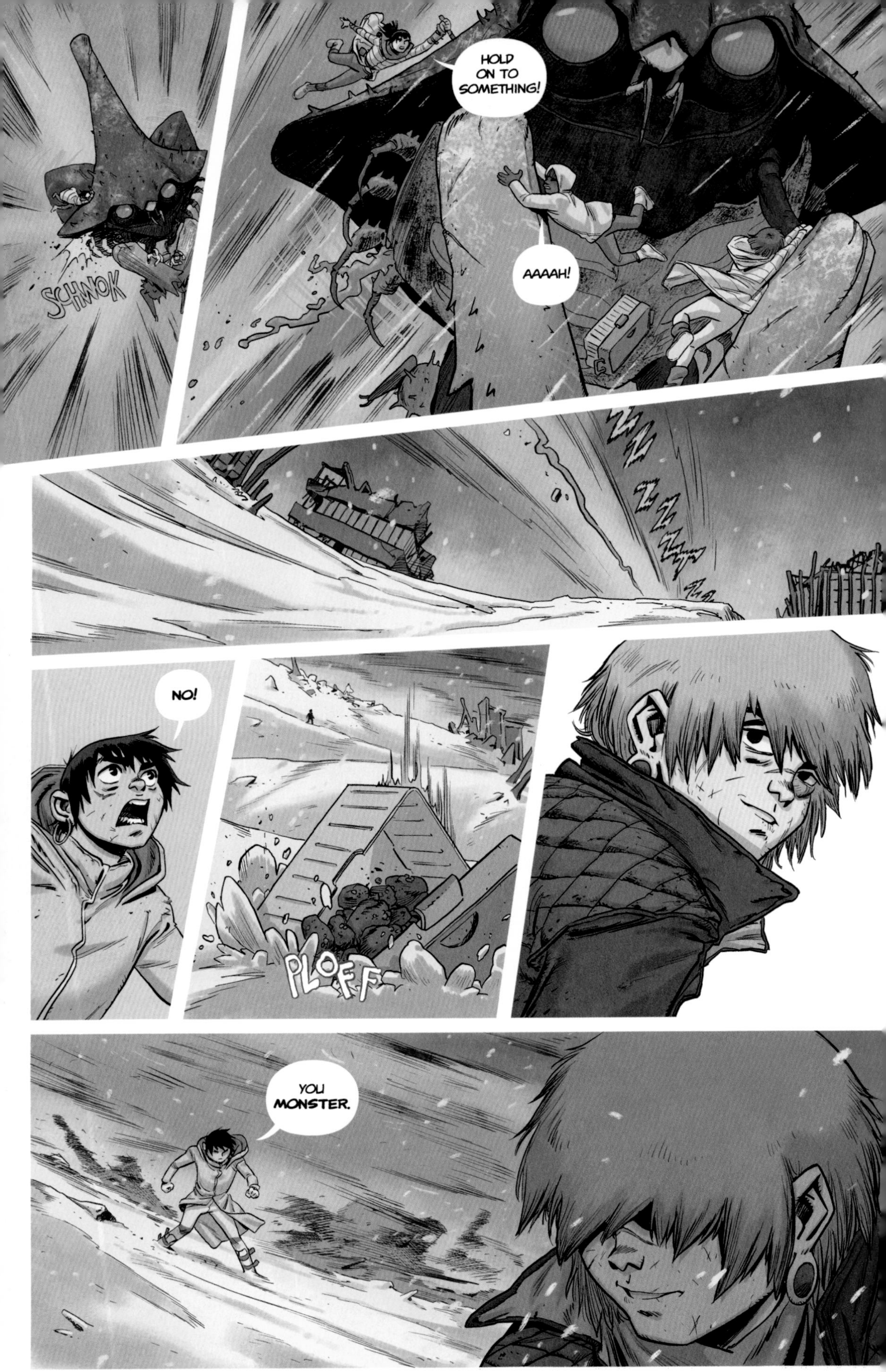
SCHNOK
HOLD ON TO SOMETHING!
AAAAH!
NO!
PLOFF
YOU MONSTER.

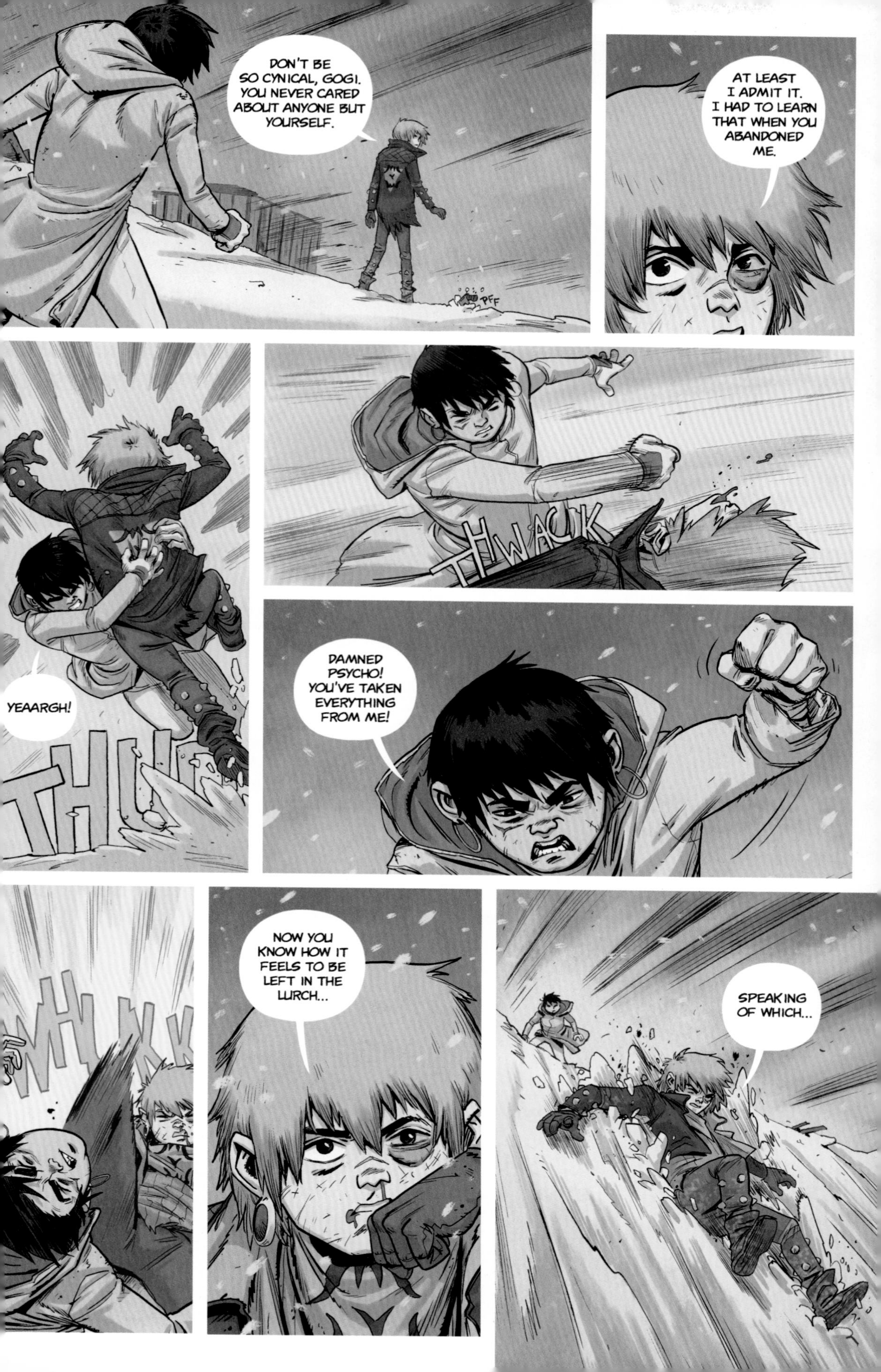
DON'T BE SO CYNICAL, GOGI. YOU NEVER CARED ABOUT ANYONE BUT YOURSELF.
PFF
AT LEAST I ADMIT IT. I HAD TO LEARN THAT WHEN YOU ABANDONED ME.
YEAARGH!
THUD
THWACK
DAMNED PSYCHO! YOU'VE TAKEN EVERYTHING FROM ME!
NOW YOU KNOW HOW IT FEELS TO BE LEFT IN THE LURCH...
SPEAKING OF WHICH...

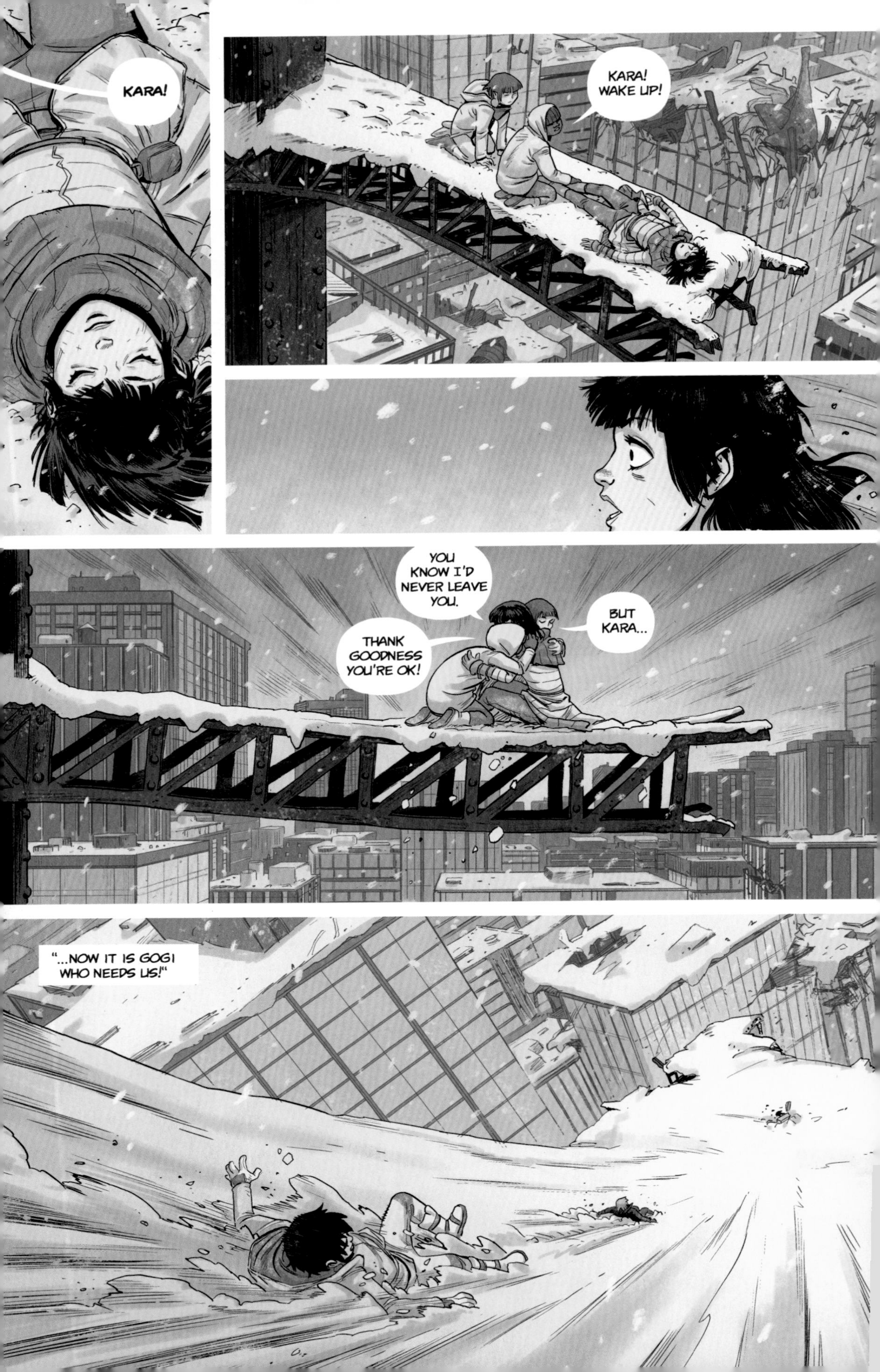
KARA!
KARA! WAKE UP!
YOU KNOW I'D NEVER LEAVE YOU.
THANK GOODNESS YOU'RE OK!
BUT KARA...
"...NOW IT IS GOGI WHO NEEDS US!"

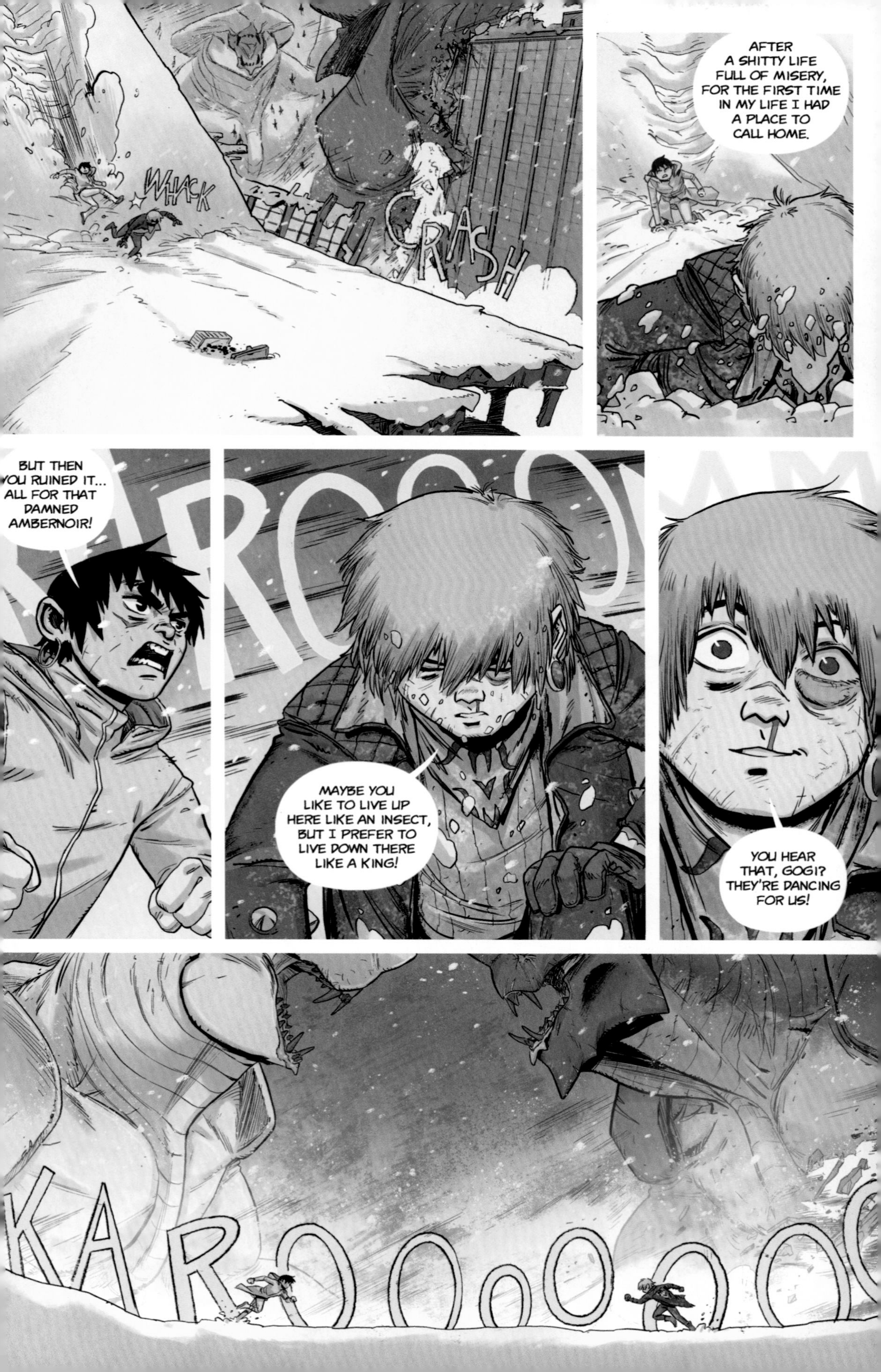
WHACK
CRASH
AFTER A SHITTY LIFE FULL OF MISERY, FOR THE FIRST TIME IN MY LIFE I HAD A PLACE TO CALL HOME.
BUT THEN YOU RUINED IT... ALL FOR THAT DAMNED AMBERNOIR!
MAYBE YOU LIKE TO LIVE UP HERE LIKE AN INSECT, BUT I PREFER TO LIVE DOWN THERE LIKE A KING!
YOU HEAR THAT, GOGI? THEY'RE DANCING FOR US!
KAROOOOOO

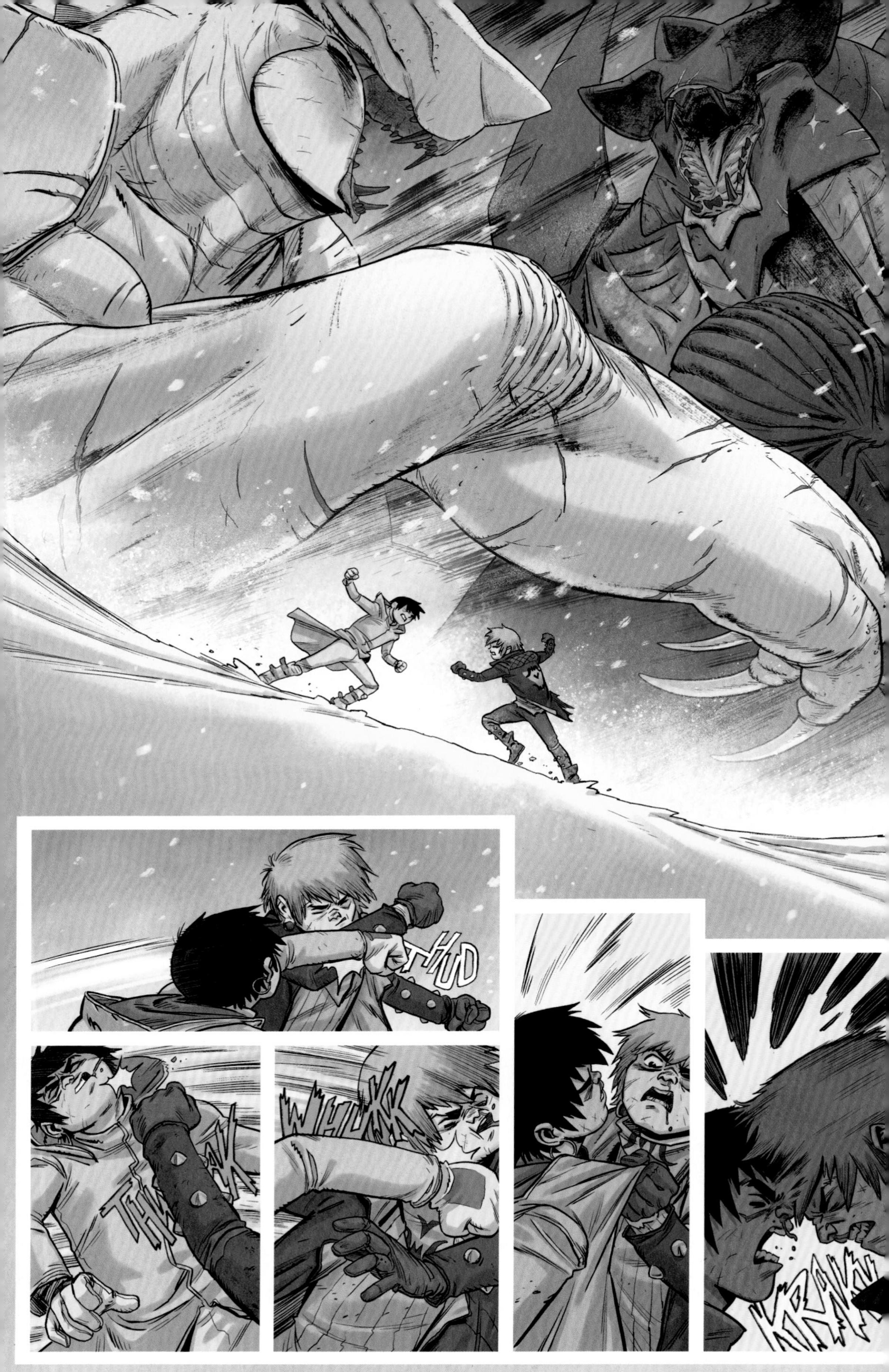
THUD
WHUKK

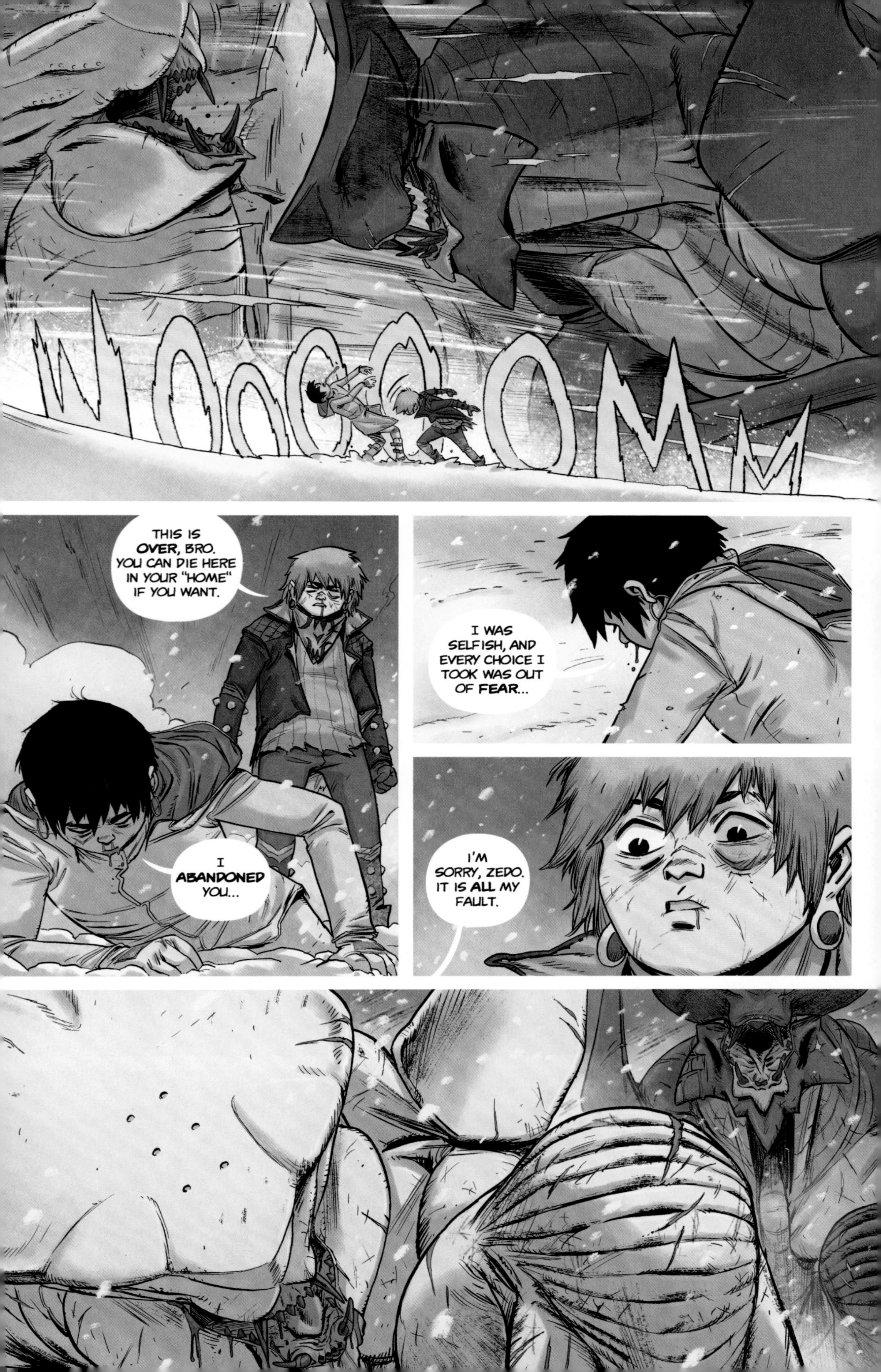
WOOOOOOMM
THIS IS OVER, BRO. YOU CAN DIE HERE IN YOUR "HOME" IF YOU WANT.
I ABANDONED YOU...
I WAS SELFISH, AND EVERY CHOICE I TOOK WAS OUT OF FEAR...
I'M SORRY, ZEDO. IT IS ALL MY FAULT.

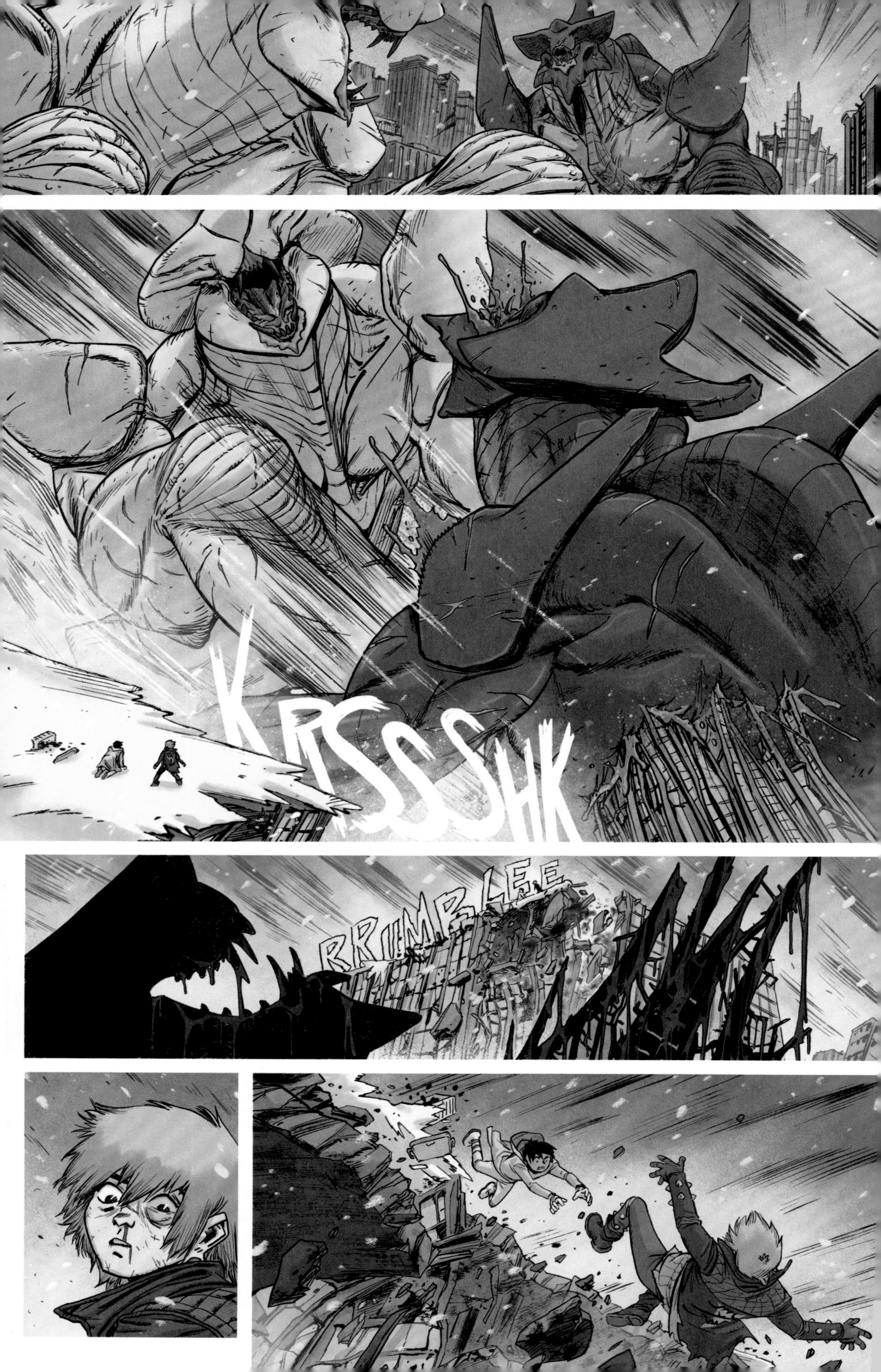
KRSSSSHK
RRUMBLEE

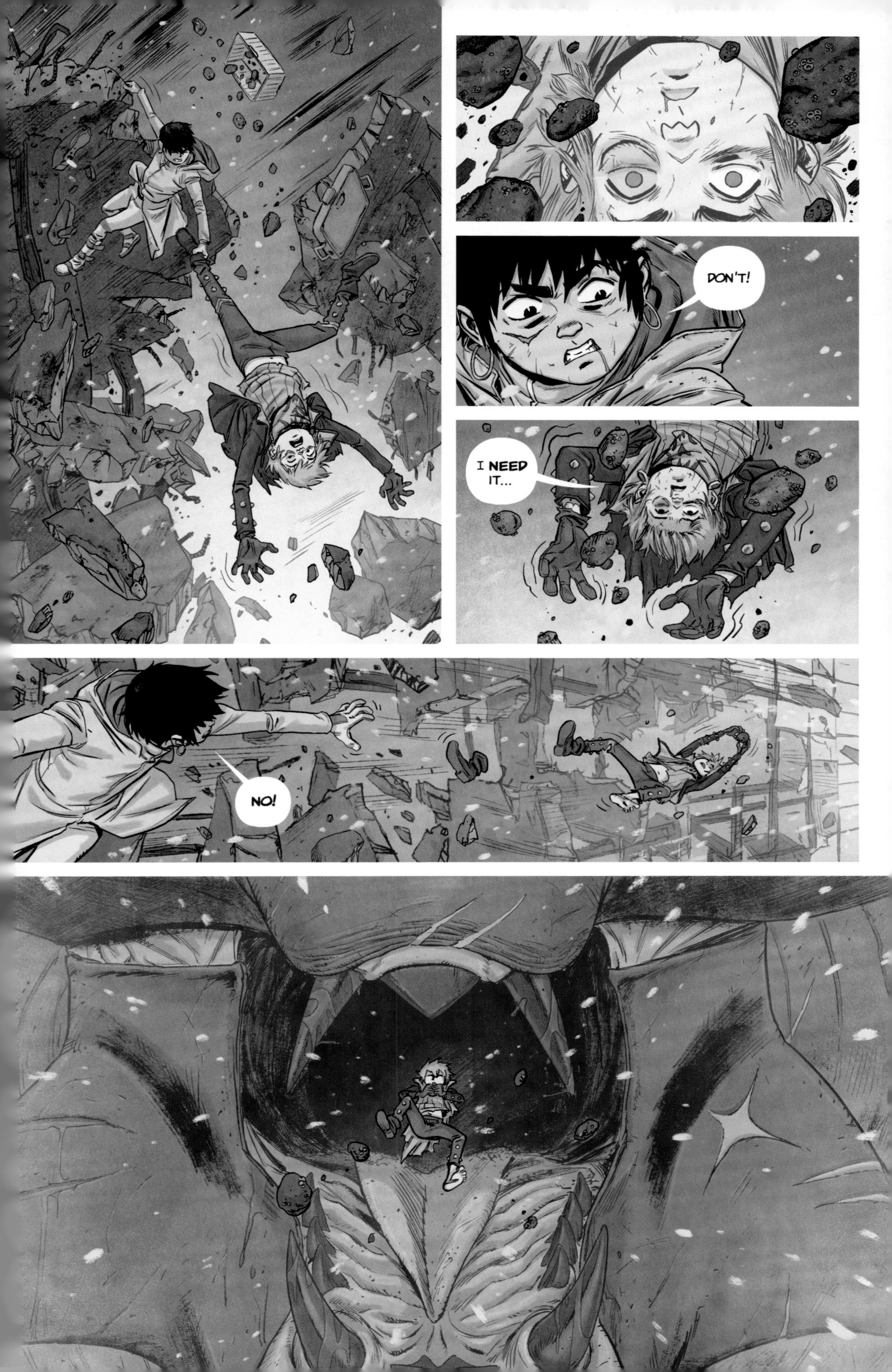
DON'T!
I NEED IT...
NO!

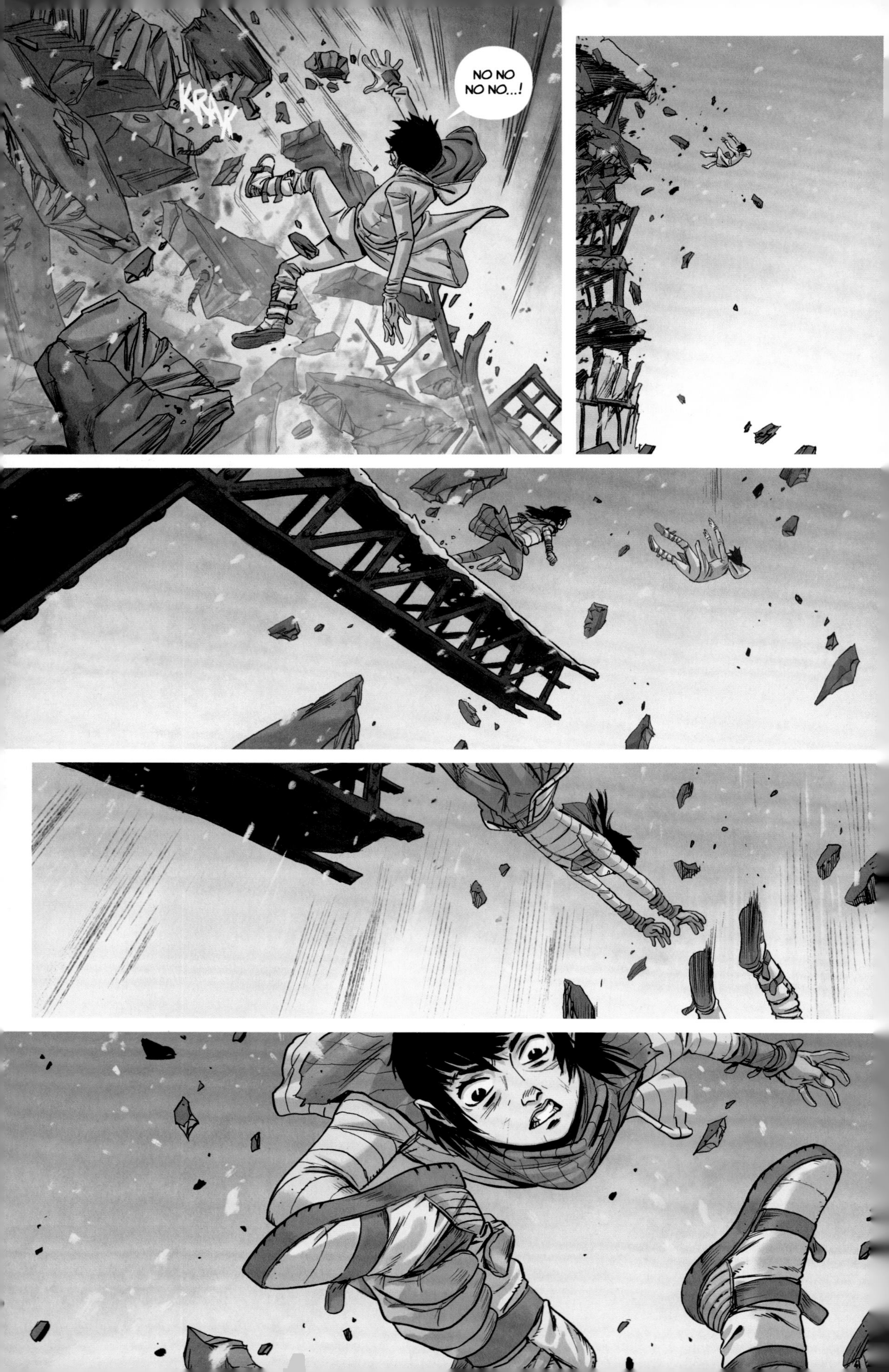
KRAK
NO NO
NO NO...!

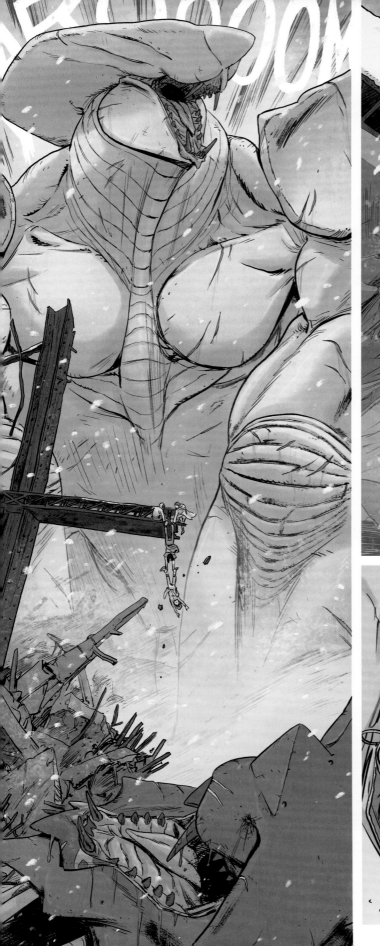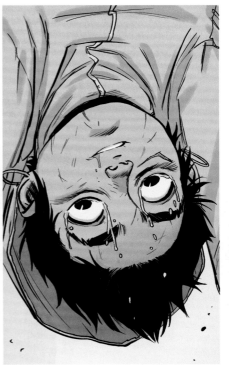

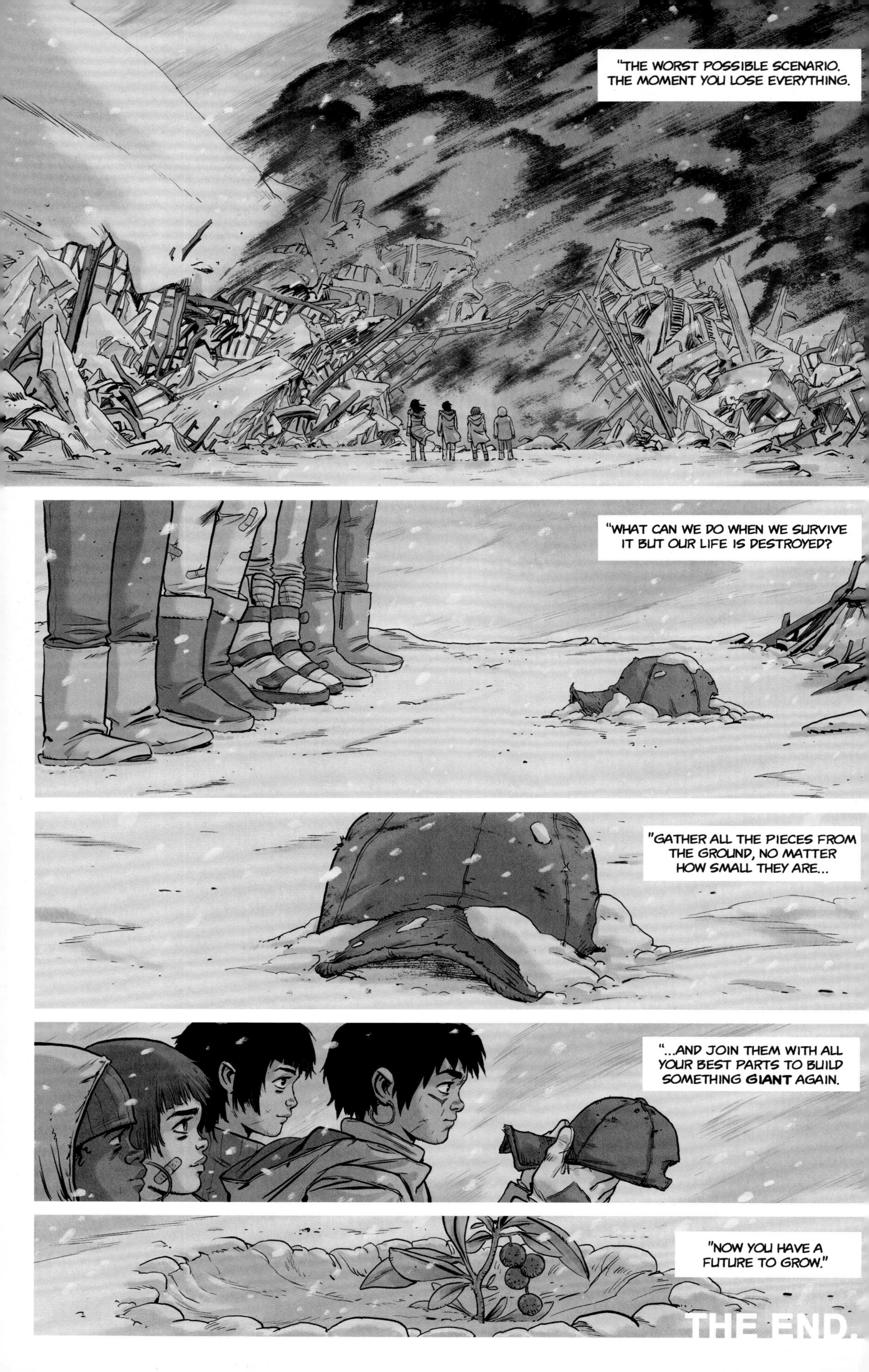
"THE WORST POSSIBLE SCENARIO. THE MOMENT YOU LOSE EVERYTHING.
"WHAT CAN WE DO WHEN WE SURVIVE IT BUT OUR LIFE IS DESTROYED?
"GATHER ALL THE PIECES FROM THE GROUND, NO MATTER HOW SMALL THEY ARE...
"...AND JOIN THEM WITH ALL YOUR BEST PARTS TO BUILD SOMETHING **GIANT** AGAIN.
"NOW YOU HAVE A FUTURE TO GROW."
THE END.

THE VALDERRAMA BROS. BIO

Carlos and Miguel were born in Marbella, on the sunny coast of the south of Spain. Since they were children, they drew their own comics inspired by the sci-fi cartoons, adventure comics, and monster films that intoxicated their young minds. After studying animation and design in Madrid, they kept on making their personal comics along with some collaborative projects.

Giants is their debut in American comics, and while it is their longest and most ambitious effort to date, it still contains the same things they loved as children.

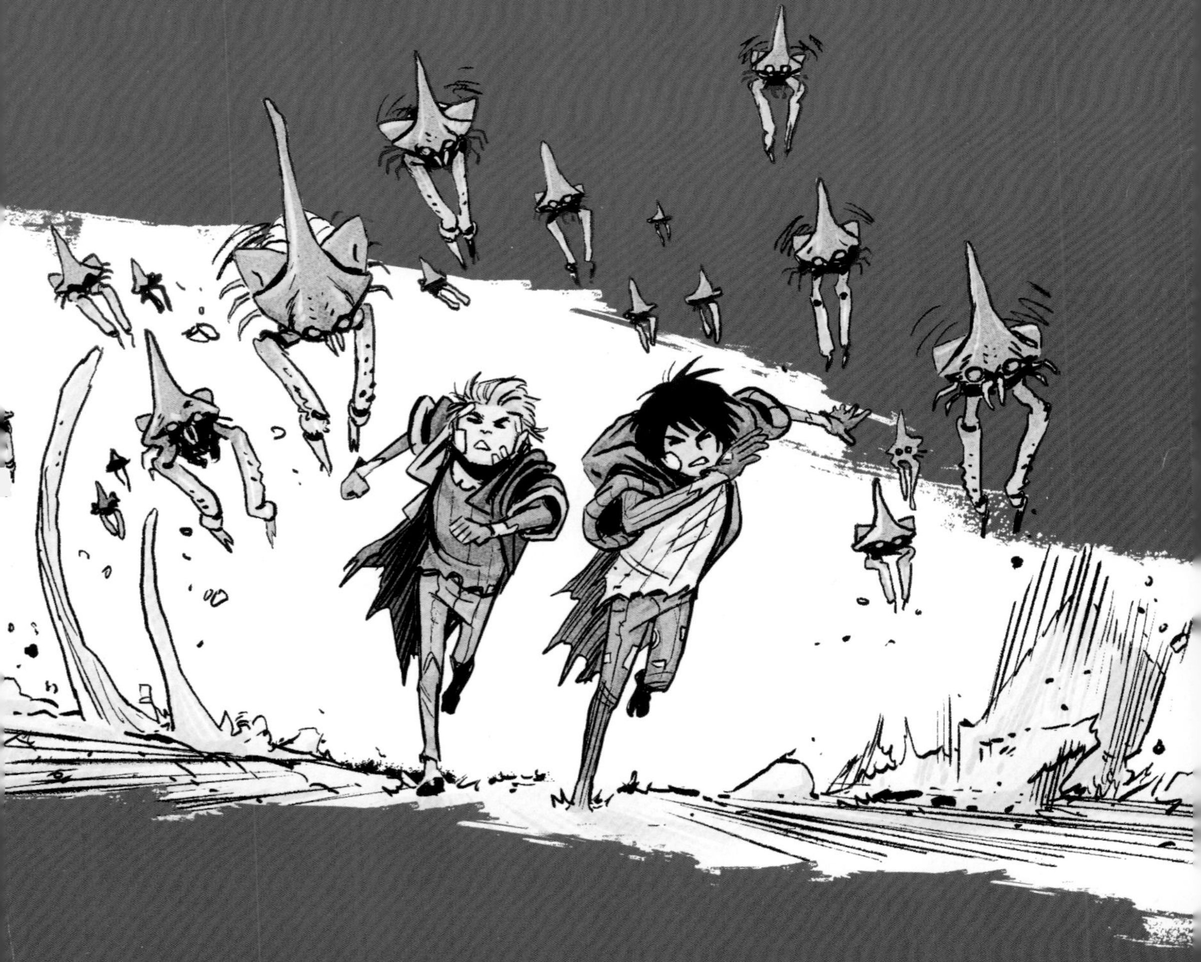

SKETCHES AND NOTES

FROM THE VALDERRAMA BROS.

When we first conceived *Giants*, Gogi and Zedo were going to be in their late teens. But as we continued to develop the story as a rite of passage, we were convinced that if we designed them a little younger, their evolution would be more impactful.

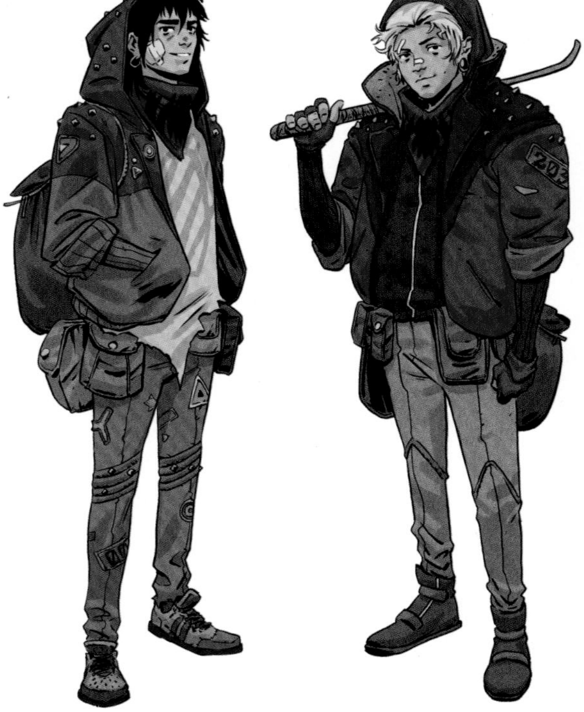

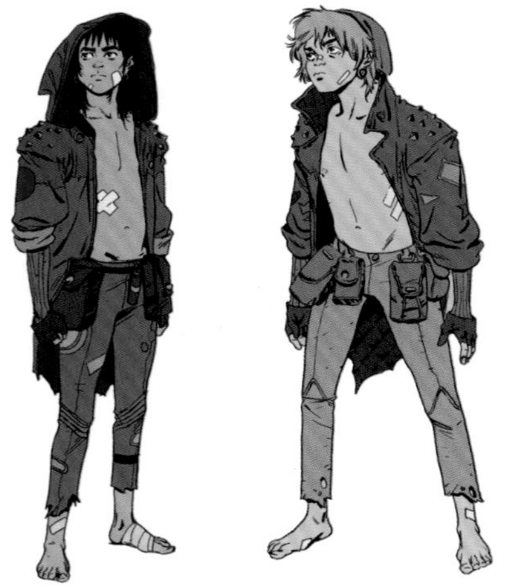

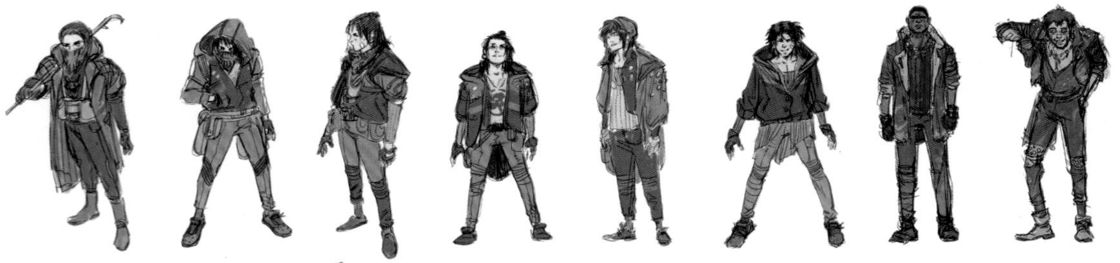

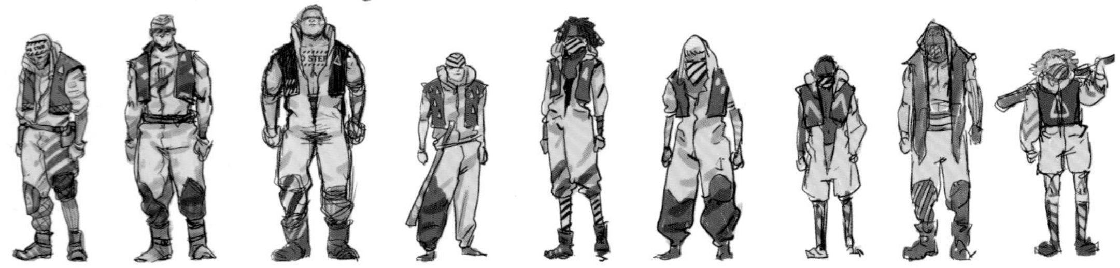

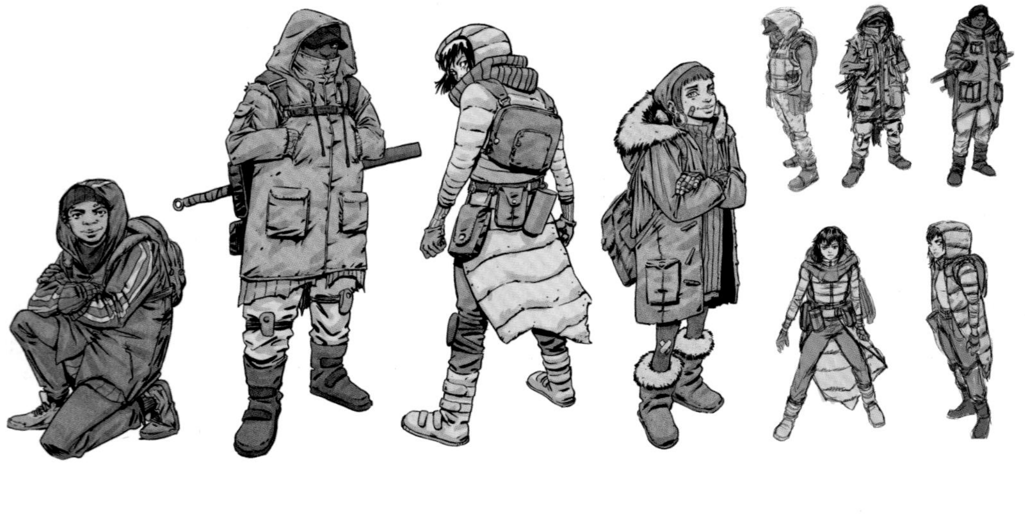